the definitive guide

BETTING ON SPORT

RACINGPOST
expertseries

the definitive guide to

BETTING ON SPORT

edited by bruce millington

Published in 2004 by Raceform Ltd,
Compton, Newbury, Berkshire, RG20 6NL
Raceform Ltd is a wholly-owned subsidiary of Trinity-Mirror plc

A catalogue record for this book is available from the British Library

ISBN 1-904317-36-7

Designed by Robin Gibson and Fiona Pike
Printed by Creative Print & Design, Wales

CONTENTS

CONTRIBUTORS

BRUCE MILLINGTON began his career as a board-marker in Mecca Bookmakers' London credit office. He then went on to work as assistant racing manager at Hackney and Catford dog tracks before being appointed greyhound correspondent of the London Daily News in 1987. He later became assistant greyhound editor of The Sporting Life before being appointed sports editor in 1995. Three years later he became sports editor of the Racing Post. He has made regular appearances on TV and radio and is regarded as one of the foremost sports betting experts in Britain.

KEVIN PULLEIN began his spectacular tipping career with The Sporting Life in 1994. Four years later he joined the Racing Post and has since established himself as the most successful football forecaster in spread betting history. His record is legendary. Between 1994 and 2004 he showed a profit on his recommended bets every season. His pearls of wisdom appear in his weekly Monday column, Pullein On Football.

JEREMY CHAPMAN has been the undisputed king of golf tipping for more than 30 years. First at The Sporting Life, where he was assistant editor until 1998, and then at the Racing Post, Chapman's golf previews, which appear every Wednesday, have become required reading for all golf punters and have provided a regular flow of big-priced winners down the years.

PAUL KEALY has been a member of the Racing Post's Sports Betting section since its advent in 1990 and is now deputy sports editor, specialising in golf, tennis and snooker.

PHIL AGIUS joined the Racing Post Sports Betting team in 1999 having previously worked at the Daily Mirror. He is recognised as the leading NFL adviser in the UK and also provides Formula One and non-league football tips.

MARK LANGDON, a former apprentice professional with Queens Park Rangers and a childhood team-mate of Ashley Cole, joined the Racing Post in 1998 and is now chief football tipster as well as the paper's rugby league expert.

ALEX DEACON is the football editor of the Racing and Football Outlook and his extensive research into the mathematics of football betting have earned him a reputation as one of the most dynamic tipsters in the business.

OTHER CONTRIBUTORS FROM THE RACING POST

GRAHAM WOODS
Rugby union correspondent

ED HAWKINS Cricket correspondent

STUART CARRUTHERS
Scottish football expert

IAN COYNE European football tipster

JAMES PYMAN Tennis correspondent

STEVE DAVIES General sport expert

ADAM SCRIVEN
Rally and Formula One expert

RON WYLLIE Bowls tipster

ANDY SMITH Speedway tipster

BETTING ON SPORT

INTRODUCTION

By BRUCE
MILLINGTON

CHOOSE A HOBBY. CHOOSE BETTING.
Choose horse racing. Choose hard-to-comprehend formguides. Choose seven-pound penalties, insufficient trips and first-time headgear. Choose mystifying terminology. Choose coming in your coat, coltish in paddock and not getting the trip. Choose stewards' inquiries, non-runners in 16-runner handicaps and jockeys dropping their hands. Choose undulating courses, mares in season and Rule 4 deductions. Me? I chose something different. I chose sports betting. And the reason? There are many reasons.

The variation on Rents's classic opening monologue in the movie Trainspotting sums up how and why so many people have come to be punters without ever partaking in what is still the most common fixed-odds betting medium in the United Kingdom.

For centuries horseracing has been not just the sport of kings but the king of sports as far as bookmakers and punters have been concerned. But that is changing. A new breed of gambler is emerging who has neither the time nor the inclination to develop the deep understanding of racing that is vital if one is to have any chance of success against the bookies.

Horseracing remains a phenomenally successful gambling activity and the intention of this book is neither to denigrate it nor to deter anyone from sampling its unique pleasures.

But the fact remains that a significant proportion of new devotees to the world of betting are attracted to it via sports other than racing, primarily because they have a well-established knowledge of football, cricket, golf and snooker but would barely be able to name half a dozen racehorses and even fewer jockeys.

These people opt not to spend the majority of their waking hours in a betting shop but enjoy using a proportion of their free time to have a punt. For them, there are now so many betting opportunities at evenings and weekends that they can become fairly compulsive gamblers without needing to possess an ability to tell one end of a horse from the other.

And it is not just the main sports like football, tennis and rugby that they can use as a vehicle to indulge in their passion. It is true to say that, with the possible exception of one or two more obscure activities such as those we see every four years in the Olympic Games, it is hard to think of a single credible sport that has not been priced up in one form or other since the sports betting boom exploded in the early 1990s.

On a typical weekend it is possible to wake on Saturday morning to find a one-day cricket international to bet on, followed by an Australian rugby league match, some golf, a live lunchtime football fixture, and then an afternoon of hardcore punting action featuring all the 3pm football, more golf, rugby and tennis. This may be followed by some tea-time football and then an evening of boxing, US golf, Spanish football and snooker before a cricket match somewhere on the other side of the world takes us through to Sunday morning, whereupon another day of action unfolds, not finishing until the final putt has been sunk in the American golf tournament. In between times there could be speedway,

Who's for hurling? It is hard to find a sport you can't bet on these days

bowls, fishing, hurling, motor racing, cycling and plenty more to get stuck into. All live on TV. All available to bet on with just a click of your mouse or a call to your bookmaker. Oh, and there will also be some horse racing as well.

And if that is not enough, you will not have to search hard to find a more trivial way of betting on a Saturday night in the form of a primetime reality TV show or competition to discover a new singing sensation.

Yes, betting is branching out. From the traditional battlegrounds of Ascot, Ayr and Aintree, through to the Oval, the Bernabeu and the Crucible and now into the realms of light entertainment.

Graham Sharpe, the voice of William Hill for more than three decades, sums up perfectly the change in public attitude towards betting.

"It is far easier to attract new customers through sport than through racing, although that is not to say we do not hope that eventually people will get to enjoy what racing has to offer," says the vastly-experienced PR man.

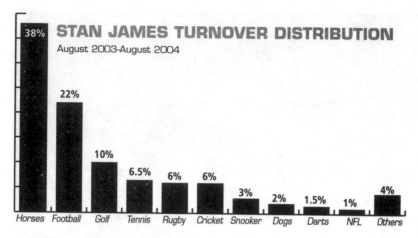

"You've got to tap into whatever people are interested in, and these days that is football, other sports and reality TV.

"My own children watch Big Brother and want to bet on it, yet it is as much as I can do to get them to watch the Grand National let alone the 2.30 at Fontwell on a Monday afternoon."

It was not always like this, of course. For many years betting shops meant races involving horses and dogs plus a brief flurry of football-related activity every Saturday afternoon. Now, you only have to scan the sport-dominated content of bookmakers' adverts to see that sport is sexy as far as the industry is concerned.

Sharpe has seen sport infiltrate the betting industry's traditional menu and is delighted.

"I had always hoped it would be like it is now," he said. "But it took a long time for the change to happen. I can remember in the early 1980s, when Channel 4 announced it was going to cover American football, I suggested in a trading meeting that we should start betting on the NFL. It was a real tumbleweed moment. People looked at me as if I was mad. Now, if you suggested not betting on the NFL people would look at you in the same way."

The bookmakers' love of sports betting is multi-faceted. Apart from the fact that it acts as an extremely welcoming gateway for novice punters who do not have a clue whether you need to be drawn high or low over five furlongs at Beverley, it is also a cheap product. Indeed, if you take football out of the equation, it costs bookmakers not a penny to price up sport, unlike racing, which rightly demands a slice of the action for the privilege of allowing layers to use it as their main revenue stream.

Above all, however, they love it because, while it is easy to be a sports punter, most people find it a good deal less easy to be a successful sports punter.

That is not to say it is virtually impossible to make sports betting pay, more that many people struggle simply because they do not make the right decisions or avoid the most basic pitfalls.

It is easy to blithely assert that there is nothing more sophisticated to betting on sport than to choose who you fancy, decide how much you want to lay out and then get on to your bookie before settling down on the sofa with a chicken tikka massala and a few beers to watch the action unfold.

Yet there is so much more to it than that. What represents value? Is the weather a factor? What is the right stake? Has the form been interpreted correctly? Where is the best value to be found – with a bookmaker? On the spreads? On an exchange? Are there any trends worth noting?

And if that all sounds a shade too much like hard work, don't worry. This book is designed to help you eliminate the bad bets and cause your betting to be more successful and thus more enjoyable. That does not require you to become an egg-headed boffin who spends all night wrestling with spreadsheets and various mathematical formulae just in order to feel comfortable about having a tenner on Crewe to beat Burnley.

Punters come in various forms. Some are happy just to restrict themselves to a couple of quid on a player to score the first goal when they go to watch their beloved football team. Others enjoy a once-a-week football coupon wager. There are regular punters who like to enhance their viewing pleasure with an investment regardless of what the sport is. And then there are the professionals – those whose whole lives are taken up with the business of carving out a living betting on anything from a Scottish Division Three match being played in front of a few dozen spectators to a World Championship darts match to a threeball in the Malaysian Open.

Whatever your punting habits, this book contains enough sound advice to ensure that you move forward as a more successful, enlightened operator.

What must be stressed, however, is that since betting began there has never been such a thing as a failsafe way of beating the bookmakers. If there was, bookmakers would very quickly cease to exist.

So if you bet simply to make money and cannot stomach the experience of handing over your money and never seeing it again, the best advice is to get a part-time job to augment your income.

It is not as hard as you might think to become a smarter punter, though. It is mainly about making the correct decisions and finding the right trees to bark up.

Take this hypothetical situation. A punter is in his shed while listening to a match commentary live on the radio.

"The ball comes across and Shearer is there. Alan Shearer knocks in the winner with what must be the last kick of the match. That's it. It finishes Everton 1 Newcastle 2."

The punter throws down his hammer in

frustration. "How unlucky can you get? I really fancied Everton. They were brilliant in their last game. I thought 6-4 was massive, although not as massive as the 13-8 that my mate got on the internet. Still, I'm not getting involved in all that online betting nonsense."

His mistakes are plentiful. He should not have been so bedazzled by how a team performed in its previous match. Many punters fall into this trap. He should have taken the best available price, yet it is amazing how often people settle for 6-4 when 13-8 is available. He should not be so dismissive of internet betting, either, especially as he ought to have at least considered protecting his position by laying Everton on an exchange as the game neared its completion.

Maybe our mythical friend (though there are many just like him in real life) is happy to view his betting strictly as a hobby and is thus content to accept that, as with fishing and stamp-collecting, he will inevitably incur some costs in the course of indulging in his hobby.

But with a little more thought, care and attention, he should be able to make his hobby less expensive. And if he does the right things he is far more entitled to dream of riches than the beachcomber scouring the sand for a gold ring.

Sports betting is exciting, jargon-free, convenient, challenging and potentially lucrative. It has the capability to make you feel ten feet tall, whether it is as a result of your team's centre-forward crashing in a 30-yard winning goal, your golfer draining a 20ft putt to seal a 50-1 triumph or the cricketer whose runs you have bought on the spreads completing his double century.

Choose sports betting as a hobby and, provided you follow the basic principles of discipline and selectivity, you have made a good decision.

It sure as hell beats trainspotting.

how sports betting soared

THE BIG BANG

THERE ARE VARIOUS THEORIES AS to why sports betting has become so popular that predictions that it will soon eclipse horse racing in terms of popularity can no longer be considered fanciful.

By BRUCE MILLINGTON

But only one carries any credibility. When Rupert Murdoch's rocket launched into the sky in 1989, it lit the blue touchpaper for an explosion of interest in betting on sport.

Before then, there had been a very gradual, but fairly insignificant increase in the amount of money wagered on events that did not involve four-legged animals, but as soon as satellite television, in the form of Sky, hit our screens a new betting phenomenon was born.

Suddenly a huge array of interesting new betting events were being beamed into our living rooms and, unlike the vast majority of horse racing, which took place when most people who like a bet were at work, these contests were being staged at times that were conducive to sitting in the armchair and having a punt.

THE DARK AGES To go back to the beginning, when betting shops were legalised in 1961, the vast majority of business was on horses and dogs. If you wanted football betting

Nerve centre: Betfair and other exchanges let punters lay as well as back

you had to make do with a fixed-odds coupon, which was extremely popular but bore little resemblance to that which the current generation of football punters is familiar with, and a pools coupon.

It is amazing that so many people were weekly players of the pools. The witless art of trying to nail eight score draws was big business and the nearest thing the average person got to a sports bet. I still wonder why between five and six o'clock of a Saturday evening we are forced to endure a man dolefully reading out the coupon numbers of the matches that finished as score-draws that afternoon when it seems interest in the pools has nosedived. But in pre-Lottery years gone by those numbers offered the general population their only chance of getting rich quick.

The difference between the fixed-odds coupon until the mid-1960s and the fixed-odds coupon today is that it did not carry any individual match odds, just prices for selecting a particular number of home wins, away wins and draws. Despite the lack of prices, something that seems so peculiar now, this coupon was big business.

But it was held partially to blame for the match-fixing scandals that rocked English football in the mid-1960s and was effectively rendered extinct when, under pressure from the pools companies, the Chancellor of the day enforced a rise in betting tax on the coupons from seven to 25 per cent. Turnover slumped from an estimated £65m in 1963 to just £5m in 1968, as Graham Sharpe chronicled in his book *Gambling on Goals*.

Worse was to come when Denis Healy increased the tax to 42 per cent in 1972, effectively killing betting on football stone dead.

It was only revived in 1974 when a Scottish company, Queen Bookmakers, brought out a coupon which bore close comparison with what we are accustomed to now, i.e., it had odds for each team and each draw.

It was argued that this constituted individual odds betting rather than fixed-odds and should therefore be subject to the standard seven per cent tax. Its originator was John MacFarlane, who went on to hold office at Football Licensing, the company responsible for charging bookmakers for the rights to bet on football.

And some quarter of a century after he rescued football betting with his new coupon, he again proved a big friend to football punters.

DEATH OF A HATED RESTRICTION For it was MacFarlane, aided by a concerted campaign by the *Racing Post*, who was a key player in the movement to abolish the minimum trebles restriction that bookmakers imposed.

The major bookmaking companies had always insisted that even if they had been prepared to offer unrestricted singles on football, as opposed to on all matches except those broadcast live in the UK, they would have been unable to because Football Licensing would not allow it.

Yet when I first contacted MacFarlane, it instantly became obvious that he was only too willing to discuss the possibility of removing the detested trebles-and-upwards-only rule.

Sure, he was expecting the bookmakers to increase their payment, but since they were paying just £666 per shop for the privilege of betting on football, he did not see why a small increase of the charge should be considered unreasonable.

Soon, the bookmakers realised that they could not blame Football Licensing, who were then taken over by Football DataCo, for the continuation of the minimum-trebles limit and gradually the wall came tumbling down.

It was Surrey Sports, subsequently renamed Skybet, who made the first move. The company had become increasingly frustrated that offshore bookmakers, particularly online ones, were offering unrestricted singles without fear of incurring the wrath of the licensing authorities.

On January 20, 2001, Surrey announced it was to accept singles on all Premiership matches, regardless of whether they were broadcast live on television.

Other bookmakers gradually followed suit until the final barrier to unrestricted singles was removed in July 2002. Coral became the first of the so-called Big Three to lift the block on Premiership singles, only for their main market rivals, Hills and Ladbrokes, to respond by dropping the minimum-trebles rule on all football matches, be they Premiership, Division One, Scottish Division Three or Italian Serie A.

Football DataCo quickly reached an agreement to make the move legal and finally, after years of suffering, punters were rid of the ludicrous requirement that they had to find two more teams to back if their main fancy was not playing live on TV.

BRANCHING OUT As well as the fixed-odds coupon in its various guises and tax deductions, it has long been possible to bet on major golf tournaments and other significant sporting events like Wimbledon and the Olympics.

But for decades the diet offered to those who wanted to bet but did not want to immerse themselves in the horserace formbook was nothing like as diverse as it is today.

However, the advent of Sky acted as an accelerant that led to the current situation whereby you seem never to be more than a minute away from another betting opportunity.

While Sky subscribers were far rarer in the immediate aftermath of the station's launch, certain bookmakers had the foresight to predict that sooner or later there would be a thriving market in sports punters and went about grabbing a piece of the action.

Foremost among these was Stan James, which began life in 1973. The Stan came from a fusion of the names of company founder Steve Fisher and his wife Ann and the James came from James Holder, another original shareholder.

Stan James were a minor player in the world of bookmaking up until the early 1990s, at which point they had just nine shops in the Thames Valley region and a very small credit operation.

But then along came Sky, and Fisher and his son Pete wasted little time spotting the potential for expansion into the sports betting market.

Pete Fisher recalls: "We detected a niche in the market and in 1993 we went for it. We made it our philosophy that if something was being shown live on TV we would bet on it.

"In the early days we had two compilers

the big bang

 Changing attitudes

Throughout the 1990s sports betting became bigger and bigger business, garnering an ever-increasing chunk of bookmakers' total turnover.

Not only were Sky dishes popping up on more walls, but then millions of non-punters were bitten by the betting bug when the National Lottery became reality. Suddenly, the idea of entering a betting shop (which were, by now, far more inviting than the dingy premises of the 1960s) and having a couple of quid on a player to score the first goal in the day's big match was not such a socially repulsive one. The Lottery had sanitised gambling.

pricing up everything. Now things have changed and our compiling department is significantly bigger."

Stan James soon built a reputation for innovation, exploring avenues that nobody had previously dreamed of.

"We have built up our business in line with Sky," adds Fisher. "The most rapid growth period was in 1995, when we doubled our turnover in one year. It has been onwards and upwards ever since and by 2004 our turnover was still expanding at an annual rate of between 25 and 30 per cent."

The company has moved its headquarters from the sleepy Oxfordshire town of Abingdon to Gibraltar, where it employs 300 people and takes bets from a staggering 25,000 different account-holders every month.

And, for Stan James at least, horseracing is by no means the be-all and end-all.

"Racing accounts for less than 40 per cent of our business," said Fisher. "The rest is sport, with football representing over a quarter of our turnover. Of the other sports, golf is the busiest followed by tennis."

NEW MEDIA And all the time it was easier and easier to have a punt. You could be the world's most compulsive gambler without ever setting foot in a betting shop. Telephone betting, while not a new concept, was made more inviting by the bookies, who cleaned up their customer service act with the consequence that their staff actually sounded like they wanted to take your bet rather than treating you as a nuisance for bothering them.

The invention of debit cards in 1991 was a major shot in the arm for telebetting. Previously it had been necessary to open a credit account in order to bet by phone, but these needed far more management than debit accounts, which were easy to open and did not require endless letters to be sent to customers who were behind with their payments. And then came the internet.

In the beginning, the world wide web was seen as the answer to every business's problems, a goldmine for everyone from magazine publishers to gardeners.

The truth, which became apparent when the dotcom bubble burst, was rather different. But, at the time, for certain industries it offered seemingly limitless scope for an explosion in turnover.

A friend of mine used to claim that the internet was useful only for betting and pornography. It has since been proved that the net has a slightly wider appeal, but he was undoubtedly correct in pinpointing betting as a growth area in the world of e-commerce.

Bookmakers rushed to chase the cyber-pound, indeed cyber-money of any currency. Suddenly there was a global market to pursue and before the turn of the millennium PC owners all around the world were able to log on and have a correct score bet on Stockport v Colchester.

Now, there is a mind-boggling array of ways to back a mind-boggling array of teams or players on the net, be it on the spreads, fixed-odds, or exchanges.

Not all the start-ups have survived. Names like Betachance, Betswap, Firststake, Netbetsports and Play121 have come and gone, while non-internet outfits Bowmans, Front Line, SP Racing and Burns have all gone bust in recent years, in some cases leaving customers thousands of pounds out of pocket.

But for those that were well established in the marketplace, business continued to boom.

YOU'VE NEVER HAD IT SO GOOD One of the most annoying sayings a losing punter will be confronted with is "if you can't win these days, you shouldn't be betting".

the big bang

Punting round the clock

A new millennium saw a new betting phenomenon – the 24-hour bookmaker. Stan James have been open for business every minute since January 2, 2000, when the firm decided to be available to take bets right around the clock.

Not only had they been taking a steady stream of evening greyhound bets until nearly 11pm but they were also accommodating a regular supply of tennis wagers on worldwide tournaments that left them of the opinion that there was no point closing.

Other bookies like Bet365, Chandler and spread firm Sporting Index have since joined Stan James in laying around the clock, while most will accept internet sport bets at all hours, although some for laughably small amounts as they strive to avoid being taken to the cleaners by punters who have latched on to a breaking story overnight.

Yet even if you are in the depths of despair on the back of a dozen consecutive unsuccessful bets, you cannot dispute that the punter really has never had it so good.

It is hard to believe that as recently as 2001 punters were still paying nine per cent on all bets and were obliged to find two other sides to perm in a treble if they fancied a football team whose match was not being transmitted live on television.

Betting tax stood at ten pence in the pound until it was reduced to nine pence by Kenneth Clarke in 1996. But, in the best news punters ever had, it was abolished completely on October 6, 2001 as Chancellor Gordon Brown ruled that bookmakers should pay tax on their gross profits rather than demanding that punters were taxed on winnings.

The effects were astonishing. In no time turnover soared as those big-hitters who were previously betting illegally on a thriving black market commonly referred to as the jungle saw no reason to bet covertly any more (although the jungle still exists to a degree to serve those punters whose money is considered too hot by the high street firms or those who want to trade in more substantial amounts than the established companies will allow them to).

Moreover, punters of all sizes had more money in their pockets and so increased their betting activity.

The result has been spectacularly good for the betting industry. In the first six months of 2002 William Hill's turnover rose by 47 per cent (and by 78 per cent online), while other firms reported similarly huge hikes.

THE OFFSHORE SWITCH In truth – and this was part of the reason why the Chancellor did punters the favour of sparing them the burden of paying betting tax – it had been possible to bet at a tax rate well below nine per cent for more than two years before the momentous decision to scrap duty.

In May 1999, Victor Chandler stunned the betting industry by upping sticks and moving his entire bookmaking operation to Gibraltar, thus enabling him to offer tax-free betting to his thousands of clients.

Actually, it wasn't quite tax free because he imposed a three per cent 'service' charge, but for many punters the opportunity to slash their tax costs by two thirds was too good to pass up.

Not surprisingly, most of Chandler's main rivals followed suit, although almost all maintained a UK presence as well, some if only to avoid the Customs and Excise ruling that offshore bookmakers were not allowed to advertise in Britain.

Since the advent of tax-free betting, more companies have opened up, especially online, thriving on the fact that technology allows risk management to be so easy and that there is abundant new money splashing around.

Another benefit of being a 21st-century bookie is that the amounts they are required to pay for the privilege of being able to lay bets on sports are so low by comparison to what they must pay the racing industry. Indeed, in most instances they are non-existent. The football authorities charge little more than a token fee, although they are now beginning to wake up to the fact that they are potentially missing a trick, while other sports do not hold out their hand to the bookmakers at all.

Many bookmakers are also delighted that much of the so-called smart money has gone to Betfair, although few will admit it.

It had been predicted that Betfair would cannibalise all but the biggest and best-established traditional bookmakers, but so far there has been little evidence of that, and as things stand punters can look to the future with confidence. Finding winners may be as tough as ever, but finding value, with so many different ways to bet and so many companies to choose from, should be a good deal easier.

SPORTS BETTING IN THE RACING POST

Throughout the evolution of sports betting, from the days when it represented a drop in the ocean compared to turnover of horses and greyhounds, the *Racing Post* has expanded its sports coverage accordingly.

Indeed the paper's output gives an interesting indicator of just how big sports betting has grown since Sky's launch.

The very first issue of the paper, in April 1986, contained a brief summary of the general sports news of the day and it was not until 1990 that the paper gave sports betting its own dedicated daily section. Edited with wit and energy by Derek McGovern, Sports Betting made everyone sit up and take notice in the summer of 1991 when it achieved a high-profile tipping double as Michael Stich won the Wimbledon men's singles after being put up at 40-1 and then Ian Baker-Finch landed the Open at advised odds of 50-1.

Since then, Sports Betting's presence in the paper has grown steadily, mirroring the public's interest in betting on humans rather than animals, and in February 1995 the section moved to its current position at the back of the paper. In April 1994, the paper carried 76 pages of sports betting coverage. In April 2004 that figure had soared to 403.

Sports Betting's primary aim is to give punters the maximum possible ammunition in the battle with the bookies. That means form, stats, news and prices. We also provide analysis and recommended bets on all the daily action, be it hurling or rallying, bowls or boxing, but are mindful that most punters have a mind of their own and thus do not need tips forcibly rammed down their throats.

the price has got to be right

VALUE JUDGEMENT

IT IS ONE OF THE OLDEST ARGUMENTS in betting: are you better off looking for value or looking for winners?

By BRUCE MILLINGTON

To me it is a no-brainer. Value is king. I am amazed anyone considers it a matter of debate, yet many do. Their thinking goes like this: what is the point of backing something because you think it is a big price if it has little or no chance of winning?

They will hold up as an example a football team that is playing away to opposition that is generally accepted to be superior. Fulham against Manchester United at Old Trafford, for example.

Fulham may be 12-1 but if you dare suggest that is too big a price, you are liable to be shot down in flames by those who believe that because the Cottagers are such big outsiders there is no point even contemplating whether or not they actually represent a value wager.

There is no point backing a string of big-value losers, they will reason.

Refrain from getting embroiled in a debate with people who think this way. They are irrational and cannot possibly be winning punters in the long run.

In betting, and in football in particular, value lies more often than not in the bigger-priced contenders.

Big-value underdogs: Fulham upset the odds at Old Trafford in 2003

This is largely because of the average punter's fixation with the very shortest prices on the weekend football coupon.

Bookmakers can usually tell whether they will have a winning weekend simply by looking at the results of the top teams in the English Premiership and Scottish Premier League.

In the autumn of 2003, Arsenal, Chelsea, Manchester United, Celtic and Rangers all won on the same weekend eight times out of 11.

This caused a drop in bookmakers' profits as punters landed some significant accumulators. By the start of December a blind £10 weekly five-timer on the quintet was showing a profit of £310. With their profits being dented, the layers reacted by strangling the match odds of the five teams that were hurting them.

Predictably, it did not prevent punters steaming in to the so-called Big Five, even when they stopped winning so regularly. And with the hotpots shortening, their opponents were offered at even longer odds, leading to some decent paydays for those punters who took the rational view that the value lay with the long-shots.

The bottom line is that everything becomes good value if the price is right. You may head out of the house one day armed with £20,000 with the intention of buying a Mercedes. On the way to the showroom you pass the Toyota dealership where the comparable car in their range is on offer at £14,000.

Your heart was set on the Merc but here is a car every bit as good for £6,000 less. You don't know why it is being offered so cheaply but it is. You buy it and, whether you bank the six grand or use it to take the family to the Caribbean, you have made a value investment.

So it is with betting. You intended to back Manchester United, but when you saw the prices and realised Fulham were so big, you backed them.

Many punters would, quite rightly, not dream of having a bet without searching for the best possible value, yet there are plenty who have no grasp of the concept of price-sensitivity and just back their fancies with the same bookmaker, be it on the phone, the net, or, more commonly, in the shop (internet punters tend to be more sophisticated and more aware of the basic premise that if you take the trouble to root out the best possible price you have a far greater chance of being successful over a long period).

I have to admit that if any such punter asked me how obsessed with value I am in other aspects of my life I would have to say I am not.

I don't bother to look at how much a filling station is charging for a litre of petrol when I need to replenish my tank, even though by failing to shop around I am probably costing myself as much money as I would if having £20 on something at evens when, if I had

 Findlay's casebook

It's not the case that hot favourites can never be considered to represent good value, of course. Harry Findlay, the larger-than-life professional punter, once offered the following nuggets on the subject of value.

"People will tell you that you can't eat value, and they'll tell you they haven't got the money to bet odds-on, but what's better – having 50 quid at 8-11 about a twos-on shot or having five £10 bets on 12-1 shots? How can people say never bet odds-on?

"If you've got Barton [top-class National Hunt star of the late 1990s] in a novice chase at Newcastle against two pit ponies, would you back him at 10-11? In terms of value there's no difference between getting 1-10 about a 1-14 shot and getting 14-1 about a 10-1 shot."

bothered to look around, I could have got 11-10.

I do not grill my wife over her shopping habits to see if we could have saved money on the weekly groceries, and I do not drink in pubs simply because their beer is less dear.

Thus, perhaps price-sensitive punters should not be too disparaging about those happy to take 5-1 when 7-1 is available elsewhere.

For me, though, the difference between getting value in betting and getting value in general life is that the customer experience is so similar with bookmaker A and bookmaker B that there is no good reason not to spend a little while detecting where your money will produce the biggest yield.

Moreover, it usually takes very little time and effort to nail down the best-available price.

In addition to the comprehensive Pricewise tables published daily on a vast array of sporting contests in the *Racing Post*, there are odds-comparison sites which offer real-time updates on which firm is the best price about your fancy.

The ease with which punters can be informed where the value lies is irksome to some old-school punters, who shed a nostalgic tear for the days when getting the best price involved a car ride around a large town centre, stopping off at every betting shop to collate the various prices.

For them, it was harder to find what the best price was, but the fact that so few people went to the trouble of doing so meant that they were able to get far more on at the prices they desired. Now, the playing field has been levelled and even the most bone-idle backer can be sure he has got the value in less than a minute with a mouse in his hand.

Whatever other beliefs you have as regards punting and all its intricacies, never forget that value is simply the most important concept in betting.

punters must be disciplined

CHASTISE YOURSELF

DISCIPLINE IS ABSOLUTELY VITAL to success in betting. You can be a master in the art of finding winners, but if you lack discipline you will struggle to avoid losing money in the long run.

By BRUCE MILLINGTON

Even if you are what could be termed a recreational punter, someone who enjoys the odd flutter with money he can easily afford never to see again, it is important to exhibit a degree of discipline. So-called fun bets start becoming a lot less enjoyable when they consistently lose.

Indiscipline can creep in both when you are winning and when you are losing. They say a football team is at its most vulnerable when it has just scored, and the same can be said of the punter who has just backed a winner.

If he is not disciplined, he is liable to start dreaming of riches. He may adopt the philosophy that he is betting with the bookies' money and that it is therefore not a major problem if his next bet is unsuccessful.

Selectivity is an important watchword and there is a strong temptation to discard it when you have just visited the payout counter. You cannot wait to get stuck in again. Playing up your winnings is an enticing concept – the belief that you are about to embark on a spree that will culminate in you winning a life-changing amount. It might happen, of course, but the far likelier outcome is that you will be back to square one very quickly.

For the punter who has just backed a loser, the equivalent of playing up your winnings is chasing your losses and is just about the most dangerous thing you can do. The difference between chasing your losses and playing up your winnings is that the journey back to square one is likely to take far longer and be far more painful.

Instead of waiting until you see a price that you genuinely consider worth taking, you bet at the next available opportunity in the hope of wiping the slate clean as quickly as possible.

If that recovery mission fails, you try again. And again. And before too long you are deep in trouble.

Overstaking is a classic trait of indiscipline and is often associated with the folly of playing up your winnings as quickly as possible instead of attempting to gradually consolidate your gains.

And in a similar vein, it is possible to understake, usually when you are treading carefully because things have not been going well. It is an understandable fault. If you really fancy something but have not been faring well, the natural inclination is to hold back a little given that you do not wish to slip further into the red.

Yet a five-star bet (or whatever terminology you wish to use to signify a betting proposition about which you are supremely confident) is a five-star bet regardless of how your recent punting history has gone.

Basically, your approach to striking a bet should be consistent regardless of whether you are in profit or behind. That means keeping a clear head, remaining confident (if you have been losing) or cautious (if you have been winning) and, above all, maintaining discipline and control at all times.

from the basics to the finer points

GETTING ON

IN DAYS OF OLD, IF YOU WALKED into a betting shop and asked the cashier to explain the basics of betting you would have been laughed off the premises.

Shops were spartan places, often manned by indifferent ladies who would sooner spend the afternoon filing their nails and chain-smoking than ensuring their company exuded impeccable standards of customer service.

Things have improved since then. Competition from other betting shop operators, internet and telebetting mean bookmakers are now far keener to ensure clients are dealt with in a courteous and efficient manner.

This is exemplified by the *Racing Post* Betting Shop Manager of the Year award, which highlights how hard a large number of betting shops try to please their customers.

It is not all sweetness and light, however. Try though they might to encourage their staff to remember their ps and qs, major bookmaking companies are not renowned as being especially generous when it comes to wages. Betting shop staff are not well paid and are often asked to work long hours to meet the demands that morning-to-evening racing provide.

So, while a novice punter is unlikely to have his initial enquiries met with a puff of cigarette

By BRUCE
MILLINGTON

No more shop horror: the modern betting shop is a more hospitable place

smoke and a curt rebuff, he should not expect to be treated to an uninterrupted seminar on the rudiments of betting either.

The following pages should contain enough information to help virgin punters grasp the basics of placing a bet.

IN THE SHOP Walk in, pick up a blank slip and a pen. Write your bet on the slip – £10 Manchester United to beat Arsenal, for example – hand it to the person behind the counter, who will write the price on it, run it through a scanner and hand you a copy of it.

It's a simple as that. Well, not quite. There are a few things you need to know.

For instance, if you are backing a football team to win a match in a knockout competition, you will be on the 90-minute result unless you specifically stipulate that you want to back the team to qualify for the next round. The odds will be shorter than for the team to win inside 90 minutes but you are a winner if your team is successful in regulation time, extra time or on penalties.

Long and short of the coupon: stick to your fancies and shun the sections

And remember that there is no starting price system on sport bets as there is in racing. The price you get is the one the bookmaker is offering at the time you place your bet.

Above all, if you are unsure about anything, don't be afraid to ask a member of staff.

FILLING IN A FOOTBALL COUPON
This might look as daunting as a tax return form at first glance, but you need not be put off.

The list on the left is all you really need to concentrate on. It contains prices for each team to win and each match to end in a draw. There is a number of blank squares to the right of each fixture. If you want to link a number of teams in an accumulator (as most punters do) you mark 1 (for a home win), 2 (for an away win) or X (for a draw) in the appropriate boxes in a vertical column.

For example, if you want a treble on Manchester City to win at home to Norwich, Chelsea to draw at home to Southampton and Plymouth to record an away win at Watford, the column of boxes nearest to the fixtures should have a 1 by the Manchester City match, an X by the

getting on

 Betting slip tips

don't be misunderstood

Remember that all bets available on coupons can be struck by writing them on a normal betting slip. So if you just want a double on, say, Liverpool and Cardiff, you can just write: Liverpool to beat (insert opponent), Cardiff to beat (insert opponent). £5 double.

It makes sense to be as clear as possible when filling in betting slips. This does not mean enrolling on a calligraphy course before entering a shop but it avoids any possible confusion over settlement if the shop staff can easily understand what your bet is. One of the problems of betting in shops, I have found down the years, is that staff occasionally do not take enough time and trouble to examine slips to see if there is a potential for confusion, and that disputes only arise after the bet has won and the customer wants to collect his winnings.

Then again, I have seen betting slips featuring all manner of complex multiple wagers that look like they have been written by a baby. How the staff have managed to understand these bets, let alone settle them, I shall never know, so do not panic too much about untidiness. Again, if in doubt, just check with the person behind the counter that everything is in order.

Chelsea macth and a 2 by the Watford match. At the bottom of the column you write your stake.

If you want another bet on the same coupon, repeat the process in the second column and so on until you have completed your bets.

Then, simply add up your total stakes, fill in the amount in the marked area and hand it to the cashier, who will give you a copy.

Be wary of the other wares on offer elsewhere on the coupon, especially the sections lists, which are basically a way of lulling you into backing teams you don't particularly fancy in the hope of landing a huge payout. There is nothing wrong with going for glory on a coupon, but if you stick to the teams you fancy, the rewards will be no smaller if they are all successful.

ON THE PHONE Opening a telepone account is easy and also instantly rewarding

getting on

 Each-way terms

it pays to know your place

For sports bets, here is a general guide to each-way terms:

Knockout tournaments Half the odds a place 1,2, ie, half the odds for reaching the final. This can change to a third 1,2 if a draw is pre-determined from a long way out. This is because you may, in the Wimbledon ladies' singles, for example, have a long odds-on favourite in one half of the draw. This could mean the prices of the runners in the other half of the draw all being big enough that punters could back each one of them each-way and guarantee a profit whichever one reached the final.

Divisions These are normally a quarter the odds 1,2,3, although some bookmakers bet a fifth 1,2,3, which is less advantageous to punters. As a division reaches the latter stages, the each-way terms may alter to a third 1,2 and then win only. Obviously, the terms that were applicable at the time you placed your bet will not change.

Golf A quarter the first four was the industry standard for many years. More recently, however, all bookmakers have recognised that it is unacceptable to operate on that basis when the field can number 156 players, most of whom have a feasible chance of winning. As of the 2004 Open it became the industry norm to offer each-way terms of a quarter the odds on the first five players for all tournaments.

It may or may not be pure coincidence that the companies that resisted paying out on each-way bets down to fifth place for the longest were those with a large number of betting shops (whose clients are often unaware of the intricacies of betting).

more often than not. If you scan the book-maker adverts in the *Racing Post* on a Saturday, you will usually find they have a free bet offer when you initiate a new account.

All you need are your personal details and a debit card to hand.

Betting on the telephone is quick and easy and if you are unsure of yourself, it is a good way of getting started as you may feel less self-conscious asking questions to a telephonist who is the only person who can hear you than in a crowded betting shop.

Remember, though, that if you want a Sat-

ODDS AS PERCENTAGES

Odds on	price	odds against
50.00	Evens	50.00
51.22	21-20	48.78
52.38	11-10	47.62
54.55	6-5	45.45
55.56	5-4	44.44
56.52	13-10	43.48
57.89	11-8	42.11
58.33	7-5	41.67
60.00	6-4	40.00
61.54	8-5	38.46
61.90	13-8	38.10
63.64	7-4	36.36
64.29	9-5	35.71
65.22	15-8	34.78
66.67	2-1	33.33
68.00	85-40	32.00
68.75	11-5	31.25
69.23	9-4	30.77
70.37	95-40	29.63
70.59	12-5	29.41
71.43	5-2	28.57
72.22	13-5	27.78
73.33	11-4	26.67
73.68	14-5	26.32
75.00	3-1	25.00
76.19	16-5	23.81
76.92	100-30	23.08
77.27	17-5	22.73
77.78	7-2	22.22
78.26	18-5	21.74
80.00	4-1	20.00
81.82	9-2	18.18
83.33	5-1	16.67
84.62	11-2	15.38
85.71	6-1	14.29
86.67	13-2	13.33
87.50	7-1	12.50
88.24	15-2	11.76
88.89	8-1	11.11
89.47	17-2	10.53
90.00	9-1	10.00
90.48	19-2	9.52
90.91	10-1	9.09
91.67	11-1	8.33
92.31	12-1	7.69
92.86	13-1	7.14
93.33	14-1	6.67
93.75	15-1	6.24
94.12	16-1	5.88
95.24	20-1	4.76
95.65	22-1	4.35
96.15	25-1	3.85
96.55	28-1	3.45
97.06	33-1	2.94
97.56	40-1	2.44
98.04	50-1	1.96
98.51	66-1	1.49
99.01	100-1	0.91

To calculate the percentage each price is worth, add a point and divide into 100. So 3-1 becomes four into 100, equals 25.

urday football bet, you may face a long wait on the line if you leave it until the busy period between 2.30 and 3pm.

ON THE INTERNET For more details on betting on the net, see the chapter on pages 66-71.

THE RANGE OF BETS

Single The easiest, and some would say only, way to wager. A single is a win bet on a horse, dog, football team, boxer or whatever. A £10 single on a 2-1 winner returns £30 (2x£10 plus the £10 stake, which is always returned to you when you back a winner), £10 on a 3-1 winner returns £40 and so on.

Calculating returns is slightly more complicated if the odds are fractional (ie, not something-to-one). If, for example, you have £10 on a 5-2 winner, that equates to £10 on a 2.5-1 winner so the return would be £35. Evens, a popular price, refers to 1-1 so £10 on an even-money winner pays £20.

Odds-on If the odds are expressed in such a way that the figure before the hyphen is smaller than the one after it, that denotes an odds-on chance, ie, one rated better than 50-50 to be successful.

A £10 bet on a 1-2 chance would return £15, £10 on a 1-5 chance would return £12, and so on. Odds-on chances are described, using the example of 1-2, as 'one-to-two' or 'two-to-one on'.

See the table on the following page for a comprehensive list of returns.

Each-way This is two bets on the same runner. One part is a straight win bet, the other is on the runner to be placed, which usually means finishing in the first three but can, in certain events, mean the first two, four or, mainly in the case of large-field golf tournaments, five.

The idea is to provide some compensation

if your selection performs well but fails to win.

Because it is two bets, your stake is doubled, so a £10 each-way bet costs £20.

A successful £10 each-way bet on a 10-1 winner would return £110 on the win part while the place part of the bet would depend on the particular each-way terms offered on that event. These depend on how many runners are in the field and, in the case of horseracing, whether or not it is a handicap.

If that sounds complicated, it isn't in reality. The place terms are usually expressed at the bottom of the list of prices. It might, for instance, say each-way a quarter the odds a place 1,2,3. So in the case of the successful £10 each-way bet on the 10-1 winner, the place part returns £35 (£10 stake plus a quarter of 10), giving a total return of £145. If the runner finishes second or third, the return is £35.

Double The most basic multiple bet. Both selections must win and your return is calculated by multiplying their odds. Thus, a £10 double on a 2-1 winner and a 7-1 winner pays £240 (£10 on a 2-1 winner = £30. £30 on a 7-1 winner = £240).

Each-way doubles are accepted, and will provide a return as long as both runners are placed. A £10 each-way double on two 10-1 winners (at terms of a quarter the odds the first three) would return £1,332.50. This is calculated by separating the win double, which pays £1,210 (£10 at 10-1 = £110. £110 at 10-1 = £1,210), from the place part, which pays £122.50 (£10 at 5-2 = £35. £35 at 5-2 pays £122.50).

The bet returns £122.50 if both are placed, or if one wins and the other is placed.

Trebles and accumulators These work in the same way as doubles.

Anything above a treble is known as an accumulator (frequently abbreviated to acca, although bets involving four runners are

READY RECKONER

	£1: Win	⅕ odds	¼ odds
Evens	2.00	1.20	1.25
11-10	2.10	1.22	1.27
6-5	2.20	1.24	1.30
5-4	2.25	1.25	1.31
11-8	2.37	1.27	1.34
6-4	2.50	1.30	1.37
13-8	2.62	1.32	1.41
7-4	2.75	1.35	1.44
15-8	2.87	1.37	1.47
2-1	3.00	1.40	1.50
9-4	3.25	1.45	1.56
5-2	3.50	1.50	1.62
11-4	3.75	1.55	1.69
3-1	4.00	1.60	1.75
100-30	4.33	1.67	1.83
7-2	4.50	1.70	1.87
4-1	5.00	1.80	2.00
9-2	5.50	1.90	2.12
5-1	6.00	2.00	2.25
11-2	6.50	2.10	2.37
6-1	7.00	2.20	2.50
13-2	7.50	2.30	2.62
7-1	8.00	2.40	2.75
15-2	8.50	2.50	2.87
8-1	9.00	2.60	3.00
17-2	9.50	2.70	3.12
9-1	10.00	2.80	3.25
10-1	11.00	3.00	3.50
11-1	12.00	3.20	3.75
12-1	13.00	3.40	4.00
14-1	15.00	3.80	4.50
16-1	17.00	4.20	5.00
18-1	19.00	4.60	5.50
20-1	21.00	5.00	6.00
25-1	26.00	6.00	7.25
33-1	34.00	7.60	9.25

All winning shown are to a one pound stake and returns include the stake. The columns are as follows: Column 1: odds taken. Column 2: amount retured for a win, including stake. Column 3: place dividend when paying ⅕ of the odds, including stake. Column 4: place dividend when paying ¼ of the odds, including stake known as four-folds, five-folds and so on).

There is no limit to how many runners you can put together, although you should be aware that bookmakers have maximum payout limits.

These can range from as little as £10,000 with smaller companies on sports like evening greyhound racing, on which they feel vulnerable to being hit by an orchestrated coup, to £1 million with the main high-street organisations.

You may, of course, be unconcerned about busting a payout limit on the grounds that you would be so happy to win that much that it wouldn't matter if you had to miss out on a few thousand more.

But it would be a shame to be left feeling that your monster win could have been even more spectacular.

Take the story of Ian Cattermole, a Kent bank worker who won £100,000 with a 2002 World Cup wonder wager that should have netted him and his friends even more.

Cattermole had an inspired £10 straight-forecast group double with Stan James on Denmark to beat Senegal and South Korea to beat the United States. Both forecasts obliged but the bet bust the firm's maximum football bet payout.

Cattermole reflected: "The £10 double on 125-1 and 100-1 winners pays £127,250, so I am not too gutted that the Stan James's maximum is £100,000.

"But my friends had the bet for a tenner each and because one of them placed it on behalf of both of them, they are each more than £75,000 worse off.

"Sure, we probably should have checked the limit when we placed the bets. But, silly though it may sound, you don't really think that sort of thing will ever affect one of your bets. Clearly, though, it is well worth checking these things out."

MULTIPLE BETS

Bet	Selections	Doubles	Trebles	4-folds	5-folds	6-folds	7-folds	8-folds	Total
Trixie	3	3	1	•	•	•	•	•	4
Yankee	4	6	4	1	•	•	•	•	11
Canadian	5	10	10	5	1	•	•	•	26
Heinz	6	15	20	15	6	1	•	•	57
Super Heinz	7	21	35	35	21	7	1	•	120
Goliath	8	28	56	70	56	28	8	1	247

Patent 3 selections, 7 bets: Trixie plus 3 singles.

Lucky 15 4 selections, 15 bets: Yankee plus 4 singles.

Union Jack 9 selections, 8 trebles from the square: A B C
D E F
G H I
ABC, DEF, GHI, ADG, BEH, CFI, AEI, CEG.

Other multiples There are ways of backing more than one selection so that you win even if one or more of them lets you down.

They are widely derided as offering poor value, but are nonetheless popular with punters whose aspiration is a big win for a small outlay and some insurance if the majority of his fancies are successful.

The betting snobs may scorn those who bet in this way but the truth of the matter is that a bad-value multiple is as damaging to your pocket as a bad-value single provided you stake sensibly and a good-value yankee is as fiscally beneficial as a good-value single. It is all about ensuring the prices are right.

If you identify four decent-value football teams, all kicking-off at 3pm, nobody should look down on you because you opt to include them in a yankee rather than have four singles.

If the prices are evens, 6-4, 2-1 and 3-1 and you have four £10 singles, your maximum possible return is £115 (for a profit of £75) if they are all successful.

A £4 yankee (costing £4 more) returns £790 (for a profit of £746) if the quartet are all victorious.

Your maximum loss is £24 if only two win

and a decent profit is ensured if three do the business.

If the odds are on your side, there is an argument that betting in multiples is actually to be encouraged, and, besides, who is to say that the man whose aim is to win big for a small outlay is wrong? It all boils down to what you want from your betting.

As I have said before, if you are driven simply by the goal of showing a profit, however small, the easiest way to guarantee one is to calculate how many hours you spend working out your bets and watching them win or lose and then working that many hours behind the counter of your local pub or burger bar.

Pick and mix Bear in mind that you do not have to choose entirely from the multiple menu listed opposite. You can tailor your betting to suit your requirements.

For instance, if you fancy six football teams, there is no obligation to perm them together in a £1 Heinz. Rather than have every combination of doubles, trebles, four-folds, five-folds and the six-fold (57 bets in all, total stake £57), you could, for example, go for 20 £2 trebles, six £2 five-folds and a £5 six-fold. You total outlay is the same and your return is greater if you manage three, four or six winners.

While multiples are not derided in these pages as being the preferred option of the mug punter, it must be stressed that there are few more annoying experiences in betting than when you strongly fancy something which duly wins but you fail to make it pay because, instead of sticking to a single, you opted to be greedy and based a potentially more lucrative multiple bet around it and all the other elements were unsuccessful.

Cross-doubles These are especially popular in golf and can result in large, if occasional, payouts.

getting on

 Related contingencies

avoid mayhem on multiples

A related contingency refers to a multiple bet in which the chances of one or more component of the bet being successful is dependent on another being successful.

One of the best examples of this came in the 2002 World Cup, when punters wanted to back certain players to be the tournament's leading scorer in a double with the team they played for to win the final.

This was an obvious related contingency in that if a team won, one of their players was automatically more likely to top the scoring charts.

Thus, bookmakers offered special double prices. Ronaldo for the Golden Boot and Brazil to win the final, which is what happened, was offered at between 33-1 and 66-1, appreciably shorter than would have been returned if the best prices on each individual component were doubled. It was still an expensive outcome for the bookmakers.

Sometimes there is disagreement over what constitutes a related contingency.

At the start of each season, for instance, fans of the big Premiership clubs will seek to back their team to win various trophies. Should the treble odds on Manchester United to win the Premiership, FA Cup and Champions League be a simple multiplication of their pre-season prices to capture each trophy or should a reduced treble price be offered on the basis that if the team is playing well it stands to reason that their chances of multiple silverware increase?

Most bookmakers treat it as a related contingency and offer 'special' prices, which are shorter than the accumulation of the individual quotes. One oddsmaker was always at pains to reject this practice.

Dermot Keelan of Bet Direct would always insist that a team's chances of winning more than one trophy were not a related contingency and so his firm's doubles and trebles prices were always bigger than the rest.

The most absurd bet involving a related contingency I have encountered was a yankee on a football match. The elements were 0-0 draw, no goalscorer, draw and half-time draw/full-time draw.

What made it even more ludicrous was that the punter who placed the bet had the temerity to ring us at the *Racing Post* to complain when the bookmaker refused to pay him what he was demanding.

Many punters like to pick two or three players in each week's tournaments on the US and European Tours and perm them in cross-doubles. For example, you may choose Tiger Woods (5-1), Jim Furyk (20-1) and Robert Allenby (50-1) in the American event and Darren Clarke (9-1), Paul Casey (16-1) and David Howell (40-1) in the European tournament.

Three players in each event generates nine cross-doubles (three multiplied by three), so your total outlay for £2 win cross-doubles is £18 or £36 if they are £2 each-way cross-doubles.

If Woods and Clarke were successful, your return on win doubles would be £120 but each-way backers could also hope to pick up some place money if more than one of his players reached the first five either side of the Atlantic.

If Allenby and Howell were triumphant, the win punter would swell his wallet to the tune of £4,182.

Cross-trebles and upwards are also accepted, although if you are taking fancy prices you should always be conscious of busting maximum payout limits, even if staking relatively small amounts.

Betting without When an event becomes uncompetitive from a betting aspect because one runner is so dominant, bookmakers often open a market that ignores the red-hot favourite. This is known as betting without.

For instance, if Tiger Woods is five shots clear of the field going into the final round of a tournament, they will bet without Woods. If your selection wins or finishes second to Woods your bet is a winner.

Sometimes, when a golfer is well clear of another at the 54-hole stage and the player in second is himself miles ahead of the remainder of the field, bookmakers will bet without the front two.

priceless punting principles

GOLDEN RULES

THE INTENTION OF THIS BOOK IS to provide you with sound advice to help you achieve the best possible yield from your betting. Each individual sport chapter will contain advice you will hopefully find useful.

Here, though, are some general principles that should stand you in good stead regardless of the sport you are betting on.

BET WHEN YOU WANT TO BET **And** not because a betting opportunity is just about to begin. Your best bets will be struck when you come across a proposition that appeals to you. Your worst bets will be struck because you are rushing to get on before it is too late. For example, you should bet on the FA Cup at the third round stage only if a scan at the best available prices throws up a team you consider to be overpriced, not because it is five minutes to three on the first Saturday afternoon in January and you feel you ought to have a punt on the competition simply because you always do.

Spend anything more than a matter of minutes in a betting shop environment and the point will be hammered home to you. The majority of punters are not betting because they have studied the form and have unearthed a horse that fits their selection

By BRUCE MILLINGTON

Don't drink and bet: it can be a hideously expensive experience

criteria. They are betting because the next race is about to start and are hastily scampering to the counter to get their slip through the scanner before the stalls open.

They are not making considered rational choices and are unlikely to be successful.

On the flip-side of having a bet for the sake of it, never commit the equally cardinal sin of not backing something you fancy.

We have all done it – watching in horror as something we intended to back wins without a penny piece of ours riding on it.

"Oh no! I was going to back that," is the usual lament. I remember saying that to a punting pal, fishing for sympathy, and was met with the following withering response: "Why didn't you, then? Did the police stop you?"

I felt two feet tall and vowed never to make this stupid error again. Not backing a winner is far worse than backing a loser.

SELECT THE BEST WAY OF MAKING IT PAY There are now so many ways of backing the same player, team or whatever that it almost seems to require an advanced mathematics degree to be able to work out how your fancy will earn you the maximum profit if successful.

You might, for instance, think Newcastle have a good chance of performing well against Liverpool. In which case you can have a straight win bet on them, side with them on the Asian handicap, back them on the double-result, have one or more correct score bets, lay Liverpool, buy Newcaslte's supremacy, buy their win index, buy their shirt numbers supremacy, buy their performance index, or sell the time of their first goal. And you would still have other options.

Familiarise yourself with the various different types of bet, weigh up the potential upside and downside and, above all, stake sensibly and in a way that accurately reflects your level of confidence in them.

For a more in-depth explanation of working out how your fancy will return the optimum sum, turn to page 160.

KEEP A RECORD OF YOUR BETS I have to admit that there was a time when I used to feel great discomfort upon hearing a punter preaching about the importance of keeping records. It was something I never did, through a fusion of innate laziness and a fear that if I had my recent betting history thrust before me in all its gory detail it would reveal that I was an even less successful punter than I suspected.

Finally, though, after a particularly bleak spell, I took on board one of the most basic rules a sensible punter imposes on himself and began chronicling all my bets.

I now wonder what I was playing at when I was not writing everything down. Examination of betting records may sound like a boring, and sometimes painful, task but it is nothing of the sort. To be able to pinpoint where

**Watching
the prices**

stay cool if the odds shrink

◇ Keep a level head if you miss the best price

It is annoying to see a price you want to take, but cannot access because it has been shortened by the time you have tried to get on.

Punters generally react in one of two ways when this happens. Some take the revised price regardless because they do not want to have missed out on a winner just because they were forced to accept 11-8 rather than 6-4; others decide not to back their fancy on the fundamental principle that if they have missed the price they were seeking, they do not want to settle for lesser odds.

The proper course of action to take in such instances – and it is hard to remain disciplined and cool-headed when you are frustrated at having missed out on what you thought was a value offer – is to reassess each situation on its own merits rather than either always steaming in at the trimmed price or always going off in a huff.

The old price is history. It has gone. Forget about it. Analyse the new price and ask yourself whether it satisfies your selection criteria.

If you still think it offers you an edge, take it. If you feel the value has gone, wait and see if the price drifts back to an acceptable mark.

This may sound obvious, but it is not always easy to think with logic and clarity when a juicy price has evaded you.

◇ The first price can sometimes be the best

Bookmakers do not issue their prices on future events simultaneously. They enter circulation in dribs and drabs until, eventually, punters have as many to choose from as possible.

Many people believe it makes sense to wait until there is a wide array to select from in the belief that more prices equals greater potential for value, and there is a solid foundation to this school of thought. But the very first prices to see the light of day are the most vulnerable because, in many case, the odds-maker who issued them has not been able to compare them to those of a rival firm.

An example of this came in at the start of the 2004 Cup Final week. IG Index began trading the bookings index (ten points per yellow card, 25 per red card) at 21-24.

It was a rare example of a wrong price from the normally ultra-meticulous spread companies.

Those with a nose for an early bargain stepped in quickly to buy at 24 and were able either to let the bet run or sell at 32, the level at which the market settled closer to kick-off, for a guaranteed eight-point profit.

you are prospering and where you are bleeding money is crucial to your future success. You can use your records to analyse precisely which type of bets are coming off and which are costing you money. Being a good punter is mainly about knowing which potential

golden rules

 Be wary of following gambles

search for the reason

This applies as much to the horse that is punted from 33-1 to 5-1 in the seller at Wolverhampton as it does to the football team that slumps from 6-4 to 4-5 in the hours before kick-off.

Don't just follow the money. Ask yourself why the gamble might have developed.

In the case of the horse, it might come from a stable renowned for landing huge touches in races of this nature, in which case it may be a significant clue as to the outcome.

Then again, it might just be that the off-course bookmakers are manipulating a weak market on a horse they consider has little or no chance in the knowledge that what they have spent on shortening its price will be recouped with dollops of interest from punters jumping on the bandwagon and backing it at vastly deflated odds.

In the case of the football team, that morning's papers may have broken a story about a key player for the opposition being injured, in which case the original odds may be wrong and the gamble could thus have a degree of merit.

Equally, and I would suggest more probably, the team is being smashed into simply because it is a free-scoring outfit in good current form and punters, wallowing in the reassurance that they are part of a large group of people backing the same team, are simply partaking in a safety-in-numbers exercise.

If you detect that this is happening, the best course of action to take is to swim against the tide. The value will invariably lie in the other team, whose odds have lengthened, quite probably for no good reason.

avenues of profit are turning into financial dead ends. You can only truly work out this information by keeping strict records and studying them at regular intervals.

If you really can't be bothered to keep your own records because you consider punting as your hobby and would get an extra job with an insurance company if you wanted to do a bit of pen-pushing, fine. All I can say is that I have found it to be a vitally important exercise, if only to keep tabs on exactly what my overall profit/loss figure is.

ASK WHETHER ALL YOUR GOLDEN RULES ARE NECESSARY **A common trait** among punters is to ban themselves from betting at certain prices. Most commonly, the self-imposed restriction is on odds-on shots, although others will not take less than 2-1.

A few years ago it was considered wise never to back Premiership teams at odds-on when playing away from home, despite a glaring lack of evidence that such a blanket ban was remotely wise. If you are genuinely uncomfortable about taking short prices on the fundamental basis that if the odds-on shot loses it will blow your bank, fair enough. But nobody can say for sure that there is no such thing as a good-value odds-on shot, be they playing home, away or at a neutral venue.

One inexplicable golden rule some punters have concerns whether to take a profit at the earliest possible opportunity. "You will never go skint taking a profit," they say.

This is an absurd viewpoint in my opinion. Religiously letting a bet run when it is going well and religiously taking the money and running when you get the opportunity are equally idiotic rules.

If you buy a cricketer's runs at 50 and the quote rises to 55-60 after a few overs, you may be happy to take the five-point profit. But to suggest you will never go skint by taking such a defensive course of action is only true if you never have another bet.

What if the next two cricketers you buy are out for a duck? Taking the three trades as a whole you are most certainly well on your way to being skint. Moreover, by jumping out of a bet early on you are playing the spread twice and are thus a loser in the value stakes.

Surely, the only golden rule concerning trading in-running you can possibly have is this: judge each trade on its merits. If you have bought a cricketer's runs at 50 and believe the new price is too high – perhaps your man has played and missed outside off-stump a few times or the ball is swinging more than you anticipated – sell. But if he has got his eye in and is looking comfortable, what is the point of closing the bet, a bet you made initially because you thought the player would get runs? The beauty of betting in-running is that you have a choice. It is crazy to deny yourself that privilege thanks to an unnecessary golden rule.

DON'T SHOW BLIND FAITH IN YOUR ANTE-POST SELECTIONS *Racing Post*
readers occasionally criticise us for tipping against a player or team we have already recommended backing for long-term success.

This is most common in snooker and tennis. For instance, we may have advised a bet on Andy Roddick to win Wimbledon but, come his quarter-final match, have reached the conclusion that the value lies with Roddick's opponent and advocated a wager on him instead. "What is that all about?" the reader will demand. "If you tipped Roddick at the start you can't start riding another horse halfway through the race."

Why not? If, subsequent to our original advice, Roddick's last-eight foe has shown better form and is overpriced it would be remiss of us not to advise getting on the best-value player.

So it is with everyone's punting. Each event has to be analysed using the most up-to-date information available and should not be clouded by an earlier trade on the same event.

In other words, if you have backed Millwall to win the Championship, you are not obliged to stick by them come what may. On a match-by-match basis they may represent what you consider to be value – this should be especially true in the early part of the season given that, if you dispute the bookmaker's assessment of the team's long-term prospects you are also likely to disagree with their match prices – but you should not wear blinkers that lead you to

golden rules

Never bet when drunk

I did it at Catford dogs one night and, when I awoke the next morning and saw the state of my wallet, assumed I had been mugged on the notoriously treacherous walk from the track to the bus stop. It was only when my memory started functioning again that I realised my potlessness was self-imposed.

the conclusion that they will always be value or, indeed, are never worth opposing.

Evaluate each proposition on its current merits. Be prepared to admit an earlier long-term wager you struck may have been wrong.

Stubbornness and intransigence are characteristics no successful punter possesses.

BE RECEPTIVE TO THE VIEWS OF OTHERS, BUT DON'T BE SWAYED TOO EASILY Just as bad as not backing a winner that you fancied is not backing a winner because you let someone either talk you out of making the bet or, worse, still, into backing something else.

It is interesting, if not always beneficial, to hear the views of others on a betting event you have an opinion on. Sometimes you will pick up a key point you had overlooked. Other times you will hear a theory you disagree with, thus strengthening your belief that you have made the right choice.

What you should never do is fall into the trap of believing the person whose view conflicts with yours is probably right.

If you have confidence in your judgement you will be immune from this pitfall, but there are times, especially when you are on a bad run, when you are vulnerable to latching on to someone else's opinion in the belief that they are probably in better form than you.

This is a particular risk when the person expresses his views in vehement tones. If you find yourself sold on a proposition other than the one you were planning to back simply because you are impressed by the way the person is stating his case, you should switch off and stick to your guns. Oh, and don't answer the door to salesmen. You are probably just the sort of person who would be coerced into spending a fortune on a set of encyclopaedias.

The best punters quietly go about their business without telling the whole world who they fancy and why.

corruption and skulduggery

IS IT SAFE?

ONE OF THE WIDELY-PERCEIVED advantages sports betting has over punting on horses and dogs concerns the issue of integrity.

Put simply, many people believe sport is less open to corruption than racing.

There are others who vehemently oppose this view. "I would much rather bet on a dumb animal," they say. But the idea that because horses and greyhounds do not have the capacity to manipulate results by themselves it must make those sports more trustworthy betting mediums than, say, a tennis match between two humans who could, if they so desired, conjure up a pre-determined result holds no water.

That is not to suggest racing involving thoroughbreds or greyhounds is rotten to the core by any means. But the basic fact is that both are organised for the specific purpose of stimulating gambling which, in itself, has to leave them open to corrupt influences from those seeking to profit from rule-bending.

Other sports have become what they are today for a different reason – the fundamental desire of one human or group of humans to test themselves against their fellow man.

Football is all about many things, according to those who spout its many clichés. It's all

By BRUCE MILLINGTON and STEVE DAVIES

Disgraced: cricket legend Hansie Cronje went from hero to villain

about the three points, it's all about winning, it's all about opinions, it's all about entertaining the fans. What nobody ever says is: "It's all about landing an almighty touch with the bookies."

The fact that football betting, and betting on a wide variety of other sports for that matter, has become so popular is partly because those who bet on it feel comfortable in the knowledge that everyone on the pitch is trying his hardest.

In horseracing, by contrast, a large proportion of the public swallow the popular theory that there is something innately fishy about it. That view is largely borne out of ignorance and a sense of suspicion that comes from backing too many losers, but it exists all the same.

It is tiresome to hear people who blindly defend racing's integrity. Yes, the sport is probably far less corrupt than the man on the street might suspect, but those who make their livelihood in the racing industry should stop and ask themselves whether something untoward has actually taken place before automatically jumping to its defence every time a whiff of skulduggery wafts across the sport.

Corruption in sport is notoriously hard to prove, as this chapter goes on to illustrate, and that applies as much to racing as to table tennis, but almost everybody who has spent a meaningful period of time working in the betting industry will have little doubt that compared to horse and dog racing other sports are, to a greater or lesser degree, far less tainted by corruption.

That is not to say, of course, that incidents of betting-related cheating in sports not involving quadrupeds have not taken place.

You would have to have walked this earth with a blindfold and earplugs for the past 15 years to avoid coverage of high-profile cases of sporting skulduggery, the common factor in which has been a desire to take the bookies to the cleaners.

And where else can one start on the subject of corruption in sport than cricket?

It was not so long ago that if you wanted to uncover corruption on a massive scale the last place you would have bothered looking was in the respectable, upstanding world of cricket.

But towards the end of the 20th century the noble sport's impeccable reputation was dragged into the gutter and beyond as a series of betting scandals rocked it to its core.

World-class players were linked with a string of allegations so serious that many punters had no hesitation in deciding they would rather burn their money than bet on cricket.

Some were cleared, others were caught. But by far the highest-profile cricketing crook was Hansie Cronje, the South African who was hailed a hero for so long by his people but died in disgrace at the age of 32.

Cronje captained his country from the age of 24 and led the Proteas to 27 victories in 53 Tests, making him the fourth most successful captain in Test cricket history.

But his love of making runs was matched by his love of making money and when the match-fixers knocked at his door, Cronje did not slam it in their face.

As is so often the case in such murky episodes as this, it took just one revelation to open the lid on a breathtaking litany of greed and dishonesty. That revelation came from the Delhi police, who claimed to have a recording of a mobile phone conversation between Cronje and an Indian bookmaker regarding the one-day series between South Africa and India in March 2000.

The voice alleging to be Cronje's divulged information about the team, including a suggestion that off-spinner Derek Crookes would open the bowling later in the series and that Herschelle Gibbs should not score more than 20 runs in a match. Gibbs did indeed score 19 in the identified match in Faridabad, while Crookes opened the bowling in the final match and later admitted his astonishment at being asked to do so.

Four days after denying any wrongdoing, Cronje admitted to not having been "entirely honest" and down came the house of cards.

Nelson Mandela personally guaranteed immunity from prosecution for Cronje if he agreed to spill the beans and his three days of testimony to the King Commission were spellbinding and contemptible in equal measure.

His international colleagues Pat Symcox and Gibbs had already tarnished Cronje's reputation, Symcox by revealing that as long ago as 1996 the Proteas had discussed taking £200,000 to throw a one-day international in Bombay, while Gibbs confirmed he had agreed to Cronje's offer of £10,000 to score under 20 runs in a match.

Cronje eventually admitted to having taken

uncommon knowledge

Notorious incidents

snooker star knew the score

Other sports have been touched by controversy down the years.

Snooker star Peter Francisco was banned for five years for his part in a betting scam at the Embassy World Snooker Championship in 1995. Betting had been suspended on his first-round duel with Jimmy White long before the players had entered the Crucible arena after a flood of money for a 10-2 scoreline. Outcome? White won 10-2.

Rugby isn't immune, either. Former Wales international Allan Bateman was offered £5,000 by a bookmaker to help fix the Five Nations match against Ireland in 1990 but he rejected the approach.

And rugby league is only now coming to terms with the extraordinary revelation that Sean Long and Martin Gleeson bet on their own team, St Helens, to lose a Super League match against Bradford in April 2004. Saints, beset by injuries to key players, including Long himself, were indeed thrashed.

Even a women's badminton quarter-final in Indonesia in 2000 was the subject of a match-fixing investigation, so the scope for skulduggery stretches right across the sporting spectrum. But, for all that, most sports punters know that the vast majority of what they are betting on is perfectly straight and above board.

around £100,000 from bookmakers for information, though there are many who believe the figure was far higher.

We will probably never know. Cronje, who left the King Commission in tears and in disgrace, was banned from all cricketing activity for life and died in a plane crash in June 2002. Plenty of people suspect he was murdered.

Cronje wasn't the only world-famous cricketer to suffer a life ban for finding the lure of easy money from insatiable bookmakers irresistible.

The same fate befell Salim Malik in May 2000 after Australian stars Shane Warne, Tim May and Mark Waugh alleged the former Pakistan captain offered them £75,000 to underperform during a Test in Karachi in 1994.

Not that Warne and Waugh were blameless.

Both men were themselves fined after receiving money from a Calcutta bookie known only as John, for information about pitch and weather conditions during their tour of Pakistan and Sri Lanka in the same year.

The unholy trinity of ex-captains banned for life was completed by Mohammad Azharuddin. He and fellow player Ajay Sharma received their punishments from the Board of Cricket Control for India after Azharuddin had admitted fixing three one-day internationals, though he strenuously denied being paid by a bookmaker to do so.

In the fall-out from that case, Ajay Jadeja was banned for five years though he later cleared his name, but more sinister was the response from Azharuddin. "Match-fixing simply cannot be a one-man show," he said. "This is a game which involves 11 players. If a team fails, it is spectacularly unfair to single out one person. What I am trying to say is that unless the entire team is part of the conspiracy, match-fixing cannot take place."

The once gentlemanly game of cricket has been severely tarnished by these high-profile episodes and the upshot of so many investigations is that many more matches, particularly on the Asian sub-continent and in Sharjah though also closer to home, have come under the microscope.

Other sportsmen and women in other sports aren't immune to the notion of getting rich by foul means as well as fair. Football, for example, can date its betting shame back to 1915 when a Football League inquiry concluded the First Division match that ended Manchester United 2 Liverpool 0 had been 'squared' by the players who had bet on the outcome. This intriguing story is brilliantly told in Graham Sharpe's book *Free The Manchester United One* (Robson Books).

Fifty years later, and far more seriously, ten players were given jail sentences for their part in match-fixing, though this time it was the bookmakers who were being defrauded.

The ringleader, journeyman professional Jimmy Gauld, organised large groups of fellow pros to bet on certain matches, throw them and then collect. In those days of bookies' coupons being printed in advance, the weight of money didn't alter the odds so the fixes were always profitable for Gauld and his cohorts, among them Sheffield Wednesday and England aces Tony Kay and Peter Swan.

The guilty men took their chances to bolster their own wages, which were nothing like the sums top footballers of today can attract.

Greed was also the motive in 1919 when the all-conquering Chicago White Sox threw baseball's World Series after accepting money from betting syndicates. 'Shoeless' Joe Jackson and his buddies earned about $5,000 from these rings and had few qualms about taking the cash because they believed they were not getting a decent wage from the club's owners.

Football's most sensational link with betting syndicates, however, came in 1997 when household names Bruce Grobbelaar, John Fashanu and Hans Segers stood trial charged with match-fixing.

The Sun said it had collected "overwhelming evidence" that the three men had been rigging matches, with Grobbelaar accused of taking £40,000 from a betting syndicate in the Far East to ensure Liverpool lost to Newcastle in 1993, and blowing a chance of making £125,000 by accidentally making a 'sensational' save against Manchester United.

Grobbelaar insisted that all he had done was forecast results, not fix them, and a compelling trial in Winchester ended with all three being acquitted.

Football in Italy and Greece has been investigated recently, with several Serie A matches the subject of suspicious betting patterns. It has reached the stage where many

controversial market ditched

Bookmakers have generally amended their rules over such incidents as floodlights going out, while another betting opportunity which it was feared could also have been exploited by the unscrupulous was nipped in the bud very quickly – time of the first throw-in.

The time of the first throw-in was among the more inventive markets offered by Sporting Index and in most matches was pitched around the 60-70 seconds mark.

But Eric Cantona's last appearance for Manchester United at Old Trafford in May 1997 was memorable as much for West Ham striker Paul Kitson kicking the ball into touch straight from the start as for the Frenchman's fond farewell.

Rumours flew that a touch had been landed but as Hammers manager Harry Redknapp furiously asserted: "Paul Kitson doesn't know how to bet. And anyway, how do you make sure you win the toss?"

The market was ditched shortly afterwards.

UK layers don't even bother pricing up matches towards the back end of the Italian season having had their fingers burned too often by mutually-convenient scorelines.

Floodlight failures have also directed the spotlight at big gambling syndicates in the Far East. Among the most notorious examples was a match between Tenerife and Athletic Bilbao in Spain's Primera Liga in 2002.

Bookmakers across Asia reported suspicious betting patterns on the game with home team Tenerife heavily opposed in match betting in the hours before kick-off. The islanders were deep in relegation trouble, knowing that only a victory for them and a loss by rivals Mallorca would keep them in La Liga.

The floodlights failed at half-time and Tenerife were left in the dark as they waited for news from Mallorca. The game only resumed once it was clear that Mallorca had won 2-1 and so Tenerife, who were themselves 2-1 up, went into the second half knowing they had already been relegated. They let in two goals after the restart to lose 3-2.

when controversy kicks in

CHAOS THEORY

ONE THING PUNTERS MUST ALWAYS remember is that the vast majority of sports were not invented with betting in mind. Indeed, kick out horse and greyhound racing and all the computer-generated virtual non-sense that bookmakers serve up nowadays, and there is not a single sport that was designed purely for punters.

By PAUL KEALY

Big deal, you might say. Actually it is when it comes to betting disputes because while there are rules that cover pretty much every eventuality with horses and dogs, that is not necessarily so when it comes to other sports, which can lead to controversy and betting disputes.

Indeed, even when there are rules that should cover a certain situation, there can still be an almighty furore, with punters quickly claiming they are being short-changed by bookmakers who make decisions that suit them best.

WHO SCORED? Goalscorer betting is a constant source of controversy and you could pick from dozens of examples down the years, but there was a landmark case in 2000 which finally forced bookmakers into action.

In January 2000 the scoring in Everton's 2-2 Goodison Park draw with Leicester, shown

Hard to tell: Uefa gave Wayne Rooney this goal but layers ruled an own-goal

live on Sky, was opened on 15 minutes when Toffees defender David Weir's 20-yard shot took a violent deflection off striker Don Hutchison to leave City keeper Pegguy Arphexad stranded.

Weir was a 40-1 shot to score first and Hutchison 8-1, and most firms ruled in favour of Weir, whose initial attempt on goal it was.

Super Soccer were the only firm to pay out exclusively on Hutchison as their rules at the time stated that goalscorer bets are settled on the player the TV company broadcasting the match decides has scored. However, Totesport, adopting exactly the same ruling, initially paid out on Weir, before eventually settling up on both. Crazy, eh?

Thankfully, the uproar that followed finally gave bookies the kick up the backside they needed.

At a meeting initiated by the Independent Betting Arbitration Service (IBAS), all major firms agreed to abide by the judgement of Britain's main news agency, the Press Association (PA), for disputed goals.

At the time IBAS's Chris O'Keeffe said: "A single criterion adopted throughout the betting industry would not actually remove the element of controversy inherent to situations where more than one player can claim a goal.

"It would, however, put an end to the immense sense of grievance felt by punters who wonder why they should be settled as a loser when other punters, with the same selection, are settled as winners with bookmakers using different settlement criteria."

It was a good decision by the industry, but it would be a lie to suggest that it marked the end of goalscorer disputes. And the water becomes further muddied when football's ruling bodies get involved. Take the Euro 2004 tournament and the match between England and Switzerland.

Bookmakers are never slow these days to come forward with special markets and some firms were offering prices on Wayne Rooney to score two or more goals in the match.

Having already bagged the first, Rooney launched a thunderous drive on 75 minutes which hit the post, struck the back of Switzerland keeper Jorg Stiel's head on the rebound and went into the net.

The PA ruled, correctly, that it was an own goal, but Uefa, quickly realising that Rooney had become one of the stars of the tournament, awarded it to the Englishman.

Their ruling had no effect on bookmakers' match settlement as the disputed strike was neither the first nor the last goal of the match, but the long-term story was different. All firms were betting on the winner of the Golden Boot for the tournament's top scorer and they had to give the contentious goal to Rooney in that market as Uefa were handing out the award.

Had Rooney gone on to score two more, he

would have had six and beaten the gambled-on Milan Baros, who finished with five. Theoretically there could have been punters who backed Rooney to score twice against Switzerland and lost because his second was an own goal, but also backed Baros for the Golden Boot and lost due to the fact that Rooney's second in the Switzerland game stood with Uefa. Thankfully it didn't happen.

But football is a long way from being the only sport to give bookmakers and punters nightmares.

UNEASY RYDER Every two years in the Ryder Cup golf punters get caught out in the singles matches on the final Sunday. Once either the USA or Europe have reached the 14.5 points they require to win the match the rest of the action becomes meaningless and there have been several early concessions from players who were behind with a couple of holes to play, or generously conceded putts on which thousands of pounds could rest, to ensure a match was halved.

The President's Cup between the USA and an International side is gaining in popularity all the time, but did little to endear itself to the betting public in 2003 when the contest in South Africa produced the one result that the rules said couldn't happen – a tie.

The match went into a play-off between Tiger Woods and Ernie Els, who were still level after three holes. With darkness falling, captains Jack Nicklaus and Gary Player agreed on a draw in the interests of fair play, causing untold havoc among Britain's layers.

Many simply voided all bets, while others settled under dead-heat rules (whereby punters are paid out at the odds they took but for only half their original stake) – bad news for in-running punters taking long odds-on.

chaos theory

 The importance of unity

punters? what punters?

The spread firms deserve plenty of credit for having done far more than their fixed-odds counterparts to ensure that bets are settled the same way industry-wide.

Shortly after the infamous Sri Lanka-India match in the 1995 World Cup, the Sports Spread Betting Association (SSBA) was formed and since then all account-holders with any of the firms have been trading under virtually identical rules across the industry.

The failure of the fixed-odds firms to adopt an industry-wide set of rules will always lead to bad feeling. I have particularly bad memories of the 1996 Pebble Beach Pro-Am, having tipped Jeff Maggert at 40-1 in the *Racing Post* and put my money where my mouth was.

The American led after two rounds, but bad weather forced the tournament to be abandoned. Under such circumstances a winner would normally be declared, but because the event was played over three different courses with varying degrees of difficulty, organisers decided against this.

Maggert was 40-1 with Hills and Stan James. I chose Hills and they, like the majority of firms, voided all bets. Stan James, however, along with Surrey, were hamstrung by their own rules and had to pay out. They nobly avoided a serious PR disaster by voiding all other bets, although their rules stated that a minimum of only 36 holes had to be played for bets to stand.

I was livid, mostly with Hills, and it took ages for me to concede that they had had no choice but to void all wagers and it was just a case of bad luck that in a toss-of-the-coin situation I had picked the 'wrong' firm.

Hills, of course, had done nothing wrong (and neither had Stan James according to their rules) but mine was typical of the immediate reaction from a punter in such circumstances, namely: those bastard bookies are settling in a manner which suits them best.

It's not true, though, because the last thing bookmakers want to do is alienate customers with unpopular decisions. But they have to abide by their own rules and it is up to every punter to know what those rules are, a lesson I learned the hard way.

I'd imagine that I am like the majority of punters in that every rule-book ever sent to me by a bookmaker has found its way into the same day's trash. It's stupid, really, as punter ignorance is often the reason behind so many disputes.

But whatever bookmakers do, there will always be cases of punters feeling hard done by and comments from some mainstream journalists do little to ram home the point that we are betting in mediums that were not designed with us in mind.

Take the Mirror's Neil Fullerton, who after the 2003 Presidents Cup wrote: "Woods and Els should have been forced to play on Monday to decide all outright bets."

No, they shouldn't have.

The Presidents Cup is a sporting event. It wasn't sponsored by a bookmaker and the interests of punters were never considered. That's how it should be and it's something we should always bear in mind.

CRICKET CONFUSION In the 1999 cricket World Cup the different settling terms for the semi-final between South Africa and Australia infuriated punters. Both sides were all out for 213 in a dramatic encounter at Edgbaston and, between them, bookmakers came up with four different ways of treating bets.

Most voided, but because Australia qualified for the final due to their finishing ahead of South Africa in the Super Six stage, there was confusion among others.

Bet Direct made the noble gesture of paying out on Australia, while voiding bets on South Africa, Ladbrokes settled bets on Australia on a dead-heat basis but voided on South Africa, while Hills made the most controversial ruling of all by deciding to pay out on Australia and treating bets on South Africa as losers.

Something similar had happened three years earlier in another World Cup semi-final in Calcutta that many spread punters are sure to remember.

Sri Lanka were on the verge of victory, having scored 251 and reduced India to 120-8, when Indian fans started to riot. With fires raging in the stands and Indian fans lobbing bottles on to the pitch, referee Clive Lloyd was left with no choice but to order the players off the field, but he declared Sri Lanka the winners.

That was how fixed-odds bets were settled, but the spread firms voided all trades, meaning buyers of Sri Lanka supremacy, who looked like picking up in excess of 100 points' profit, were left empty-handed. Sellers, of course, got out of jail.

This caused almighty uproar with punters, but at least the spread firms were consistent and they were covered by a rule which stated that all bets would be void if a team did not complete 90 per cent of their overs (India had faced 34.1 of 50).

easy betting just a click away

ON THE INTERNET

IF YOU PREFER TO TRY TO MAKE reasoned betting decisions without the banal chatter of numbers games in the background, an aged bore telling you of his infallible BAGS system and a curious aroma of cigarettes and alcohol filling the air, then internet betting might be for you.

By PHIL AGIUS

But the clichéd reasons why some are happy to desert the happy camaraderie of betting shops for the solitude of their own homes is only a tiny factor why smarter bettors are better off using the net to strike their wagers.

Net betting has grown with the web itself. That is to say, from humble and unheralded beginnings in the mid-1990s it has spread like wildfire to become a major influence on our lives. Bookmakers' early attempts to utilise the net came largely as a vehicle to advertise their wares, listing prices and providing the contact numbers for their telebetting services and addresses for those pokey old shops.

As the technology improved the first tentative steps towards online betting were taken and since the turn of the millennium it has been downhill all the way, with internet turnover going through the roof and accounting for an ever-increasing percentage of firms' turnover. The whole process has now gone full circle with Blue Square, originally an

Clicking the winners: betting on the net is the method of choice for many

enterprising net-only bookmaker, first opening a phone service and then branching out into betting shops and even taking up rails pitches at racecourses.

So now that almost every traditional firm has a live website, why should uninitiated punters start moving their mice rather than lifting a receiver or popping down the high street?

PRICE COMPARISON SITES Arguably the best offshoot of internet betting is the development of odds-comparison sites which enable punters to obtain the best available price for their chosen selection.

These sites simply show every event currently being quoted by their participant firms, rather like the *Racing Post*'s Pricewise boxes, and highlight which company offers the best odds on each selection. In the long run this alone should improve the return of all online investors.

Four principal sports odds-comparison sites are www.racingpost.co.uk/sport (formerly

on the internet

**Betting
in peace**

nobody to watch over you

Believe it or not, some people don't want the world to know they are betting. It's hard to comprehend, but some husbands and wives would rather their partner didn't find out exactly what percentage of the weekly budget (however reasonable) they are staking on a bet and, more to the point, some people think it's none of anyone else's business what they choose to spend their money on.

From the comfort of your own home, there will be no-one else looking over your shoulder at your betting slip or listening as you read out your bet.

Instead you can quietly type in the details of your selected wager and the transaction will go through. Neither will a cashier make a funny remark when you collect your slip (have they ever made a really funny one?), nor will the computer change its tone if you request a particularly small or unusual stake.

Best of all, net betting affords you the opportunity to have a silly, maybe small-stakes, maybe potentially life-changing multiple or to back a rank outsider without having to summon up the courage to state your intentions out loud to another human being.

known as Smartbet), www.oddschecker.co.uk, www.easyodds.com and www.bestbetting.com. At the time of writing, the sites compared between ten and 24 bookmakers' prices, plus betting exchange and spread quotes. All contain some level of editorial content as well as mere prices. A feature of these sites which is mutually beneficial to punters, comparison sites and bookmakers is the click-through feature. This simply means that punters can click on the price in the table they are interested in, enter their login details on a form and place a bet straight away without having to visit the firm's site independently.

SPEED It's arguable whether net betting is in fact quicker than phone betting but there's no denying it's a lot faster than hotfooting it to a betting shop in your hour of need.

Depending on how user-friendly the site is you should be able to find the selection you

on the internet

 The cooling-off period

As quick as it can be, all internet bets give you a chance to change your mind after requesting the bet. Every site asks you to confirm your selection and stake and requires a secondary click of the mouse before your funds are committed. You can, in theory, wait as long as you like before deciding whether to proceed, although you might run into a change in price of your selection or even the start of the event if you dally too long.

want to back, enter your stake and confirm your bet within a minute or two.

An advantage of net betting is that the speed of the transaction is largely down to you, the user. While a simple single bet by phone can be faster, around 35 to 45 seconds even allowing for bank clearance, that does depend on the lottery that is getting a call centre employee who can spell your name, find the event you are interested in and get your stake right first time. Computers are much maligned by some but they seldom have a problem with regional accents either!

RESEARCH OPPORTUNITY What better place to do last-minute fact-checking or extra research into your event than the internet? If it strikes you in the middle of a crowded betting shop that you haven't checked the course form of a certain golfer or looked for the team news of a rugby league side there's not much you can do about it except abandon the bet entirely or place it without knowing the facts.

If the same thought occurs to you while placing your web-based wagers, simply open up another browser window, select an appropriate site and the missing information will be at your fingertips.

WE NEVER CLOSE The names of some sites give you a clue as to their opening hours and, as Bet247 (now part of Bet Direct) and Bet365 suggest, you can bet on the net all day, every day of the year. Save for occasional short periods of routine maintenance (usually during the small hours of the night) the opportunity to place a bet will always be there. Some firms' phone operations, notably Stan James, Chandler and Bet365, are open around the clock but all-day betting is largely a web-based phenomenon never dreamed of in the days when shops ruled the scene.

on the internet

 Getting the right site

keeping safe and secure

Established name or big-value new boys? Who you choose to place your online bets with is, ultimately, solely at your own discretion. Find a site or group of sites you are comfortable with, in terms of value, security and ease of use and get to know them as well as you can in order to find what you want in a hurry should the need arise.

A valuable tip is to make sure you can remember your passwords. Obviously keeping your passwords and usernames written together in the same place is a big no-no for security reasons, but take whatever steps you can to keep on top of your various login details.

Failure to get your password right in three attempts can result in you being locked out of some sites, whose security systems will be triggered as they think you are trying to gain access to the account illegally.

And getting your locked account back online can be more trouble than you might anticipate, necessitating an exchange of emails and probably a phone call too to confirm your credentials. The time taken to get back into your account could, of course, result in you missing out on the bet.

SPOT A WINNER Merely browsing around a website can help you find the opportunity to back a winner you might not have known existed if you were betting by the more traditional methods. Hundreds of bets are listed on the sites, with prices constantly updated. In shops the range of prices you see is limited to the number of monitors available and the number of markets the public address system can mention.

INSTANT PAYOUT Reaction times vary across the betting village but some firms are particularly quick at putting returns back in your available-to-bet pool after the event has finished. Better still, it takes seconds to discover if you have been paid, while phone punters are left to rely on the arrival of bank statements and shop clients might have to wait until morning to collect what is due to them.

on the internet

Correct connection

The reliability of your internet connection is a rather important factor as a crash of your browser or the betting website at a crucial time can lead to frustration all round. The problems are not as serious as in the formative days of net betting but some site servers can still be slow at particularly busy periods. The advent of broadband has improved the reliability and speed of internet links compared to the slower dial-up method and if you can afford it, broadband is advised for net punters, particularly those who want to make the most of the betting exchanges.

Not everything is hunky-dory in the world of internet betting, however. Here are some reasons why punters might prefer to keep modern technology out of their betting.

IT'S NOT VIRTUAL, IT'S REALITY The antiseptic atmosphere of a PC could lead some to forget that it is real money they are betting with rather than some abstract commodity which rises or falls on a computer screen with no real impact on their lives. Net punters would be advised to think of handing over the amount they have selected in ten pound notes each time they prepare to click the 'confirm bet' button. If you wouldn't hand it over to a shop cashier, don't bet it on the net.

WHO ARE YOU? Beware of betting with any old firm whose website you happen across. There are quite enough well-established companies in business online now for punters not to have to chance their arm with some small-time cowboys who might disappear as quickly as they came. Several net betting enterprises have fallen by the wayside and though such happenings are now more scarce, you don't want one taking your funds down with them when they sink.

A BALANCING ACT The only way to ensure you will have funds in your accounts when you might need to place a bet in a hurry is to have a serviceable amount of cash in your account, presumably at least up to the level of your usual maximum bet. But assuming that most value-seeking punters would want to have a choice of firms to bet with in order to get the best price for their selections, that means leaving what could be a sizeable amount of cash lying dormant in sites across the globe. And all of it is sitting in the firms' bank accounts, making money for them, rather than in yours, working for you.

simply a better way to bet

ON THE EXCHANGES

EXCHANGES HAVE ALTERED THE punting landscape forever and for those of you who have yet to embrace this relatively new but now hugely successful and popular concept the message is simple: you don't know what you're missing.

By PAUL KEALY

I know several people who declare no interest in ever getting involved in exchange betting, their reasons varying from a general distrust of betting by computer, to not wanting to get picked off by the shrewdies, to the 'I'd much rather take the money from a bookmaker' mentality.

All these standpoints are complete nonsense and serve only to ensure that punters swerving the exchanges are at a disadvantage to the rest of us. Those not prepared to take the risk of putting their bank details into a PC are the same people who for years have been happy to stick their bank cards into a computer in the middle of a high street to withdraw cash.

The preference for winning money from a mainstream bookmaker is almost too stupid for words. For while contempt for the high street layers is all very well, you are in fact trying to take on people who have spent their lives in market-making and, unless you are extremely good (in which case you risk having

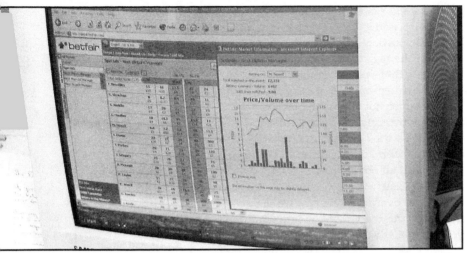

New face of betting: how Betfair presented the Blackburn manager market

your account closed down or your bet size limited), you are going to lose in the long run, no matter how much pleasure you get from the occasional pick-up.

The theory about being picked off by those who are more knowledgeable than you has been given some weight by Betfair, the largest exchange, who early in 2004 adopted the rather daft slogan Sharp Minds Betfair. The implication is that you need to be a pretty cute operator to be an exchange punter.

And though Betfair probably won't be worried about getting the odd thing wrong during their spectacular transformation from tiny internet start-up to giant of the betting world, the suggestion could not be more ridiculous. Yes, there are users out there who have made vast sums out of exchange betting, but they do so only because they are betting against a large number of punters who adopt the same flawed characteristics (poor judgement and lack of discipline) that made them losers with the high street firms.

For people to win, others must lose, and while a figure of 15 per cent winners to 85 per cent losers has been bandied about, I would not be surprised if the losers made up an even bigger proportion.

One of the biggest advantages of exchange punting is that you sometimes find yourself betting against mugs that otherwise would have no option but to lose their money to bookmakers. Obviously an exchange doesn't want to advertise the fact that the majority of its users are losers, but it is true all the same – as it is with all bookmakers.

Examples of stupidity and greed reveal themselves every day and now we can exploit them like the traditional bookmakers have done for decades.

There really is no argument for not becoming an exchange player and once you start to become a more sophisticated user, the numerous advantages will soon make themselves clear.

A BRIEF HISTORY OF EXCHANGES

A creationist would have it that because the world we live in fits us so nicely it must have been designed by a superior being. Well, if there was such a thing as a punting god, his starting model would have been a betting exchange.

Instead, we had to wait for the brilliant mind of Andrew Black, who is considered something of a deity by punters whose lives have been turned upside down since his concept, Betfair, arrived on the scene in June 2000.

There are other betting exchanges like Betdaq, Sporting Options and Backandlay fighting for your pound, but they are mere plankton to the big blue whale that is Betfair, and until such time that the company's market domination is threatened we can supplant the word exchange with Betfair.

HOW IT WORKS Once you have opened an account, simply by following the easy-

---

on the exchanges

 The price is right

However good or bad you are at betting, you will be better on an exchange even if you ignore all the extra advantages and remain a backer pure and simple.

The main difference between betting with a bookie and on an exchange is the prices you will get.

The vast majority of the time an exchange price will beat that of a bookie hands down. If you win big, you will win bigger. If you lose big, you will still lose big, it will just to take you longer to run out of money. It really is up to you how you fare.

to-understand instructions, you are ready to go. At first the process of placing a bet may be slightly daunting, but it should not take a lot of getting used to. And once you have cleared stage one, one of the main beauties of exchange betting – the number of options available to you – will become apparent.

Here is a simple guide to placing a bet on Betfair (the other exchanges work in roughly the same way):

TAKING A PRICE Once you have navigated your way to the event you are interested in, you will be confronted by a list of runners with six columns of prices next to each contender (see illustration on page 73).

The first three, reading from left to right, are the 'back' prices, with the furthest right of these (on a blue background) showing the biggest price currently available to back and, beneath it, the amount of money on offer at that price.

The next three sets of prices are the 'lay' prices, but this time the one on the left (on a pink background) shows the shortest price being asked for (best available to layers).

If you are looking to back and the price on the blue background is acceptable, simply click on it, type in the amount of money you wish to place where prompted, press submit and away you go. Betfair will then process your bet and tell you whether or not it has been matched. Usually it will be, but sometimes the price will have been snapped up by someone else in the short time it has taken for your bet to be processed. Always check that your bet has been matched.

ASKING FOR A PRICE You can also ask for a better price than is available in the blue box if you believe your selection is under-priced or think that it will drift. Just click on the blue box price and then insert your chosen odds and stake. Again, this needs to be monitored. If you have asked for a price, your selection has to drift in order for your bet to be matched. If it does not, your bet will not count once the event starts.

LAYING SELECTIONS TO LOSE You may

have an opinion on a football match, a golf event or any other sport that does not involve picking a winner. You may simply believe that a certain runner is too short and on Betfair you can back that opinion with hard cash simply by laying it. If you want to lay £20 at 4-1, £80 will be deducted from your betting balance, with that sum, plus the £20 stake, paid back in if you are proved correct.

The term 'play bookmaker' is often used when discussing the laying of bets on an exchange and has led to calls from the big bookmaking firms for all individual layers to be licensed. Betfair's Tony Calvin believes this is a red herring, though. He said: "We are the bookmakers. We just allow punters to bet on something not to happen as well as to happen. The definition of a bookmaker is someone that takes people's money at a given price and then pays out after the result is known. Betfair does that, and we are the book-maker. Even the Government has admitted recently that laying and bookmaking are not the same."

CALCULATING THE BEST ODDS All

bets on Betfair are subject to commission, so though you will get better value more often than not, it will not always be the case. Depending on how much you bet, commission ranges from two to five per cent. You have to be a huge punter or a professional bookmaker to get anywhere near two per cent, and most Betfair punters will pay between four and five per cent commission on winning bets.

All Betfair prices are shown in decimals, so

on the exchanges

The key advantages

margins in punters' favour

Why, some may ask, should exchange players pay commission at all? The days of taxable betting are long gone. If I place a bet with a bookmaker I get paid in full to the odds I have taken.

The answer is pretty simple. A bookmaker's intention is that you lose, and he will frame a market around a profit margin, which means if he manages to lay an even book, he will win whatever the result.

For instance, if all three outcomes in a football match are equally likely, the true odds should be 2-1 home side, 2-1 away side, 2-1 draw. A bookie would go something like 7-4 home, 7-4 away, 7-4 draw. Odds of 7-4 equate to a percentage of 36.4 so this gives a book of 109.2 per cent or a 9.2 per cent profit margin for the layer. If three different punters had £40 on the separate outcomes (£40 at 7-4 returns £110), the bookie would face a payout of £110, having received total stakes of £120. He wins £10 whatever happens.

On Betfair, your fellow punters set the odds. The market is super-competitive, which means profit margins are almost non-existent. In an event with three equally possible outcomes it would be a surprise if all three were not backed at some stage at better than 2-1, while big-field events like snooker and tennis tournaments still feature books of around just 102 per cent compared to up to 200 per cent with the average bookmaker.

That is why exchange betting on Betfair is so successful. You are offered prices that bookmakers could not afford to give you, while Betfair have no interest in whether you win or lose, only that you bet. If you win, they take their commission from you, if you lose they take commission from the person who took your bet.

If you suddenly find yourself a six-figure winner, Betfair will love you for the commission you generate. They may well offer you some corporate hospitality as an expression of their gratitude. A bookmaker would likely as not have turned away your business long before your profit reached five figures.

2 is evens, 3 is 2-1, etc, and it is simple to work out your true price. All you do is multiply the price by 0.95 if your commission rate is five per cent (up to 0.98 if you are on two per cent). For instance, let's say 20-1 was available with a bookmaker, but 22 (21-1) on Betfair. The calculation is 21 multiplied by 0.95 = 19.95, which shows that you are better off with a bookmaker in this instance.

Remember, though, that all deductions are

on the exchanges

Betting in-running

so much freedom of choice

Bookmakers have been jolted into action and now you can bet in-running with most major firms on most major events, but they still require you to back a winner and quite often adopt a defensive pricing policy, with huge over-rounds.

In-running betting was, of course, around long before betting exchanges hit the marketplace, and the most proactive firm in this department have been Stan James, who say that around 40 per cent of their sports betting turnover now comes from in-running trade.

But betting in-running on Betfair gives you more options. As well as simply placing a bet after the event has started, you can trade your way out of a position if things are going well or cut your losses if they are going badly.

For instance, if you have backed a 2-1 chance in a football match and your selection is in front with ten minutes to go, you might be able to lay them back at 1-3 to guarantee a profit. There is an ongoing argument about whether it is right to hedge out of positions, but we will come to that elsewhere.

The other great advantage of in-play betting is that you are pitting you wits against fellow punters in an environment that puts professional market-makers under pressure, let alone the novices trying to make it pay. Split-second decisions are made all the time and the upshot is that prices sometimes materialise that are totally wrong.

Trading in-running is not something you can jump into straight away because it's a dangerous game, but if you watch a football match and check the market moves immediately after a goal, you will see how some people can be sucked into a bad bet. The scoring team is virtually always matched at a shorter price than will be available a few minutes later once the market has settled down.

made on profits only, which makes odds-on betting attractive. Thus, a bet of £100 at 1-5 (or 1.2) returns a profit of £19 at five per cent commission (20-5%=19).

TYPES OF USER There are many different ways in which you can use Betfair and the types of punter can probably be split into three loosely defined groups, although many will cross over.

The punter Whether professional, casual, or mug, the punter uses Betfair as he would any internet betting site or bookmaker, but just takes advantage of the better prices available.

A professional is unlikely to have formed an opinion until confronted by the odds. The prices on offer will determine his selection and he will not necessarily content himself with being a backer if something is obviously too short. A professional may use computer models, excel spreadsheets, anything to help him find an edge.

The casual punter will already have formed an opinion, but is likely to make sure the price on offer is the best he can get. He is more likely to concentrate solely on live events as fun is his main objective.

A mug knows exactly what he is going to bet on before logging on and will take a price regardless of whether or not it represents value.

The layer Laying bets is far more sophisticated than placing them and, believe it or not, it takes a good deal more effort to make money being a Betfair layer. If it is widely accepted that the marketplace heavily favours the backer, it stands to reason that the layer faces an arduous task. Anyone attempting to lay a full set of runners will have to work hard to ensure their book just creeps over the 100 per cent mark. This proves how hard it is to be a bookmaker and shows that the term 'play bookie' is wrong. Most punters would find it nearly impossible to make a book, so in essence they are just punting on one or more selections not to win.

The professional layer operates in the same way as the professional punter. If his figures say the prices should be bigger he will lay it, whether it is 1-2 or 100-1.

One of the advantages a layer has is that the market is rarely static and he can pick and choose when to lay.

A casual layer is far more likely to

concentrate on the favourite or a team or individual near the head of the market. The reason for this is purely risk-related as the casual punter is far happier laying at short prices than long ones. He is not interested in risking £100 on a golfer he does not think will triumph just to win £10. In general there are enough mug punters around to ensure that even if the pro and casual layers come to the same conclusion about the favourite there will still be plenty of value in laying.

The trader He could not care less about finding a winner. His unique skill is not in knowing what a price should be, but what it will be. One of the well-known sayings among traders is 'don't tip me a winner, tip me a price'.

If you have an insight into how other people will bet (how the market will react), it can be a licence to print money on Betfair, whether you identify an upcoming gamble or a drifter in the betting. The strategy behind it is simple enough, although it takes a fair degree of skill.

Let's say you have identified a 4-1 shot which you are pretty sure will shorten throughout the day and may start at around 3-1.

You place £200 at 4-1, wait for it to shorten and then lay it back. You could lay £200 at 3-1 and give yourself a free £200 bet, or simply lay £250 at 3-1 and show no more interest in the event safe in the knowledge that you have made £50 whatever happens. Remember, commission is only taken from profits on any particular market, so if your selection wins, you do not pay five per cent on £800 winnings because your lay at 3-1 has cancelled out most of the profit.

Obviously that is a rather simple example and in practice it is rarely that easy, but there are many traders who make a comfortable living by never taking a position and they can do so even if the difference in price is only a few hundredths of a point. All you need is plenty of money in your account and an ability

on the exchanges

Trading carefully

practice makes perfect

Many traders make big profits with in-running betting and if you want to practice becoming a trader, it may be worthwhile to try to hone you skills in a market that lacks liquidity.

A Premiership football match features very few fluctuations unless there is a goal (betting is suspended anyway then) and in any case you are almost constantly up against pros. But an event with a lower profile, like a live rugby union or league match, attracts fewer punters and deters big-money traders because there is generally not enough cash to go round.

These can be the perfect mediums to practice trading as more scoring opportunities mean more fluctuations and there are no market suspensions after a try. I know someone who routinely bets to 130 per cent in rugby union matches, making a small profit most of the time. Be aware, though, that sometimes in a market lacking liquidity you can get stuck with a position you cannot escape from as even a generous price will not be taken if no-one else is playing against you.

to call it right. However, the advantages far outweigh the negatives, especially for live sport, as Betfair's telephone customers can often be relied upon to snap up whatever price is there regardless of the value.

The problem with in-running telephone punting on the exchanges is that you have to make your decision pretty quickly. Punters sitting in a pub watching the afternoon action are less likely to want to leave a request up without knowing whether it has been matched, so often they'll just take what is available.

Which category of punter you fall into depends on what you want from your betting. For some there is no greater feeling than backing your opinion and being proved right. It's all about an adrenalin rush. For others making money is the be-all and end-all and if they can do so without any risk then so much the better.

on the exchanges

 **Closing:
the deal**

to hedge or not to hedge?

Laying off is by no means a new concept. The possibility of closing out a position has been available to spread punters since the early 1990s, but the argument against doing so is pretty strong because of the layers' built-in profit margin. You pay for the margin when you place your original bet and then you pay again when you close out.

But with Betfair there is little or no margin to consider either on your first or second bet, so is it now correct to hedge or not? The idea of not letting a bet follow its full course is anathema to some of the most respected punters around, but that doesn't necessarily mean it is the right thing to do.

My colleague at the *Racing Post*, Nick Fox, has a strong opinion on this. He says in Betting on Horses: "It's wrong to take a profit unless you are sure the second bet is a good one. If the horse you backed is still over-priced why lay it? If anything you should be having more on."

That seems pretty much like commonsense, but there is a counter-argument that goes along the lines of: you've done all the hard work and put yourself in a position to make money, so why not take a profit and get rid of the risk? If you can consistently ensure that you can't lose, you must win in the end.

Both seem equally powerful arguments and I think it is purely a matter of choice. What you should do whenever you consider taking a profit is to make a note of how you would have fared by staying in or closing out. My own suspicion is that those continually taking a profit will prove better off in the long run.

Whether you intend to become a punter, layer or trader, identifying the mugs is one way to maximise your profit potential. Let's face it, most of us are not going to beat the pros but there is plenty of silly money out there and if we can spot it we have a chance, not only to make money, but to make sure we don't fall into the same trap. Obviously, you can't actually identify anyone, because all punting is anonymous (at least at the person-to-person level – Betfair can trace every bet themselves) but there are particular traits of mugs and the traps that they fall into.

Avoid these and you are on the way to success.

DOS AND DON'TS

Don't be a cliff-jumper This is someone who watches the market, sees something shorten and jumps in at the lowest point in the belief that everyone else must be right. I'm sure temptation to do this exists in almost everyone. Humans are essentially pack animals and you can see evidence of this in everyday life. At Waterloo rail station, for instance, there are a couple of down escalators side by side. Yet rarely, if ever, do anything like the same number of people travel on each one at the same time. The first person (the Alpha male, as David Attenborough would call him) on is usually followed by the second and so on and usually one escalator will be three times as busy as the other (yes, I've watched it happen and yes, I am that sad).

It is a safety-in-numbers mentality that is bred into all of us and it manifests itself in the world of punting all the time.

The advantages of travelling on a less busy escalator are a more comfortable ride and an easier walk, the advantage of opposing the majority view on Betfair is a value bet. Swim against the tide and you will make money in the long run.

One of the best examples of the cliff-jumping mentality is in markets on who will be a football club's next manager. Such markets don't show tabloid newspapers in a great light but do give an indication of how people are prepared to believe anything they read.

Tabloids love to give you an exclusive and are quite prepared to present even the flimsiest rumour as the truth, especially if there is no chance of them getting sued for doing so.

The 2003-04 Tottenham manager market featured no fewer than five different odds-on favourites (not to mention Chris Hughton at 11-10), all influenced by what people read in the papers and all wide of the mark until Jacques Santini finally got the post. Start a rumour and you quickly provide the environment for the cliff-jumper to make his leap. Somewhere out there is a punter who was lulled into placing £10 at evens on Terry Venables to get the Leeds job in 2003. A few hours later El Tel was more than 100-1.

Don't overreact In desperation to back a winner, the mug can take some truly horrendous prices by overreacting, whether it is to an item of pre-event news, a goal, a putt or whatever.

This happens all the time and to prove it here are just a couple of examples from Euro 2004.

As Roonmania was taking Portugal by storm, many mug punters were taking leave of their senses. Immediately after Rooney scored his second goal (giving him four in total) against Croatia in England's final group match punters rushed to back him at evens to be the tournament's top scorer. Those taking the price probably did so in the belief that the person offering it was not watching the action.

But the opposite was almost certainly true. The person offering evens knew exactly what was going on and was sure that someone would fall into his trap. He put up an artificially short price knowing that someone would take it in the belief that they were availing themselves of a price that nobody else would have access to. They were right in the sense that nobody else would access the price but only because it was so short. By the following morning, the market had calmed down, reached its correct level and Rooney was back out to 7-2.

In the same tournament more than £20,000 had been matched at evens or shorter on the tournament producing fewer than 75 goals.

The initial trading price in a market of four possibilities (fewer than 75, 75-80, 81-85, more than 85) was 2-1 and by quarter-final time it was 150-1.

And after Greece shocked Portugal in the opening match of the tournament (as they would in the final itself), Otto Rehhagel's men were backed at 2.14 to beat Spain in their next match. They were back out to 6.2 by the time that game kicked off. So while the advice

on the **exchanges**

 **Betfair
chatroom**

nuggets amid all the dross

The Betfair chatroom is a source of many things – good advice, bad advice, humour, information, false information, smut, wit, vitriol, and, of course, sauce.

Once you learn to quickly bypass the feeble threads about which racing presenter has the nicest breasts, the woeful examples of after-timing and of losing punters talking through their pocket, you will be left with a useful tool for gathering information.

The forum is divided into various different sports and also has sections for general betting, speciality bets, minority sports and chit-chat.

It doesn't take long to discover that there is a hard core of users who are responsible for a large proportion of the postings. Some talk good sense, others utter nonsense.

In betting you should always be your own person and never be swayed by the opinion of others, but that is not to say you should not be prepared to take on board what others think, especially as they may bring up a salient point you had overlooked.

The forum will often throw up interesting views on lower-division football from fans who support a team you are thinking of backing or opposing, and however hard you may try to keep up to date with team and injury news from the 92 league clubs, you will never know as much as the diehard fans.

Beware of rampers, though. These are contributors who deliberately post false information with the intention of swaying the market in their favour.

In a next manager market, for instance, someone may submit a posting that appears to be a cut-and-pasted red-hot story from a news agency, complete with technical matter like catchlines, claiming the potential candidate who is currently odds-on for the vacancy has ruled himself out. Gullible chatroom users may quickly jump in and lay the man in question, enabling our hoaxer to back him at inflated prices.

Far and away my favourite ever post came in response to a person who had used the phrase "in my humble opinion" before he proffered his view on a particular event.

"Sorry, mate," came the reply. "No room for humble opinions on this forum. All views must be expressed with total vehemence and there must be no hint of remorse or humility if the opinion is proved to be completely wrong."

in this section is not to overreact, it must also be to look to take advantage of people who do overreact.

Beware the good thing I once passed on a tip for a horse to a friend, who had a tenner on it at 8-1. "Thanks for that," he said

on the exchanges

 If you don't ask . . .

when crazy prices are laid

The time to ask for unrealistic prices, whether you are attempting to back or lay, is when a market is reopened for in-running betting. You will never cease to be amazed at the prices that some of your fellow bettors will accept and the reasons for this will be found elsewhere on these pages. They are the cliff-jumpers, the mugs who overreact and the greedy favourite-backers who see only the profit and not the risk.

Crystal Palace fans were not the only ones celebrating the Eagles' unlikely return to the top flight in May 2004. Two minutes from the end of 90 minutes' play in their semi-final second leg with Sunderland, Iain Dowie's men were backed at 1,000 and 970 to make it to the Premiership. A last-minute goal from Darren Powell forced extra-time and the rest is history.

after it had bolted up. "If it had been 6-4 I'd have had £100 on."

I was astounded by his reaction, but the truth is that a large group of punters consider favourites to have a divine right to win. The betting shop mug does not stop to consider that a 6-4 favourite is actually odds-on to lose.

It took me a long time to realise that betting at odds-on is not necessarily a bad thing, but because something is a short price it doesn't mean you should step in without weighing up all the possibilities.

At the end of 2002, Betfair provided the *Racing Post* with a list of all the events in which at least one contender had traded at 1.01 (1-100) in a particular three-month spell. Basically, they gave me details of virtually every market that they trade in-running (or turn in-play, as they say) as at the end of any event the winner is almost always backed at 1.01.

However, so are many losers. And after totting up almost £40m worth of bets, it was found that backers at 1.01 were actually down to the tune of £350,000. Most of us find it hard to believe that people could be so stupid as to back a 1-100 loser, but it happens on a frequent basis for the simple reason that the vast majority of punters have no idea about true market value.

Greed also plays a part in in-running trading. There is a clamour to get on as an event nears its climax which often results in a price shortening up prematurely. I am pretty sure there are some punters who make a decent living purely from betting at long odds-on, but to do so you need an extraordinary strike rate. It is certainly not for the novice exchange punter.

Don't be afraid to be unrealistic Because the market is rarely static, the price you are originally offered may not be the best you can get and purely by asking for something bigger and monitoring the situation you can squeeze out that extra bit of value.

All unmatched bets are cancelled before a market is turned in-play anyway, so you are not doing yourself any harm by leaving it until the last second, unless your selection is being heavily supported beforehand and you miss a price you probably would have considered acceptable had you not opted to go for even bigger riches. It is a question of judgement.

The next tactic will appeal only to bigger punters, but if you want to ask for an unrealistic price you can set a trap for telephone punters by requesting bets in units of £50.

Unlike online players who can bet as little as £2, phone punters are restricted to a minimum bet of £50. Strange as it may seem, a telephone punter can lay £100 at 1.01 for a potential loss of £1 but can't lay £20 at 5-1 for the potential loss of £100. He or she has to lay a minimum of £50.

Telephone punters are far from stupid, but they have to make a decision on the spot because a Betfair phone operator is not going to sit and provide a running commentary on the state of the market until such time that his client sees fit to place a bet. They are, therefore, more likely to be forced into rash choices. But if only £20 is up there, your bet can't be taken by them.

Don't trust your TV When you are sitting on your couch at home watching a football match or a golf tournament, you are probably under the impression that what you are viewing is live. It is not. All transmissions are subject to some time delay.

When you are talking about a matter of a couple of seconds the difference is irrelevant, but if it is more than that there is a chance that someone is in a position to know more than you.

It should be well known by now to horse-racing punters that some cable TV is behind digital TV, which is behind SIS, which is in turn behind terrestrial analogue coverage. My own calculation of the difference from cable to analogue in 2002 was five seconds – that's about 100 yards in a race.

In other sports there can also be people in a position to know more than you. The best example is golf. It is pretty obvious that a lot of the coverage you see cannot be live as at any one time there are at least two groups of people on any one hole (except par-threes). And that doesn't take into account the frequent ad breaks.

In America there is quite often a delay and many people have been taking advantage of the PGA Tour's Tourcast service, which gives real-time positions of everyone on the course right down to the details of what lie an individual has in the rough or the exact distance of a putt.

Tourcast is not easy for everyone to subscribe to because payment is only accepted from a credit card registered to an American address, but having used the service I can vouch for the fact that it is often, but not always, well ahead of both the PGA Tour's regular website and the TV.

With a bit of lateral thinking, you can get by perfectly well without Tourcast. All you have to do is watch the market. When there is a significant shortening in price before you see any pictures, you can be sure that Tourcast punters are getting on. So what do you do now?

You certainly don't become a cliff-jumper and follow the money in. Instead, offer to lay at an even shorter price than is now available because when that putt hits your TV screens there will be a second wave of punters itching to get on. Moments later the market will settle and you will be in a position to lock in a profit.

Keep an eye on all related markets You may be sitting in front of your TV trading a football match without realising that value can lie elsewhere once a goal is scored. Tournament betting provides good illustrations of this, as Euro 2004 showed.

Remember, when a goal is scored, in-running 90-minute match betting is suspended, but outright markets are not. A classic example came in the final batch of group D matches in Portugal, with Holland needing to beat Latvia and then hope that Germany failed to defeat the already-qualified Czechs.

The Germans took the lead, at which point Holland were backed at 80 outright, while Ruud van Nistelrooy touched 100 for the Golden Boot. The Czechs turned it around, though, van Nistelrooy bagged a brace against Latvia and by the end of the night you could have laid the Dutch at 6 and van Nistelrooy at 1.8, even though, of course, neither won.

CORRUPTION Much has been made of the potential for corruption on betting exchanges and the subject cannot be ignored, even though an awful lot of hot air has been spouted by jealous bookmakers.

You can take it as read that if a bookmaker moans, he is not doing it out of concern for the punter or a sport's integrity but for his own potential for profit, and, whatever the mainstream layers may say, the exchanges have had an impact on their turnover.

Many of the bookmakers' concerns surround horseracing, but it would unwise to think corruption starts and ends there as there are few sports that have gone untainted by the whiff of scandal over the years.

The truth is that in any sport where prize money is relatively low there will always be the potential for someone to pull a fast one if they can make more money out of losing than they can by winning.

Bookmakers can spot an attempted coup a mile off and will quickly react by suspending betting but that doesn't happen on exchanges so in a sense it is true that fixing a result for profit has been made easier.

However, Betfair have done their level best to address the integrity issue. They have a memorandum of understanding in place with the majority of sporting governing bodies, which allows them to pass on details of anyone (all punters have to agree to having their names given to regulatory bodies if requested) involved in suspicious betting patterns.

Of course, anyone can open an account using somebody else's name, but money still has to be deposited via a bank card, so people are easy to trace.

Proving corruption is virtually impossible – there have been several cases of sportsmen getting bans in different disciplines, but quite often the offence is deemed to be nothing more serious than unprofessional conduct – but at least market transparency gives punters the freedom of choice.

on the exchanges

Men in the know

piling on the certainties

There were several irregular betting patterns in tennis at the end of 2003 and early in 2004. The most high-profile of all concerned Yevgeny Kafelnikov's match with Fernando Vicente in Lyon in October 2003.

The Russian was quoted at 1-6 by fixed-odds firms for the match, but by the start he was the underdog, with Vicente trading at as short as 1-10 on Betfair.

With an example like this, it is clearly obvious that someone knew something, although, of course, it doesn't mean the match was crooked.

If you knew everything was right with both players, you would happily mortgage your house to lay Vicente (a loser in all six previous meetings with Kafelnikov) at 1.1, but the fact he was that price should have set alarm bells ringing.

As it happened, Kafelnikov lost 6-2 6-3, citing a foot injury. Next time out he retired in Madrid, complaining of the same injury. One tournament later, he had quit the sport altogether.

What almost certainly happened in that instance was that sources close to Kafelnikov knew he was hopping lame and as soon as word about his injury hit the grapevine there was a wholesale gamble.

The truth is that corruption in sport is still very rare and that those who attempt to pull off a coup very often get caught because of greed.

The beauty of exchanges is that there is a much better chance of cheats getting caught thanks to the willingness of the exchanges to cooperate with sport's regulators (something the high street layers failed to do for so long), while the transparency of markets at least acts as an early warning sign for punters.

In the final analysis, for every negative there are a dozen positives and if you are serious about making money you will find the odds more in your favour on an exchange than anywhere else and even if you are not serious you will still find your money lasting longer than it would with any regular bookie.

And that can't be bad.

no reason to fear spreads

LIMITING THE RISK

A THRILLING INTRODUCTION TO the official receiver. That's how *Racing Post* columnist David Ashforth once brilliantly described spread betting, and while he was doubtless using a certain amount of journalistic licence, there is no doubt that when you play on the spreads you are playing with fire.

The spread firms' own ads carry a statement that warns: "Spread betting is volatile and carries a high level of risk to your capital. It may not be suitable for all investors. Ensure you fully understand the risks involved. Seek advice if necessary and speculate only with money you can afford to lose. You may lose more than your initial stake."

But, just as the big rectangular warnings on cigarette packets have not wiped out smoking, so the wise words from the firms themselves do not deter an ever-increasing number of punters from sampling the thrills (and hopefully not the meeting with the official receiver) that spread betting provides.

In truth, spread betting has an aura of menace about it that it doesn't really deserve.

Sure, spread betting is volatile, but so is any form of gambling if you are such a compulsive punter that you cannot control yourself.

There is no one factor that will make you a successful spread punter, but there are a couple

By BRUCE MILLINGTON

Strife of Brian: Lara's quadruple-century left some punters on their knees

of basic rules that will help you avoid financial armageddon.

First, stake properly. In spread betting some markets are perceived to be more volatile than others – a cricket team's runs compared to a football team's goals, for instance – but if your unit stake is ten pence per run and a grand per goal, the goals become far a more volatile proposition.

Getting your staking right is essential – and if you have never spread bet before it is one of many reasons why you should have a lengthy dry run to see if you are comfortable with it before deciding to take the plunge.

The other absolutely crucial thing to remember is never to chase your losses on the spreads. It is a risky enough thing to do in more traditional ways of betting, but if you lose control on the spreads you are liable to clean yourself out in double-quick time.

However, if you exhibit due care and attention and adhere to the basic principles of selectivity and sensible staking there is no reason why spread betting should not represent another worthwhile string to your punting bow. I remember a colleague from my days at *The Sporting Life* leaving to join IG Index in the firm's early days as a sports spread betting company.

"I hope they have made you an offer you can understand," read one of the messages in his leaving card. That summed up the general feeling towards spread betting in those days. It was viewed as a complex form of betting indulged in only by loaded City boys.

Those who scoffed as our man traded a successful career in journalism for the then fledgling world of spread betting were laughing on the other side of their faces when, a decade later, he cashed in his IG share options and walked away with more than £6m.

It must be said that down the years I have contributed to his windfall. Spread betting has not always been lucrative for me but nor have I committed financial suicide.

And if I look back on my most exciting betting moments, many have involved spread wagers.

I fell in love with spread betting the moment I got to grips with how it worked. And if you still don't understand the ins and outs, here's the answer.

England prepare to bat on the first day of a Test match and a spread firm quotes their total first innings runs at 300-320.

If you think England will do badly and will score fewer than 300 runs, you sell. If you think they will do well and exceed 320 runs you buy.

If you sell you are trading at the lower figure, in this case 300. If you buy you are trading at the higher figure, 320.

If you sell England for a pound at 300 and England make 260, you win 40 times your stake (300-260=£40). If you sell England for a pound at 300 and they make 372, you lose 72 times your stake (372-300=£72).

If you buy England for a pound at 320 and

spread dread

1994 West Indies v England

Lara buyers laughing The perils and delights of dabbling on the spreads were starkly highlighted as Brian Lara blitzed his way to a then record-breaking Test score of 375 in Antigua. Punters who bought his runs at 55 before he received his first delivery were in seventh heaven. Some of those who sold have probably only just recovered. Sporting Index traders could only sit and suffer as every Lara boundary cost the company £1,200.

spread knowledge

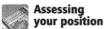 **Assessing your position**

take a profit – or cut losses

One of spread betting's many virtues is that you have the option of closing your bet before it has reached its natural conclusion, either to secure a profit or to take a loss to nullify the risk of having to absorb an even bigger loss later on.

For example, if you bought Stoke's points at 61 at the start of the season and they make an excellent start, winning seven, drawing two and losing three of their first 12 matches, the spread, which is updated after each set of fixtures, may rise to 72-74. You then have the option to sell for the same unit stake at 72, thus guaranteeing an 11-point profit (72-61).

Likewise, if you sold at 59 at the outset you might feel more comfortable buying for the same unit stake at 74, thus taking a 15-point loss. This is a painful course of action but if you believe Stoke are playing so well that they might go on to amass a really huge points total it may be a prudent move.

What you should remember when trading in-running (and the same principle applies in a 90-minute situation – if you have bought the time of the first goal and it is 0-0 after 20 minutes you have the option to close your position with a profit) is that you are playing the spread twice and are therefore automatically getting worse value than if you let the bet run. For example, if a team's points are quoted at 62-64, the true price is 63. If you buy at 64 and the revised quote two months later is 73-75, the true price is 74. By selling at 73 you are locking in a profit, but are paying a one-point premium for the privilege.

England make 260, you lose 60 times your stake (320-260=£60). If you buy England for a pound at 320 and they make 372, you win 52 times your stake (372-320=£52).

The spread firm makes its money by trading at either end of the 20-point spread they have quoted.

Ah, I hear you say. That is all very well but what does it mean when a football team is quoted at 0.3-0.6 against another. This is what foxes many people and is probably the single reason why spread betting took a while to catch on. If the companies had had the chance to reinvent spread betting I wouldn't mind betting they would have given considerable thought to operating football supremacy on a basis of ten points per goal to avoid this major point of confusion.

Once you get your head around it, of course, you wonder what the fuss was about. Here is the easy way to understand football supremacy.

You see a price on an advert, teletext page or in the *Racing Post* that says 0.3-0.6 Liverpool/Everton.

What it means is this: Liverpool's supremacy over Everton is rated at 0.3-0.6 of a goal. It is at this point that the following question is always uttered: how can you have 0.3 of a goal? You can't, but nor can you measure one team's supremacy over another in whole goals. Football is too low-scoring a sport for such a vague assessment.

What happens in this instance is that if Liverpool win 2-1 the make-up (final total) is 1 (2 minus 1). If it ends 0-0 the make-up is 0 and if Everton win 2-0 Liverpool supremacy makes up at minus 2.

So, as with our cricket example, if you sell Liverpool for £20 at 0.3 and they draw 1-1, you win 0.3 times your stake (0.3-0=0.3 or £6). If you sell Liverpool for £20 at 0.3 and they win 4-0, you lose 3.7 times your stake (4.0-0.3=3.7 or £74).

If you buy Liverpool for £20 at 0.6 and they lose 4-2, you lose 2.6 times your stake (2+0.6=2.6 or £52). If you buy Liverpool for £20 at 0.6 and they win 5-0, you win 4.4 times your stake (5.0-0.6=4.4 or £88).

Understand this and the rest should be easy.

THE MOST POPULAR MARKETS: FOOTBALL Apart from goals supremacy (see above), there are scores of football markets. These are the main ones.

Total goals For the same reasons as for goals supremacy, this market is quoted in tenths of a goal. A typical total goals quote

spread dread

1997 Open, Troon

Off the rails
Sporting ran a market entitled the Railway to Hell, which focused on the notoriously brutal par-four 11th hole at Troon. Working on the basis of six points awarded per double-bogey six, seven for each seven recorded at the hole, eight per eight and so on, the firm opened up at 170-190 and buyers immediately steamed in.

As a gale blew and the hole became nearly unplayable, the struggling field contributed a mammoth 219 points on the first day alone. Sporting were forced to push the spread up to 490-510, and though the wind relented and the scoring improved, the damage was already done as most buyers closed their position with a 300-point profit. "It was a disaster," claimed a Sporting spokesman.

between two sides renowned neither as prolific scorers nor as inept defenders is 2.4-2.7. If the match finishes 1-0 to either side the make-up is one and sellers at 2.4 win 1.4 times their stake while buyers lose 1.7-times theirs. If it is a 3-3 draw the make-up is six and sellers at 2.4 lose 3.6-times their stake while buyers win 3.3-times theirs.

Shirt numbers This is the aggregate of the goalscorers' shirt numbers and could be quoted at around 36-39 depending on the scoring prowess of the teams involved and their squad-number details. It makes up at zero if the match ends goalless and can occasionally total as high as 150 or greater. Sellers are always fearful of a late substitute with an astro-nomically high shirt number coming on and banging in a late goal.

Corners Typically pitched at around the 11-12 mark, corners are a fundamentally unappealing market simply because the make-up rarely strays far from the opening quote and the one-point spread (the gap between the sell price and the buy price) is too wide. Some punters specialise in corners, however, focusing, for example, on teams that play with a lot of width or those that statistically concede an unusually large or small number of flag kicks.

Bookings A fascinating market that works on the basis of ten points per yellow card and 25 per red card. Depending on the historical behaviour of the respective teams and the referee's penchant or otherwise for brandishing cards, the bookings may open at 38-42 for an average match. This could rise to as high as 70-74 for an Old Firm derby or typical Spanish league fixture.

Goal times These take the form of a market for the first goal in the match (typically quoted at 36-39 minutes) as well as one for each team (in the region of 42-45 for a well-fancied team rising to around 69-72 for a big underdog).

First goal markets make-up at 90 if no goal is scored. The time of the last goal is also quoted by most firms. This makes up at zero if the match does not feature a goal.

Player goal minutes Extremely popular after taking a surprisingly long time to come into being. The main attackers and midfielders of each team are priced up, with a striker like Ruud van Nistelrooy, playing at home for Manchester United against mid-table opponents, being given a spread of around 32-35. If he does not score he makes up at zero. If he scores in the 19th and 53rd minutes he makes up at 72 (19+53).

Win indices A very basic market in which the punter knows exactly what his potential profit/loss is when he strikes the bet. A team's win index makes up at 25 if they win, 10 if they draw and zero if they lose.

Performance indices These are like win indices with added extras. Each firm has a different scoring tariff, but, taking Sporting Index's as an example, a team is awarded 25 points for winning, 15 per goal it scores, 10 for keeping a clean sheet, 10 per woodwork strike (the ball must rebound into play), 3 per corner, minus 5 per yellow card and minus 10 per red card. Thus, if a team wins 3-0, gains nine corners, hits the bar once, has two players booked and one sent off, its performance make-up is 97.

Performance indices are offered on all televised matches. Mini-performances are also offered for every other game. These work in a similar way but have less sophisticated scoring systems and use components that enable punters to keep tabs on what the current make-up is without having access to live pictures.

Long-term football markets The main type of long-term football spread bet is the team points market. The market-makers estimate each team's total points for that season and punters have the choice to buy, sell or agree and make no trade. At the start of a season, Arsenal points might be quoted at 75-76.5. If you think they will do well, you buy at 76.5 and if you think they will struggle you sell at 75. Firms also operate indices on each division. An index is a list of runners with a pre-determined scoring system, thus offering the punter peace of mind in that he knows his maximum possible upside and downside. A typical Premiership index will award 60 points to the team that finishes first, 40 to the eventual runners-up, 30 for the team that is third, 20 for fourth place, 10 for fifth and 5 for sixth. Chelsea might be quoted at 25-28. If you buy at 28 and they win the title you make 32 times your stake (60-28=32). If you sell at 25 and they finish fourth you win five times your stake (25-20=5).

GOLF

Finishing positions The leading players in every tournament are given finishing position spreads with a maximum make-up of 50 if he finishes outside the top 50, although in certain tournaments there are also unlimited make-up quotes offered, where the most a player can make up is the total number of players in that event.

If you win, your finishing position is one. If you are the runner-up it is two and so on. If two players share second place their make-up is 2.5. If five players share 19th place their make-up is 21 (the average of finishing positions 19, 20, 21, 22 and 23).

Indices There are two types – leaderboard and restricted. The leaderboard index includes the entire field and operates with a similar scoring system and in an identical way to a Premiership index (see long-term football markets). The restricted index comprises a selected number of players, usually ten, and may award 50 points to the golfer who finishes best of the ten nominated players, 30 to the one who is second best, 20 for the third best, and ten for the fourth best. This would be expressed as a 50:30:20:10 index. Only these ten players matter for the purposes of the index.

Supremacy There are match bets over either 18 or 72 holes. They are very different and the 18-holers are particularly volatile. An example: you buy Mickelson/Singh at 0-1.5 over 18 holes. Mickelson loses by four shots. You lose ten for the loss and three per shot margin, a massive 22 points in total, plus, of course, the 1.5 that you pay for the buy. Very expensive. Over 72 holes it's more straightforward. The offer margin this time will be wider, 0-3, and say Mickelson shoots 281 to Singh's 288. You win simply the difference, seven shots, less the three you have paid for the privilege. The volatility here comes if either player misses the cut, in which case both players' 36-hole scores are doubled. Maximum make-ups apply but it is foolish to have a supremacy bet without working out what you will lose in the worst-case scenario.

RUGBY (BOTH CODES)

Supremacy Nice and easy to understand. No tenths of a goal, just basic whole-point supremacy. Thus, England may be put in as 7-10 favourites over Ireland and if they win 32-12 buyers at 10 win ten-times their stake and sellers at 7 lose 13-times their stake.

Hot Hands A similar market, known as Hotshots, exists in football. Four players from each team are bracketed together and these four earn 25 points per try they score. Their Hot Hands might be quoted at 38-41 and will make-up at zero if none of the quartet scores a try or at 100 if they manage four tries between them.

OTHER SPORTS Most markets in others
sports will work on the same basis as in the

---

spread dread

 1996 Monaco Grand Prix

City's field day
The perils of getting short, especially at a low level, were drilled home by the experience of a City Index client who thought he was picking up money in the street by selling the field in City's Monaco Grand Prix index.

The leading drivers were given individual quotes with the remainder lumped together as 'the field'. These longshots were being quoted at 0.5-2 on an index which awarded 50 points to the winner, 25 to the runner-up and ten to the third driver over the line.

The unfortunate punter sold for £250 at 0.5, expecting to boost his account by £125, but it all went horribly wrong. The heavens opened and the slippery streets of Monaco turned the race into a lottery. Olivier Panis, one of the 'field', won at odds of 300-1 and another unconsidered driver, Johnny Herbert, was third. The field made up at 60 and our man was £14,875 out of pocket.

various examples quoted above. If you do not understand any aspect of spread betting it is imperative that you gain clarification from your spread firm (and if you are at all serious about making spread betting pay, you should have accounts with all the companies in order to always get the best possible price).

Above all, never get cocky with spread betting. It is a perpetually risky business and if you start thinking it is easy after two or three successive winning trades you can be in for a rude awakening.

Always contemplate the maximum amount you could lose. And if there is no stipulated maximum (if you sell a batsman's runs he can theoretically keep going for five days) do not be afraid to overestimate the potential damage.

It sounds almost ridiculously simplistic, but spread guru Kevin Pullein's oft-quoted mantra – the worst thing that can happen is the worst thing that can happen – should never be forgotten when it comes to spread betting.

THE TERMINOLOGY Spread betting, like all sports betting, is mercifully free of jargon, but there are certain expressions you will become familiar with if you spread bet on a regular basis.

Arbitrage Cases of arbitrage, or arbs as they are better known, occur when two spread firms take conflicting views on a particular event. IG might quote West Indies runs at 300-320 whereas Cantor might go 330-350. So if you bought at 320 for £5 with IG and sold at 330 for the same amount with Cantor you would guarantee yourself a £50 profit (330-320x5) regardless of what total the West Indies made.

Arbs also exist in conventional fixed-odds betting. If one bookmaker goes 4-6 Roddick, 11-10 Hewitt in a tennis match and another offers 4-7 Hewitt, 5-4 Roddick, you can ensure a profit by having £50 on Hewitt at 11-10 and £50 on Roddick at 5-4.

Some people carve out a living purely by hunting down and exploiting arb situations. They are disliked by bookmakers as they are usually the first to pounce when an arbitrage arises, thus denying those customers who simply want to trade at a price they consider attractive the chance to do so. Then again, it is hard to blame someone for trying to do something which is, in most cases, as simple as picking up money off the pavement.

Obviously life as an arb shark, as these people tend to be known, is not without risks. Using the cricket example, you may have bought with IG only to find that by the time you dial through to Cantor, the price has dropped, although generally the arb shark will still be able to sell at the same level at which he bought or, if the worst comes to the worst, take an occasional loss.

Getting long and getting short Getting long means buying and getting short means selling. Also known as being with and being against.

Bid and offer The bid price is the price at which you can sell (ie, you may hear bookings quoted at 32 bid, which means 32-35) and the offer price is the price at which you can buy.

Thirty-four seven and all variations. This is merely the way traders tend to quote prices. Thus, if you ask for a shirt numbers spread and are told "thirty-four seven" it simply means 34-37.

Upside and downside The potential for winning and the potential for losing. Buy total points in a rugby league match at 63 and the maximum downside is 63.

Feel price A spread based on a market-maker's instinct rather than one derived as a result of thorough research of relevant stats.

THE PSYCHOLOGY The shrewdies sell and

the mugs buy. That's the rule of thumb anyway, and while it may not be as true now given that spread punters have evolved and become more canny in the main, it is still largely the case that the successful punter will sell more often than he buys.

This is almost certainly due to two things.

Firstly, many spread punters trade sentimentally, backing what they hope will happen rather than what they think will happen. Take shirt numbers. The quote is 40-43. Do you really want to sell and have to sit through a match you want to watch hoping attacks break down on the halfway line, players go down injured and the referee fails to allocate sufficient injury-time and shots soar into row Z rather than bursting the back of the net?

Secondly, many spread punters are scared of an unlimited downside. If you sell the shirts at 40 you know the most you can win is 40 points. You also know you could, however implausible the threat, lose 250 points. For the cold, calculating spread punter, this is not a risk he cares remotely about because he knows that statistically it is virtually impossible that he will suffer this fate.

For the less dispassionate spread punter, the danger plays on his mind. The last thing he wants is to sell at 40 and spend the last hour of the match in a state of panic following early goals from number 25 and number 15.

This is why, as Karim Fatih goes on to explain in the next chapter, spreads are frequently pitched artificially high.

Nothing illustrated this better than when Sporting Index issued the first ever corners spread. They did not have stats to hand and came up with a feel price of 23-26, more than double what the average corners quote is now. And guess what. They saw far more buyers than sellers. ▪

spread betting: an inside view

TRADE SECRETS

WHEN KARIM FATIH JOINED IG INDEX in 1996 his arrival swelled the sports trading team from five people to six. Within eight years six had become 40, reflecting the rapid explosion of interest in spread betting.

Fatih, now customer experience manager at IG, reflects on the differences between then and now and gives an insight into clients' betting habits and where the punter may have an edge.

By BRUCE MILLINGTON

THEN AND NOW Of the many changes that I have seen in my time in the spread industry, one of the biggest is the extent to which minimum stakes have plummeted.

When I began, the minimum unit stake for double card numbers (the aggregate of the saddlecloth numbers of the winning horses at a race meeting multiplied by two) was £30. That market can easily make up some 40 points away from the spread so the minimum bet was effectively around £1,200. Now you can trade double cards for a pound.

It is a similar story with all our markets. Generally the minimum stake is now 50 pence for everything except low-volatility markets like total goals in a football match.

In the early days we traded nine markets on live football matches and that didn't include

Karim Fatih: Football is king of spreads

corners. You could fit the spreads on to one teletext page and still have room for other things. Now the spreads for one TV game fill three text pages and we still can't cram them all on. The growth of spread betting has been in close parallel with the rise of Sky television.

HOW TURNOVER IS SPLIT

Football is by far and away our most important element. Roughly speaking it accounts for 60 per cent of our business. I would estimate that rugby union and league are responsible for a further eight per cent between them, about the same as for cricket and golf.

Racing's proportion of total turnover was once in excess of ten per cent but has probably dropped marginally below rugby, cricket and golf, while the rest is split between all the other things we bet on, of which tennis, snooker and American football would be the biggest.

HOW THE MARKET HAS CHANGED

It used to be the case that if a football match was exciting it would automatically spell bad news for us, and that if a football match ended 0-0 we would almost certainly be laughing all the way to the bank.

Shirt numbers, goals, corners – you name it we would be short of it. Now, that is no longer the case every time, even if to some degree we are generally happier if matches are dull, well-behaved affairs.

It used to be the case that the wagons (rhyming slang term derived from wagon-shunter, punter) bought everything and the professionals sold. Now, though, they are more clued up. They have access to stats via the internet and are no longer instinctively looking to buy absolutely everything.

This is partly due to the fact that they have learned from experience that there is no mileage in buying, say, shirts obsessively. And they are also well guided by Kevin Pullein.

trade secrets

 Post man always delivers

the pullein factor

Kevin Pullein was the person who changed the way the spread industry went about pricing up football.

Before his articles started appearing, first in *The Sporting Life* and then the *Racing Post*, we would be fairly casual in how we went about coming up with prices.

The bookings is the best example. When we first started doing the market, we didn't even consider the referee to be a factor, which, looking back, is laughable. We would just take the rough average make-ups of the teams and add a few points on, knowing that the vast majority of clients wanted to buy. These days, of course, we would walk over broken glass to find out the identity of the match referee.

We had one particular client who cottoned on to the fact that the quotes were invariably too high and sold religiously. He made a lot of money out of us but we didn't really mind as he helped balance the book sometimes.

But it was Pullein who rumbled us and spread the word that the bookings prices were artificially inflated above their true value. In days gone by, we might have estimated the bookings to be worth 30 and gone up with 32-36. Now, if they are worth 30, we go 28-32.

It is the same with other football markets. Pullein finds an edge, tells his readers about it and we have to react. I have known us to hold emergency meetings to discuss how to alter our pricing policy if he uncovers an edge.

Pullein has been a pivotal figure in shaping how football markets are priced and have evolved down the years.

HOW PRICES ARE MADE After the supremacy and total goals prices have been decided upon, our computers statistically generate prices for all our other standard markets, although the market-makers will always look at them to see if they need tweaking to reflect probable market trends.

With player goal minutes, for example, Thierry Henry's true price when Arsenal are at home to Everton might be 30, but we would probably look to offer 32-35 in anticipation of a majority of buyers.

Similarly, when Tiger Woods was at his peak, his finishing position for a Major would be worth around ten or 11, but we would have to go 6-9 simply because far more people wanted to sell than buy. The shrewdies could see the price was too low and bought yet still did their money.

RELIGIOUS SELLERS We used to have a lady who would sell multi-corners (first-half corners multiplied by second-half corners) before every match. She would trade in anything up to £10 a point. We thought nothing of it until we looked at her account and saw that within a matter of months she had won more than £3,000. She was exploiting the fact that the price was always too high because people generally wanted to buy, although if she did the same thing on that particular market now she would probably do no better than break even. We were happy for this client to help balance our books but we became acutely aware that there was a growing number of what might be termed ex-wagons willing to buck the trend and go against the grain.

There is, however, one truism that has always existed in spread betting and still does. Namely, that cricket runs – both for teams and individual batsmen – are still pitched too high almost every time.

Cricket is perfect for spread betting and many clients' first bet is on a team's runs. Being short of runs has been a mainstay of our business from the outset and it is only recently that a meaningful number of people have begun to detect the value in selling.

Even then, though, we will still pitch England runs at 300-320 at the start of an innings when we know they are worth 300 or just a shade over. And we know most clients will want to be long at 320.

THE LARA EFFECT The reasons we see more buyers than sellers in cricket are varied. Instinctively, though, people probably can't help but think of Brian Lara's innings of 375 and 400. Not everyone wants to sell a guy like Lara at 50 when they could conceivably lose 350 times their stake.

His then record-breaking innings of 375 in 1994 was a massive long-term boost for the spread industry, if a short-term disaster for Sporting Index. They did their money but I have no hesitation in praising the way they milked it so well from a PR perspective.

The publicity they received really opened people's eyes to spread betting and was beneficial to all the companies. It was the same when New Zealand thrashed Japan 145-17 in the 1995 rugby World Cup and with their total wides quote in the 1999 cricket World Cup. Those were terrible results for Sporting but they managed to get valuable publicity out of it.

Lara's 400 against England in 2004 provided me with the greatest escape of my punting career. I am an habitual seller of cricket runs and would undoubtedly have got short of Lara as he walked out to bat.

Thankfully, though, I was on a stag weekend in Copenhagen and could not get on. A weekend in Copenhagen is an expensive business, but nothing like as expensive as it would have been if I had stayed at home.

VULNERABLE SPOTS Anything that is not big enough to warrant us employing a full-time specialist will be traded very cautiously for fear that we know less than the clients.

We do not price up things like Big Brother, the Olympics, cycling and speedway blind. We put as much thought into the prices as we can, but it stands to reason that we are not going to be as hard to beat on things like that than we would on football. We employ nine football specialists, each of whom spends upwards of 40 hours every week analysing matches, poring over stats and discussing various markets. It takes a hell of a punter to get the better of these guys in the long-term.

trade secrets

 My highs and lows

apathy in the uk

My worst price I got the 2001 General Election badly wrong. I am a great believer in focusing on stats and ignoring hype and it usually stands me in good stead, but not on this occasion.

The media was full of predictions that voter apathy would cause the total turnout percentages to hit rock-bottom but I wasn't having it.

The lowest turnout since the beginning of the 20th century had been 72 per cent and the weather forecast was good so I disregarded the theory that large numbers of voters would stay at home and went up at 66-69. It made up at 59 per cent and we lost a massive amount of money. If I was guilty of anything it was that I did not weigh up the stats and the hype and get the balance right.

My best price It's said that any dealer can make money by being short but the real test comes when he gets long and that the mark of a great dealer is that he can win even when a football match finishes 4-3.

A dealer always gets more satisfaction from winning on a high-scoring game, and the one that sticks in my mind was when Newcastle played Tottenham in December 1999. I'd done my research and thought that what we had were two high-scoring sides who were likely to produce plenty of goals between them. I went up with a total goals price of 2.6-2.9 and was amazed that the other firms were going 2.3-2.6.

At first I thought I must have missed something but held firm, even though all the derivative markets – shirts, goal times, etc – were all over the place. Newcastle hammered Spurs 6-1 and it was a fantastic result for the company.

THE FUTURE The advent of betting exchanges and the removal of betting tax for fixed-odds punters have undoubtedly made it harder for us to grow the business, but we are still managing to do so, even though new accounts are opened less frequently than they were during the boom of the 1990s.

Improved customer service is crucial. The days of our staff talking to customers in an aggressive 'city boy' style are long gone. And having a website that allows punters to bet in real time on the net is also a massive advantage. I believe spread betting remains an adrenalin-pumping experience and will continue to thrive.

inside the mind of a pro punter

BEATS WORKING

MAKE NO MISTAKE, KELVIN
Richardson knows the time of day. So said
a prominent figure in the betting industry
of a man who took Nick Leeson's job after the
infamous squanderer of money was rumbled
but did not inherit Leeson's ability to kiss
fortunes goodbye.

By BRUCE
MILLINGTON

One time of day Richardson doesn't know
any more is 5.30am, which is when he used
to leave the house to go to work in the City.

Life in the Square Mile was good to him
and the fruits of his career are a large house
in a leafy Home Counties town which oozes
affluence from every bistro and patisserie.

But while his life as a handsomely paid
employee of some of the most prestigious
finance houses in the world has provided
the 41-year-old, his wife, two children and
dog with a home to die for, Richardson's
champagne lifestyle – not to mention the
children's school fees – are funded by the
career path he has elected to tread for nearly
five years. He is a professional punter.

Here, he lifts the lid on the highs and
lows of earning a crust out of betting.

LIFE BEFORE PRO PUNTING I was born
in Liverpool and came down to London when
I was 15. After getting a law degree I worked

**Kelvin Richardson:
no more early starts**

beats
working

What I
bet on

When I was working
I had to completely
write off horses. It is
impossible to keep
tabs on form when
you are in full-time
employment.

Now I am back
studying the form
properly again and
I would say horses
and dogs account
for around half my
bets, with the other
half being divided
up mainly between
football, rugby
league, American
football, cricket and
golf. Of those five,
I do my own work
on the first three and
rely on an associate
to mark my card on
the other two.

I don't believe it
is possible to be able
to focus on any more
sports than these.

I reckon I do
marginally better
on sport than racing.

for Warburgs, in London and Paris, but in
1997 I decided I wanted to stop working
for someone else and punt for a living.

I did this for three years but was then made
a great offer to return to the City, which I did
for two years.

Then, after a drunken night in a casino just
outside Deauville, I ended up dancing on a
table in a nightclub. I fell off and shattered
my arm. I was given six weeks off to recover
and in that time I put £2,000 into my Betfair
account, which I played up to £102,000. It
felt great to be back punting all day again
so I decided to resign from my job and give it
another go. I have not worked for anyone else
since and have absolutely no plans to do so.

A TYPICAL DAY Take a busy Wednesday
in, say, September, when there is a lot of sport
on the go. I will take a call at 10am from
my golf man. He will give me the names to
back on both that week's tournaments, both
outright and on the threeballs and match bets.

After I have placed the golf bets, I will crack
on with the day's racing, using the *Racing Post*,
the internet and various connections in racing.

Having got my bets lined up, I will then
have a look at the evening's football before
the racing starts.

After racing I will have a break before
the football starts and only once the matches
are over does the day end.

FOOTBALL This is a mainstay of my betting
and I am particularly active on ante-post
markets. I will look to get £100,000 a season
out of long-term points markets on the spreads,
and usually manage to do so. In the 2003-04
season I finished £180,000 up. That's quite
a decent tax-free income!

I like trading teams' points because the old
cliché about bad luck evening itself out
over the course of a season is generally

true, and a team's ability will be reflected far more accurately over the course of a number of games than in one 90-minute period, during which they can hit the post, have shots cleared off the line, have players wrongly sent off and any number of other misfortunes that can result in them failing to win games they deserve to.

I always look to trade teams dynamically. In other words, if I have bought a team's total points at 61 and the team keeps winning, I will keep buying – at 65, 68, 71, whatever – because they are proving me right and I want to maximise my position.

By the same token, If I have bought at 61 but the bet goes wrong – the team might be failing to sell out their home games, there could be reports of discontent in the dressing room, their key players are rumoured to be up for sale and results go wrong – I will sell them and keep selling them.

It goes wrong from time to time but the policy leaves me in strong positions more often than not.

As far as individual matches go, I would say my average bet is around £3,000.

I don't bet on sports I dislike. I must have an intuitive feel for something. Take a football match between Leeds and Manchester United. I know that if that game takes place at 8pm on a Wednesday night it is a completely different fixture to what it would be if it was kicking off at noon on a Sunday, yet the prices are highly unlikely to reflect that.

RUGBY LEAGUE The advantage of being a punter in rugby league is fairly obvious: bookmakers have to price up around 12 matches every weekend but I can choose how many I want to bet on.

As far as deciding which matches I play on, there is no magic secret to it. I just feel I have

beats working

 Golden rules

I have surprisingly few hard and fast rules. I have maxims on various things but I will often ignore them. For example, I'll look to oppose a dog over hurdles if it is odds-on. But then if such a dog is 4-5 and you make it 1-3 you can't not back it.

Of the various types of pros, arbers are the ones with golden rules, but they operate in a completely different way to me.

They always take a profit when they can and such like, but to my way of thinking they aren't gamblers in the true sense.

They may delude themselves that they are professional punters but all they are doing in reality is guaranteeing a particular sum of money every week so are basically little short of office workers on wages.

I know others who are pro punters in that they do not work for a living, but they bet when drunk, chase their losses and do all sorts of things that are fundamentally wrong. That doesn't mean they are not winners though.

an edge on the compilers in many cases, especially once team news has broken or weather conditions have changed after the prices have been made. Often these factors are not reflected sufficiently in the prices, even when changes are made.

Where the industry has the edge over punters is, of course, with the handicap draw. It is a scandal that bookmakers do not use half-point handicaps to eradicate the draw. I lose count of the times I have been undone by the handicap draw. What is especially galling is that, not only will the bookmakers be 5-6 each team, they also have the extra percentage from the draw price on their side.

AMERICAN FOOTBALL Again, ante-post betting is my main source of profit on American football. I like to have a good look at the divisions right through the regular NFL season. I am not sure the prices always change as much as they should after each week of matches. I mainly do singles, although I have been known to get stuck in with anything up to a five-timer if one firm is out of line on a number of matches I fancy. I am an avid watcher of NFL and will go over to see Tampa around five times a year. I also try to get to the Super Bowl when I can.

GOLF My golf man is superb and puts in phenomenal amounts of research work. For a Major he can easily do eight 18-hour days of preparation. He places great importance on weather conditions, which are often not reflected in the market, and is an excellent judge of weather conditions and knowing which players will be suited by going out in the morning or the afternoon.

CRICKET Another sport in which I rely upon other people for information. My cricket contact does the donkey work and I put on for him. Whatever winning bets we have I split with him on a 25/75 basis.

HOW MUCH I WIN All I know is that with the mortgage, school fees, travel and everyday living expenses, I need to make at least £150,000 every year and I have never failed to reach that figure.

I have bad days and bad weeks. Very occasionally I have bad months, but never a bad year. I would say that in my least successful year I still made £150,000, although I need to given how much I spend on watching live sport.

I like to go to at least one live event every week, be it horses, dogs, a football match, cricket or whatever, just to get me out of the house and in touch with the outside world. On top of that I will get the sports diary out every so often and book trips here, there and everywhere to watch live sport.

Whether it is racing in Dubai or Dublin, a live NFL game in Tampa, the African Nations Cup or cricket in St Lucia I get a terrific buzz from watching great sport in the flesh, especially when I know it is being funded by my betting. My profit margin is less than ten per cent, probably nearer eight, and I am turning over well in excess of £2m per year.

DISCIPLINE I am pleased to say I have never had a boredom bet since I stopped working for other people. Nor do I chase my losses, although I know plenty of pro punters that do.

They will probably deny this but I know for a fact that many, because they compile day-to-day profit/loss figures, will have a disproportionately large bet on the last horse or dog race of the day.

I do around half an hour of accounting work every day, but I have to admit it is pretty chaotic and I am not constantly aware of my current profit/loss situation. There are

beats working

 The bubble never bursts

Napoleon once said of champagne: "In victory we deserve it. In defeat we need it." That applies perfectly to punting. I drink two bottles of champagne every day. Tea before 11am, champagne after. It helps with my temperament, especially when I back a horse that gets chucked out and am in danger of feeling so down that it knocks my confidence.

It is no good being too big a worrier in this game. You can't lose £400 on a dog and start thinking that you could have bought a new TV with that money.

Then again, nor can you get too complacent and kid yourself that you are simply playing a numbers game. If I am having £15,000 on a football match, the figure merely reflects how much I fancy a particular team. But it is also an amount of money and you must not lose sight of that.

When all is said and done, though, I am confident that I'll always win in the long run, even if I am on a bad run.

beats working

 Excellence of exchanges

the only way of getting on

There is no way I would have contemplated taking the plunge and giving up my job to go punting had it not been for Betfair.

The idea of being able to get such value and be able to have as much on with the traditional bookmakers is absurd.

These companies have now effectively given up trying to compete for the big punters' business. They are all about virtual racing, slot machines and numbers games. There are occasions when I can get a £5,000 football bet on with a big-name fixed-odds firm, but generally they don't want to know.

Personally, if I was pricing something up I would like to think I had enough faith in my price to stand a few big bets, but they don't seem to care about things like that.

times when I will get a bill of a few thousand pounds and will rummage through a drawer to find a cheque or two from other bookmakers to settle it.

I am not as disciplined as I could be, that's for sure. There are times, for instance, when I am at the races and have told everyone to back my nap of the meeting and I will be the only one who did not get on because I was getting a round of drinks in instead.

And I also let emotion seep into my betting which is, I know, ridiculously indisciplined. As a lifelong Evertonian I will never lay them and never back Liverpool. It is different with England. I want the national teams to win everything but will not hesitate to lay them when the price is wrong, which it often is.

A good test of a punter's discipline comes when there is a live event on television. The usual dilemma exists of whether to have an interest bet or not. I think the two rules that I adhere most to are never to change stakes to chase losses and never to bet on an event simply because the Sky cameras are present. After all, it's not like the bad old days when we only got about five live football matches a year and felt obliged to have a punt – there is live sport 24 hours a day, seven days a week. It also helps that my big ante-post books mean that normally I automatically have a long-term financial interest in most live NFL, rugby league and football matches.

The serious approach to betting on live sporting events where you have no opinion on the prices before the start should be to watch it for a possible in-running bet or at the very worst simply to pick up clues for future matches.

HEDGING Betfair has been fantastic for hedging, but in certain areas it is not as good as it was simply because things have evolved.

There was a time when, having backed the draw at 9-4 in a football match, you could lay it back at 1-5 with 87 minutes on the clock. These days you are having to offer 1-2 if you want to cover your position. It's crazy. Three minutes plus probably another three minutes of injury time and the draw is 1-2. There is no way you can possibly lay at that level.

SPREADS When they came on to the scene they were a breath of fresh air. While fixed-odds betting still entailed paying nine per cent tax, the spread firms came out all guns blazing and looked like they would be the future face of betting.

Then they changed. Sporting Index shut me down and the others limited my stakes to such an extent that I became disillusioned with them.

If you had told me in the mid-1990s that I would struggle to get on with the spread firms and that fixed-odds betting would be everyone's god I would have laughed myself silly. But that's the way it has gone.

I am, though, extremely encouraged by what I see of Spreadfair. Now, there will be no getting knocked back for the bets I want and the margins will be as small as they are on Betfair. I expect a lot of disenfranchised spread punters to get back into this form of betting thanks to Spreadfair.

GETTING ON I believe a number of professionals like to remain anonymous because they do not want bookmakers knowing who they are as it might affect their chances of getting the bets they want on. But I have long given up trying to get on with the majority of bookmakers in my own name so I am not remotely bothered who knows what I do.

I can get accommodated to my desired levels on many events on Betfair, but there are certain markets where there is not enough liquidity to enable me to get what I want on. If I want a £6,000 threeball bet on the golf, for instance, I have no choice but to use satellite accounts. I have various accounts in friends' names with each fixed-odds and spread firm which has shut me down. The problem, of course, is that these people are not always available at short notice so it involves a lot of time spent on phone calls and money transfers.

PERKS OF THE JOB There are many. I do not have to be up at the crack of dawn, walking to the station in the pitch black, and not get home until 8pm five days a week.

If I want to miss a race and pop down to collect the children from school I can. I have the freedom to go racing, go to the dogs, go to football, fly to Australia to watch the Ashes series whenever I want. I am never bored. I have not had a single boredom bet since I stopped working for other people.

I can crack open a bottle of champagne when other people are going for their morning coffee break, and best of all I can see my kids growing up every day of the week instead of just at weekends.

getting it all figured out

RATINGS FOR ALL

FROM THE MOMENT WE COME INTO this world, ratings exert a profound, though almost always invisible, influence on the way we live our lives.

This process starts within minutes of popping out of the womb with newborn babies subject to a series of observations called the Apgar Test that rates their breathing, pulse, activity and appearance with scores on a scale of 0-2. When these individual ratings are added together and applied to an overall scale this quickly calculable and, critically, objective figure provides medical staff with an effective solution to determining a baby's health and the most appropriate response to it.

This rating process continues through childhood with various methods of ratings being used to determine the extent and depth of our education and thus having a very large impact on the rest of our days.

If only it stopped there. By the time we're adults, in just about every walk of life, the effects of ratings are all-pervasive. Your behaviour is reduced to a number by those people or organisations seeking to try to objectify, or simplify, an aspect of you. Whether you're being rushed through a hospital emergency ward on a stretcher or trying to buy a new television, behind the scenes will be in

By ALEX DEACON

Ease surface tension: ratings help you tell who thrives on which terrain

place a system that its creators hope will provide the best indication of how to deal with you and your current situation.

WHY MAKE SPORTS RATINGS? That the everyday rating of our lives is important to sports punters may not seem completely obvious to those who go about their betting exclusively from the perspective that personal knowledge, as well as one's ability to sift through the masses of pertinent information, is sufficient to come up trumps.

Given the amount of data and the increasing sophistication of sports markets even the traditional reading of form as an exclusive method of finding your bets has become increasingly irrelevant as we seek to make the most objective and accurate decision.

The amount of data, much of it contra-dictory, surrounding a single sporting event, whether it be a football match, horse race or the latest round of F1, is the most obvious reason why those interested in sports betting turn to using ratings, either their own or a third party's, as a means of getting an objective handle on a sport with relatively little fuss.

Horseracing provides an excellent example of why punters need to simplify all of the available data. With each new angle that is found in racing eventually entering the public domain and thus becoming common currency to every punter, the picture becomes ever more confusing to those punters trying to catch a winner by taking in all the information at hand.

Where does a punter start? Is it with collateral form, draw bias, official ratings, speed ratings, trainer records, jockey form, the going or the course itself? Bearing all of those things in mind it's no wonder that many confused punters' methodology is little more elaborate than a blindfold and pin. The list is as endless as it is ultimately perplexing and is no less complicated when looking at sports other than racing.

For those who've avoided the route of pinsticking, it doesn't take many bets before a pattern develops as to what factors a punter considers when making their choice. Usually this happens as a consequence of a bet winning and, people being people, they naturally repeat the exercise in anticipation of a similar outcome, if not the next time then certainly within the foreseeable future.

Pretty soon a pattern is set in their punting and while there is a consistency to what they're doing, for most it will prove insufficient to see them coming out on top in the long run.

This strikes at the very heart of how ratings can help by rationalising all of the available information; you not only free yourself up from time-consuming form studies but also create a consistent framework from which to make your decisions and your bets. It's a fact that the worst punters are those who are entirely inconsistent in the way they go about looking at a sport. Ratings bring a consistency to your betting and, while their modification

RATINGS FOR RUG RATS THE APGAR TEST			
Score	0	1	2
Heart rate	No heart beat	lower than 100 per min	higher than 100 per min
Respiration	Not breathing	Weak crying	Strong crying
Muscle tone	Limp	Some movement	Active
Reflex	No response	Grimacing	Grimace and cough or sneezing
Colour	Blue or pale	Good colour with blue hands or feet	Completely pink

Total score 7-10, infant in good health
Lower than 7, infant is monitored and retested

and refinement can over time see them adjust to new ideas and changes in sport, they do provide a very satisfactory way to set about finding winners.

THE DISSENTERS Despite so much evidence in favour of objectifying one's impression of a sport and broad acceptance of the benefits that they can bring to your betting, amazingly there are still those punters out there who give ratings a very wide berth on account of what are usually far from convincing reasons.

The most common of these excuses has to be, aside from the fact that they take some work of your own that doesn't involve scanning the newspaper, is that they in some way remove the 'human' element from betting.

Nothing could be further from the truth. A good rating is achieved by those who can look rationally at a sport and decide what counts when trying to forecast it and how each of those aspects of the sport relates to the others. If that isn't putting a personal touch on your betting, it's hard to know what is.

My own objection, however, is to losing and the bad feeling that that leaves in me. Quite frankly, every punter should see it as their duty to themselves to do whatever is possible to minimise the risk of that happening. Better that than rejecting something out of hand simply on account of it being seen as some kind of slur on your punterhood.

About the only reasonable excuse is that you've already got yourself a functional and profitable methodology to start with, but this isn't exactly the situation that most punters find themselves in. Even so many continue to resist taking any help from ratings, preferring instead to continue to rely on their, more often than not, fatally flawed judgement.

WHAT MAKES A GOOD RATING?

Like skinning the proverbial cat there are any number of ways that an accurate rating can be calculated. It's merely a question of what type of rating you want to create.

Many ratings exist with the sole reason of establishing a 'true' order of ranking. We will go on and look at this in the Elo rating, which not only creates an accurate figure but can also be used to prescribe probabilities and thus odds to those sports that it is rating.

Before looking at the creation of your own figures, for the purposes of betting, any really useful rating has to be able to be taken further and used as part of the process of calculating odds. There's little point in doing all the work behind devising even the simplest ratings method if, once you're done, it doesn't in some way or another provide a reasonable approximation of the 'true' odds.

ELO RATINGS

The easiest way into the world of sports ratings has to be what are known as Elo ratings, which, while comparatively ubiquitous in providing the origins for many ratings systems across a range of sports, have nevertheless remained a powerful tool in the hands of a competent ratings fiend.

Having originally been conceived as a way of rating the ability of chess players both past

ratings for all

 You don't have to be a boffin

pinpointing the key factors

In talking to punters, both successful and otherwise, it's clear that there are any number of ways that one can set about approaching the problem of forecasting a sport. From within that variety of methods it's equally clear, regardless of the diversity of ideas and approaches, that each of these has its merits and disadvantages. The measure of success is, however, determined between those punters who are going about their business intelligently and consistently and those that are in real terms just guessing.

One of the great myths about creating ratings is that you need to be some kind of egg-headed freak with a postgraduate maths degree in order to get even relatively close to having a handle on the topic.

As someone who struggled at a horrible level with school maths before throwing in the towel for many years, I can vouch that this is complete nonsense, however difficult it may appear at the onset

of sitting down and figuring out how to start making ratings.

As with ratings in the real world, sports ratings only attempt to distil all the available and relevant information into a concise, yet representative, form that can be easily interpreted and used for the purpose you intend. In our case, making money.

Speed ratings in horseracing are the obvious example of this as they look purely at the particularly fundamental aspect of a horse, namely how fast the beast can run.

However, the skill in making speed ratings comes in determining which factors you use to adjust the original time by.

From then on it's up to the individual creating the rating to determine how they will take that actual time and create a relative speed figure from it by factoring in variables such as the going, race distance, weight carried and weight allowances for the age of the horse.

and present, the Elo rating system lends itself very well to the purpose of sports betting in that it can be used not only to determine the relative strength but also to calculate probabilities and thus odds.

In addition to that primary reason it is also a useful system in that it can be easily subjected to modifications that can be made to fit one's own ideas as to what elements of a sport a rating should reflect.

The first adaptation of the Elo system in the UK for betting purposes came in Drapkin and Forsyth's seminal book *The Punter's*

Revenge, to which various modifications have been made over the years – some public, some not. The Elo version described here has in time become the most popular starting point for the system and the example used is the most basic interpretation and so allows for the greatest modification.

A further plus in using an Elo-based system is that unlike other types of ratings it doesn't necessarily require the use of a computer to calculate the match-by-match changes.

The system works in the following manner: each team/player has a point value that is calculated on a match-by-match basis with the average rating of all sides in the system being 1,000 at any given moment. In order to calculate the ratings change for each game both opponents provide a proportion of their points total to a match 'kitty'. The amount that each opponent supplies is determined by, in the instance of football (or those sports with a home/away bias), whether they are the home or away side, with the home side providing seven per cent of their current points total and the away side five per cent. When taking the system over to sports without a home or away split this figure is, in the case of our example, six per cent for either opponent.

The points in this kitty are then redistributed according to the match result with the winning side receiving all of the points while a draw sees the total redistributed with 50 per cent of points going to either side.

A simple example shows the basic method in operation. The match illustrated below is set at the start of the system so that each team's rating is set at 1,000. To rate an entire division each side would initially be set at 1,000 and the same calculation applied to every game, with the most recently played matches the last to be entered into the system.

The table shows the changes that occur

to the distribution of the kitty with each possible result type and the resulting change to either side's rating. This figure is then carried over into their next game and used as their new rating value. Once this calculation has been repeated for each club, so that all have about 15-20 games behind them

ELO, ELO, ELO WHAT'S GOING ON HERE THEN?

Home	Current	7%	5%	Current	Away
Man United	1000	70	50	1000	Birmingham
Result	New home (Man Utd) rating		New away (Birmingham) rating		
Home win	1050		950		
Draw	990		1010		
Away	930		1070		

in the system, it's quite likely that you'll be in possession of a figure that provides a reasonably accurate reflection of each side's ability relative to the other sides in the system.

Before setting out to rate a sport it is important that you know you will have sufficient data to process for the system to settle the ratings at the correct level. For a situation such as creating grass-only ratings for tennis players or cup match-only ratings for football teams, the rater has to look to making a modification to the system given that it's almost certain that the games being rated happen much less frequently. It's not difficult to find sides that regularly get knocked out of cup competitions in the first or second round and so attention has to be paid to the accuracy of their figures in these circumstances, with the figure changing at a comparatively slow rate.

In terms of making basic modifications to the method, by far and away the easiest is to modify the proportion of points added to the kitty by the home and away side. By making the smallest changes it is possible to make significant improvements to the original method.

For example, by making changes to the original seven and five per cent proportion of points that are added to the match kitty it is possible, by increasing the figures, to give more prominence to recent form. Similarly, by reducing the proportions taken, each side's rating will change at a slower rate.

Further simple additions could also be made, for example by factoring in the margin of victory by looking to add or subtract further points from the system to reflect this extra detail from the game. Similarly in tennis ratings I've found it useful to make a similar adjustment by calculating the difference in set totals at the end of a match. In other words, extra points can be added to and taken away from the modified ratings by looking at the winning margin in a game so that a one-set victory adds an extra percentage point into the calculation, while a two-set margin adds two per cent. Using such a method also helps to create a distinction between the quality of competitions, as with Grand Slam events being five-set affairs players have a chance of winning and losing by bigger margins with the maximum margin being three rather than two per cent.

LOOKING AT SPORTS

Having sat and made ratings for a wide variety of sports, the first myth that's worth dispelling is the one that says you should bet only on those sports that you have a genuine interest in and thus have some enthusiasm for. Better still, I say, to have an enthusiasm for ratings in general and a belief in what good ones can achieve. As a consequence of this, you will have plenty more opportunities to bet on.

Outside of my published football ratings it's fair to say that I have little, if any, affection for most of the sports that I've tried to create

ratings for all

 Record collecting

vital to analyse your results

It's important to analyse your ratings by keeping records of them. The most useful and simple method is to record the match, game or race results against your ratings together with some idea as to the best available prices. In time the value of having done so will be worth its weight in gold, whether your ratings are working or not.

What you choose to record depends to a large extent on the time that you have available to maintain your ratings but, regardless of the particular sport that you're looking at, there is a minimum standard that you must adhere to if your ratings are to be of any use for punting:

◇ Date of event.

◇ Competition name. In addition to the name of the competition it's also sometimes worth recording additional information about it that may help in modifying your ratings. For example, it is essential to find somewhere to note down the par score for a golf tournament.

◇ Team or player names.

◇ Final match score. For example, the final score in football, the set score in tennis, the total shots in golf or winning position in F1.

◇ Additional scores. In football one would look to record half-time scores or in the event of extra time those after 90 minutes, while in

tennis it would be useful, in addition to having recorded the set scores, to also record the scores of individual sets. Golf raters are also well served by keeping the individual round scores of players in addition to the final shot total.

◇ Pre-match ratings for each player/team. These show the ratings that each player or team brings into the game and from which your pre-match forecasts are derived.

◇ Post-match ratings for each player. These reflect the change that has taken place to the pre-match rating as a consequence of the outcome of the match.

◇ Bookmakers' odds. It's hard to underestimate the importance that one has to attach to recording the odds for each game or contest that they're rating. Without doing so it is impossible to ever know how your ratings fared against the bookies and how much money you would have won or lost.

As a minimum it's worth taking down the best available prices. However, it is time well-spent to look at recording the prices of a consistent group of bookmakers so that you can identify which are perhaps weak in pricing up the sport in question. I keep the prices of three high street firms as well the most traded price of the betting exchanges.

ratings for, although that's far from saying that I don't experience the same pleasure from rating and betting on them as I do when looking at football. In fact there's a reasonable argument to bei made that suggests specific

ratings for all

Other ratings methods

more to life than elo

Aside from Elo ratings there are many other types of ratings in an ascending order of complexity. It's probably true to say that the more mathematically complex a system becomes the more potential there is for the ratings to be more accurate.

Nevertheless, the necessity for involving complex mathematics can be met head-on by those punters who show themselves to be adept at correctly identifying and weighting the importance of the elements that make up each sport.

My own preference over the years has been to continually develop my original derivation of Elo to the point that it is barely recognisable. Nevertheless, in that time I've tried to look into as many other systems as possible to see if there are any useful ideas that I could possibly take across to improve my own figures.

Rather than look to specific differences between the mathematics of ratings, I feel it's more useful to look at the factors, many of them common, which are used in the creation of ratings.

knowledge about a sport can, from a betting perspective, be a hindrance as preconceptions almost always override the less obvious or merely hidden 'facts' that ratings can show up. Having watched football for more than 25 years it's fair to say that what it taught me about betting on the sport can be etched, with plenty of room to spare, on top of the pinsticker's weapon of choice.

The growth of betting exchanges and the ability to easily play both sides of a proposition can also be exploited by those playing such markets as 'pick a winner' type betting can be consigned to the dustbin by those playing a ratings-based game. All that appears to be required is the knowledge that you don't have to be anything other than a fraction more accurate in your prices and a bit more objective than the next guy to come out on top. In this situation ratings are a positive boon. Despite this the vast majority of punters feel they like to use their own knowledge and judgement to get ahead in their betting.

Aside from horseracing, the next most popular sport to bet on in the UK is football. However, the national sport's popularity means that it is much easier to determine the odds of a football match than, say, a 20-runner handicap and that the opportunities to bet to a big advantage on football are increasingly few and far between.

For those football punters wanting to turn over more money from their betting banks, the only solution is therefore to look to other sports where the information overload doesn't mess things up by over-informing the market to the extent that the lines are so tight. The consequence of not doing that, unless you're turning over a lot of money on football, is that without a considerable measure of skill and luck on your part it's unlikely to be vastly rewarding without significant risk.

In looking at rating sports other than football we'll focus on a selective group of three. Each not only presents decent betting action but can also be used to highlight key points as well as certain pitfalls that are of the utmost importance to those making ratings.

GOLF In addition to all the usual US sports, punters across the Atlantic have for many years made good use of golf ratings, unlike those in this country. I've never quite worked out why, given how readily the sport lends itself to ratings, this should be the case, particularly given the number of opportunities that exist, week in, week out, across an ever-increasing range of outright as well as match-based markets.

So while the popularity of golf betting in this country continues to grow at a slow but steady rate, the sophistication of many of the methods that punters use to try to get inside the game appear, in most instances, to have originated in the sports betting dark ages. That is not to

GOLF 2004 US MASTERS RATINGS
Actual par 72, adjusted par 72.75 (average of all scores)

	Actual score		Adjusted
Phil Mickelson	279	-9	-12
Ernie Els	280	-8	-11
K.J. Choi	282	-6	-9
Bernhard Langer	285	-3	-6
Sergio Garcia	285	-3	-6
Fred Couples	286	-2	-5
Davis Love III	286	-2	-5
Nick Price	286	-2	-5
Kirk Triplett	286	-2	-5
Chris DiMarco	286	-2	-5
Vijay Singh	286	-2	-5
Paul Casey	286	-2	-5

say that punters can't have success doing so – just that from my perspective golf does appear to be one of the great untouched areas in which punters could seriously prosper by looking to develop their own ratings system.

At the simple end of things the creation of a tournament par score can serve as a basis for a form rating for each player. This is achieved by averaging the final scores in a tournament for those players who beat the cut and offsetting each player's score against the tournament par. For example, in the 2004 US Masters, the tournament average score was 291 against the course par of 288. Thus, Phil Mickelson's tournament score is recalculated from his final score of -9 to -12. Similarly, Tiger Woods' 288 changes from a course par to an adjusted 2.4-under.

Having adjusted the scores it's possible then to take them further by adding them to those from previous tournaments to create a considerably more useful value than would be the case if one were looking purely at raw scores. Depending on the number of tournaments that you look back over, such a method has been shown to be a very useful indicator of player form.

THE SAGARIN METHOD In the US, sports ratings guru Jeff Sagarin has been rating golfers for many years using a 'pure' ratings approach similar to the Elo system as well as a more general type of analysis to come up with a final figure. In doing so Sagarin has been able to take this further and create decent figures across a wide range of sports and from the perspective of a consistent approach, this appears to be an excellent example for aspiring ratings creators to follow.

It is interesting when looking at ratings to see what factors the person behind them is employing and while it is rare for them ever to divulge the calculations involved in the final figure, it is nevertheless easy to get a general idea of where they're coming from. So it is with Sagarin's golf figures, which are composed of three key elements – power ratings, the strength of each player's schedule relative to other players and overall records.

The power ratings aspect is the one most similar to the Elo ratings.

Like the Elo figure it doesn't provide a representation of what score the player will shoot, rather it forecasts the expected difference between the player's score and those of the other players in the tournament. What this means is that rather than the ratings saying that Player X is going to go out in his next match and specifically shoot a 70 in each round and Player Y a 72; the ratings merely provide an idea as to how many shots better or worse off player X is to player Y. In this case Player X is two shots to the good over his opponent.

As we've seen previously, this is a useful figure to get hold of, but Sagarin then looks to improve the original power figure by modifying it in accordance with some other important factors.

Sagarin provided a good example of how to take a rating forward in that his method highlights which are the most important additional factors with which to improve an Elo-style rating.

From my own experience the factoring in of previous opponent strength is perhaps the most important of all modifications that can be made to a set of ratings. In fact it's essential to all those sports where teams or players over the course of the season might not have met the same group of opponents as their rivals.

This is at its most obvious at the start of a season when, for example, one team might have met three of the tougher clubs and another three of the weakest. At this juncture there is no point in drawing a distinction between the two on account of their results without factoring in the fact that one has had it easy and the other hasn't. Over time and as the season progresses the strength of their schedules will broadly average themselves out so this becomes less of a factor, but until that has happened you have to work out a way in which you can reflect the differences.

In golf the situation often arises when players who are highly rated from performances in smaller tournaments take that same figure over to play for the bigger money. As a consequence a way needs to be found to account for the fact that whatever the rating, it has almost certainly been compiled from results achieved against a weaker set of rivals.

A similar problem also occurs when trying to rate most team sports as it is not usually until around the halfway point of the season that every team has played each other. In some respects the Elo rating deals with this factor as, when adjusting a player or team's score, it does so in accordance with the strength of the opposition. Nevertheless, the fact that one team might have played significantly tougher opponents than another does mean that the rating changes are potentially not as representative of their true strength as they might be.

In such instances one simple solution to this has been to record and then average the Elo ratings of opponents that each side has met to create a generalised previous schedule strength rating in addition to the overall rating. While yet another figure to refer to, a schedule-strength rating serves as a fine check-and-balance tool for any overall rating.

Aside from those specific factors the key to looking at Sagarin's numbers, or for that matter any rating system, is to focus on the broad factors that each individual sports-rater believes are necessary in order to make the most accurate forecast for the given sport.

The beauty of making ratings is that the choice is yours. If you don't consider it relevant to determine the overall strength of a team's previous opponents in calculating that team's worth then it's quite easy to ignore it and concentrate on those factors that you do consider important.

FORMULA ONE While not necessarily the best medium for betting, due to the relatively small number of grands prix in any one season, the increasing number of markets now available over the course of a grand prix weekend is sufficient to warrant some investigation by those interested in sports ratings.

As with all of the sports discussed in this chapter, Formula One can be easily rated on a relative level by using the Elo method. Similarly to the use of Elo ratings in golf, Formula One can be rated in this manner with every driver in the race assessed independently against each other driver. In so doing, over the course of one race, his rating is calculated as though he has had as many one-on-one races as there are other drivers in the race.

While this is useful, given the comparatively small number of cars in each race, together with the fact that they are as often as not the same driver/car combinations it's not exactly difficult to establish an accurate pecking order from a simple study of form.

Where I have tried to deviate from this in the past has been to try to take many of the ideas I have used in developing speed figures for horseracing on to the F1 circuit in order to establish an objective measure of the speed differences, particularly in the mass of middle-to-bottom-ranking cars.

This task is made relatively simple given the precision with which F1 is timed, unlike the 'one-Mississippi, two-Mississippi' style timings that a lot of horse races still appear to have been timed by. Together with masses of sectional times to play around with, the opportunities for time-based punters, particularly betting in-running, are quite significant.

As with speed figures for horseracing, the best way to set about creating F1 speed figures is to establish standard times for each circuit. This is a task, as in horseracing, that is easier said than done given the regularity with which changes are made to the layout of a circuit or course.

From that standard time, which needn't be much more than an average lap time, a base point can be established from which it is possible to start relating the times a driver is putting in during practice, qualifying or in the course of a race.

Similar principles can also be taken over to other race-based sports, although, however nice it is to have your own ratings for cycling or athletics, the number of times in a year that you can use them to have a decent bet is very small.

FORMULA ONE BRITISH GRAND PRIX 2004

	Driver	Laps	Time beaten	Seconds raced	Seconds lost per km	Rating
1	Michael Schumacher	60	0	5034	0.000	100
2	Kimi Raikkonen	60	2.1	5036.1	0.007	93
3	Rubens Barrichello	60	3.1	5037.1	0.010	90
4	Jenson Button	60	10.6	5044.6	0.034	66
5	Juan Pablo Montoya	60	12.1	5046.1	0.039	61
6	Giancarlo Fisichella	60	12.8	5046.8	0.041	59
7	David Coulthard	60	19.6	5053.6	0.064	36
8	Mark Webber	60	23.7	5057.7	0.077	23
9	Felipe Massa	60	24	5058	0.078	22
10	Fernando Alonso	60	24.8	5058.8	0.080	20
11	Takuma Sato	60	33.7	5067.7	0.109	0
12	Marc Gene	60	34.3	5068.3	0.111	0
13	Cristiano da Matta	59	+1 lap	0		0
14	Christian Klien	59	+1 lap	0		0
15	Nick Heidfeld	59	+1 lap	0		0
16	Gianmaria Bruni	56	+4 lap	0		0

Retired Giorgio Pantano (47 laps, spin), Jarno Trulli (39 laps, accident) Zsolt Baumgartner (29 laps, engine) Olivier Panis (16 laps, accident)

Rating = 100 – (seconds lost per km x 1000)

TENNIS Like each of the sports looked at in this chapter, tennis provides an excellent opportunity to rate with a basic system such as Elo. However, while experience suggests that an overall figure of each player's ability in relation to another is certainly a useful indicator when going on to forecast a game on a general level, factors such as the differences in surfaces have to be accounted for in some way.

The most obvious call is to simply apply the basic rating method across each surface by only rating those matches on specific surfaces. This is easy enough when looking at the most prevalent surfaces such as hard-court or clay. However, it's less simple when we come to look at the game on grass which, unfortunately for tennis punters given that Wimbledon still perseveres with an organic surface, is about the one time in which there is plenty of money sloshing around to bet against.

A problem arises here, which is the case with potentially all ratings, as there are an insufficient number of grass events each year. Therefore any figure you create will, by its very nature, be less accurate than those for surfaces which dominate the season's schedule. To this end, performance ratings on a game-by-game basis have to be created in the knowledge that you must have sufficient data in the first place with which to create your figures.

In the example of tennis, one of the more interesting aspects to come out of creating surface-specific figures is that while on the face of it they should create more accurate figures, the analysis of them, at least from the point of Elo ratings, suggests that punters are better off concentrating on creating a general figure that represents players' performances across all surfaces.

Partly this is due to the all-surface rating being more reflective of recent form. However, it also suggests that the tennis betting orthodoxy in the distinction that is made between a player's ability on different surface types is, on a general level at least, perhaps over-emphasised.

Again ratings can serve to quantify many of the things we take for granted when we look at a sport.

CONCLUSIONS It's a measure of how hard it is to win at sports betting that many of the world's finest poker players seem to lose much of what they grind out on the baize tables when they take their very considerable gambling skills over to the world of sport.

If such hardened and knowledgeable people can't make it work, with their in-built sense

TENNIS ALL-SURFACE RATINGS

My tennis ratings during the 2004 season for games played on all surfaces

	Weekly rank change	Current rating	Seasonal change	Season start rating	Tnmnts played
1 Roger Federer	0	1060	40	1020	19
2 Andy Roddick	0	1026.8	10.8	1016	23
3 Guillermo Coria	0	982.4	8.4	974	22
4 Carlos Moya	0	977.2	56.2	921	23
5 Tim Henman	0	968.4	71.4	897	20
6 David Nalbandian	0	959.2	16.2	943	16
7 Juan Carlos Ferrero	0	946	-38	984	19
8 Rainer Schuettler	0	938	-29	967	28
9 Gaston Gaudio	2	929.2	10.2	919	22
10 Lleyton Hewitt	-1	928	2	926	17

of odds-calculation and gambling knowledge developed over many years sat at the table, then what hope is there for the rest of us who have also got regular jobs to think about and mouths to feed, in addition to attempting to fulfil our betting dreams?

The answer is that there are sports punters out there making a regular profit, some using ratings, some not, but all being consistent in what they do and with a sharp eye for knowing what really matters when it comes to finding decent bets.

Making your own ratings is as much to do with consistency as it is to do with finding the winning blend of factors and can unquestionably become the most powerful tool in your arsenal.

The most important thing to bear in mind at all times regarding your thought-processes and assumptions is that if they are in any way correct about the sport in question, it's almost certain that you'll end up creating decent ratings. Equally important, they will be good enough to help you bet successfully.

the apple of bookies' eye

FOOTBALL BASICS

THE THREE MOST IMPORTANT
sports outside of racing are, if you ask most
bookmakers, football, football and football.
Inside many football fanatics there has always
been a punter waiting to come out. It was only
when around-the-clock live football was
brought to our TV screens that he emerged.

Now, football is such big business that
new betting concerns – the spread betting
exchange Spreadfair comes to mind – are not
even covering racing.

And the jewel in the football crown as far
as the betting industry is concerned is the
Premiership, the most bet-on league in the
world. From Calgary to Calcutta, Hornchurch
to Hong King, astronomical sums are bet
on every game in the top tier of English
football. The players, not just the Henrys and
Keanes but the Dodds and Radzinskis, are
world famous.

Punters love Premiership football because
they know so much about the teams, coaches
and players.

Bookmakers love it because it is a reliable,
trustworthy medium which they know they
have under control in the long run even if short
sequences of results go against them and
certain shrewd punters have an edge over
them.

By BRUCE
MILLINGTON

It is also cheaper to bet on football than horseracing, whose authorities demand a larger slice of their turnover.

Gone are the days when betting on football meant the pools or nothing. There is a rapidly expanding menu from which football punters can select. The basic elements are these:

THE RESULT A simple bet on whether team A will win, team B will win or a match will be drawn.

THE DOUBLE RESULT Otherwise known as half-time/full-time betting. Nine different outcomes are quoted: home side leading at half-time-home side leading at full-time, home-draw, home-away, draw-home, draw-away, draw-draw, away-away, away-draw and away-home. Worse value than straight match result betting and little, if any, more scientific.

THE CORRECT SCORE Self-explanatory. Great for bookmakers when there is a freak result. Who bets on a 6-2 victory? Just remember to back no goalscorer instead of 0-0. Own-goals do not count for first-scorer purposes so if it is 1-0 and the goal was an own-goal, you still win.

FIRST SCORER Also self-explanatory. The first-scorer prices also act as last-scorer prices, which some punters prefer as they feel they are getting a better run for their money.

It is galling, though, to back a player to score the last goal and he nets the first, only for someone else to complete the scoring. Totesport have recently introduced each-way first scorer betting, which pays a third the odds the first three scorers. This sounds like a far better deal than most each-way punters are offered, but it must be borne in mind that in many matches fewer than three goals are scored.

ASIAN HANDICAPS AT A GLANCE

Favourite			Underdog		
H'cap	Result	Payout	H'cap	Result	Payout
0	Win	Win	0	Win	Win
	Draw	No bet		Draw	No bet
	Lose	Lose		Lose	Lose
0, -0.5	Win	Win	0, +0.5	Win	Win
	Draw	Lose half		Draw	Win half
	Lose	Lose		Lose	Lose
-0.5	Win	Win	+0.5	Win or draw	Win
	Draw or lose	Lose		Lose	Lose
-0.5, -1	Win by 2 or more	Win	+0.5, +1	Win or draw	Win
	Win by 1	Win half		lose by 1	Lose half
	Draw or lose	Lose		Lose by 2 or more	Lose
-1	Win by 2 or more	Win	+1	Win or draw	Win
	Win by 1	No bet		Lose by 1	No bet
	Draw or lose	Lose		Lose by 2 or more	Lose
-1, -1.5	Win by 2 or more	Win	+1, +1.5	Win or draw	Win
	Win by 1	Lose half		Lose by 1	Win half
	Draw or lose	Lose		Lose by 2 or more	Lose
-1.5	Win by 2 or more	Win	+1.5	Win, draw	
	Win by 1, draw or lose	Lose		or lose by 1	Win
				Lose by 2 or more	Lose
-1.5, -2	Win by 3 or more	Win	+1.5, +2	Win, draw or lose by 1	Win
	Win by 2	Win half		Lose by 2	Lose half
	Win by 1, draw or lose	Lose		Lose by 3 or more	Lose
-2	Win by 3 or more	Win	+2	Win, draw or lose by 1	Win
	Win by 2,	No bet		Lose by 2,	No bet
	Win by 1, draw or lose	Lose		Lose by 3 or more	Lose
-2, -2.5	Win by 3 or more	Win	+2, +2.5	Win, draw or lose by 1	Win
	Win by 2,	Lose half		Lose by 2	Win half
	Win by 1, draw or lose	Lose		Lose by 3 or more	Lose
-2.5	Win by 3 or more	Win	+2.5	Win, draw,	
	Win by 2, 1 draw or lose	Lose		lose by 1 or 2	Win
				Lose by 3 or more	Lose

PAYOUTS

Win *You win your stake multiplied by the price.*
Win half *You win half your stake multiplied by the price. Half your stake is returned.*
No bet *The bet is void. Your stake is returned.*
Lose half *You lose half your stake. Half is returned.*
Lose *You lose your stake.*

ASIAN HANDICAPS **Another fast-growing market. As the name implies, they originated in Asia, where the punting culture is for bets to be as close to even money as possible. This system of handicapping football teams**

football basics

 Too good to refuse?

Certain bookmakers offer regular, great-value specials which you would be daft to ignore. Blue Square, for example, refund all losing correct-score and first-scorer bets in matches which end goalless. Some people try to exploit this by backing each team to win 1-0 rather than back fewer than two goals, knowing that they will be reimbursed if the match ends without a goal.

Bet Direct, Paddy Power and sometimes Ladbrokes refund losing bets if a certain player scores the last goal in a televised encounter. This is an excellent offer which should always influence which firm you do business with, especially if most layers are offering identical prices on the team you fancy.

can seem complicated at first but is not. The table shows what each handicap mark represents, and if you place Asian handicap bets online, the site should provide final clarification of what your bet entails just before you press the confirm button.

It is in every punter's interest to get their head around Asian handicaps. Because they are two-runner contests (normal match betting has three possible outcomes with the draw) they are priced up far more competitively and are invariably the best value method of supporting a football team.

HANDICAPS A far less appealing sibling of the Asian handicap. The favourites are asked to give up a start, usually one goal, which still makes a handicap draw possible. Far better to take the Asian route.

HALF-TIME BETTING Some punters like to bet on who will be ahead at the interval, although unless you have a convincing stat-based argument it is hard to know why.

THE SCORECAST Favoured by those who want a big return for a small outlay. A combination of a certain player to score the first first goal and a particular scoreline. For instance, Alan Shearer to score the first goal in a 2-0 Newcastle win might be 20-1. Seldom do these represent good value.

DRAW NO BET A couple of firms offer these prices. Each team is shorter than on the normal match betting but the punter gets his money back if it is a stalemate.

OVER/UNDER An increasingly popular bet, having established itself as one of Betfair's key football markets. Punters must guess whether a match will produce fewer or more than 2.5 goals.

the last word on football betting

PULLEIN POWER

YOU SHOULD NEVER PLACE A BET

By KEVIN PULLEIN

unless you are satisfied, beyond reasonable doubt, that the odds are wrong.

You cannot win money, in the long run, unless you bet only when the odds are wrong – in technical parlance, when your prospects of winning are better than is implied by your prospective winnings.

You will have read elsewhere in this book how the odds are supposed to express the chances of something happening. For example, evens implies a 50 per cent chance.

If the probability of that event occurring is really greater than 50 per cent, you have a good bet. If not, you have a bad bet.

If you accept only good bets, you will win sometimes and you will lose sometimes. But overall, you will win more money than you lose.

And vice versa. Sometimes bad bets cop. But not often enough to yield a profit over a substantial period of time.

In theory, it all sounds so simple, doesn't it? In practice, of course, it is anything but.

Before placing a bet on any event, you need to know two things. You need to know how to work out what the odds should be. And, where appropriate, you need to know why the odds you are actually being offered are different.

You know all about Arsenal, but how much do you know about Macclesfield?
(This is Tommy Widdrington, by the way)

The second is an essential cross-check of the first.

We are all human. We all make mistakes. Unless you know why a bookmaker is offering the odds he is, and are confident that he is wrong to be doing so, you cannot be convinced that your own assessment of the odds is right.

A PERSONAL ODYSSEY I have been writing about football betting for more than ten years – until now, if I say so myself, with some success. I got into it in a rather unusual way.

I was a journalist. In those days, reporters were told – I guess they still are – that their news stories should tell readers who did what, where, when, how and why.

I was always most interested in the how and why. I was also fascinated by football.

I wanted to find a way of writing about football that was different from anybody else's. And I decided to try to analyse the game statistically. In those days, nobody else did.

Who would want to read a statistical analysis of football? Bettors, I thought.

The odds, as we all know, are expressed in numbers. Our stakes are defined in numbers – pounds and pence. The result is declared in numbers – 1-1, 3-2, whatever. Our winnings, or losses, accumulate in numbers – pounds and pence again. The decision whether to bet, it seems obvious to me, should only be reached after, among other things, a rigorous examination of numbers.

We live in an age of supposed saturation television coverage of football. Yet it is still hard to find live broadcasts of many games outside the Premiership.

We all know how Newcastle play, and Manchester United. But what about Northampton? Or Macclesfield Town?

You could follow a local Football League team around the country and get a good first-hand impression of how they play. But you would still not be able to watch the other teams in their division more than twice a season. And teams in the other divisions you would never witness at all, unless they happened to be drawn against your team in a knockout competition such as the FA Cup.

In short, it is almost impossible to build up a detailed first-hand knowledge of the individual playing styles of most of the teams we are able to bet on, even in England and Scotland. All we have to go on, in most cases, is their results.

But what do these mean?

It is all very well saying, as television commentators so often do, that a team have won their last so-many games. What does this tell us about their prospects of winning the next game? We might know that a team from the top of a table are likely to beat one from the bottom. But how likely?

It was questions like these that I wanted to answer. I should add that I am not a formally trained statistician. Nor am I, despite the impression some *Racing Post* readers seem to have of me, a particularly clever man or an especially well-educated one.

I am just someone who found when he started to ask questions about the mathematics of football and betting that the answers required a greater knowledge than he then possessed. So I improved my knowledge. I went to the library and borrowed mathematical textbooks, and read them over and over again until I understood them.

We are all different. I have some characteristics which I know have hindered my football betting. I also have two that I think have helped. I will mention them here because I believe they are useful. Try to accentuate them if you have them already. Try to encourage them if you do not.

Originally, as I explained earlier, I was not a punter. I do not have a compulsion to bet, to have a flutter for its own sake. I can wait patiently for an occasion when I believe the odds are wrong. I can wait as long as it takes.

I can also be contrary. If everyone says something is right, I will begin to wonder whether it might be wrong, if only because that would give me an opportunity to be different. I know: this is very silly – and probably speaks of some deep-down psychological disorder. But in betting it can help.

When the odds on a football match are wrong, it is nearly always because they express not the chances of a result occurring but a commonly-held misconception about the chances of that result occurring.

But more of that later.

WHAT IS THE RIGHT PRICE?

1. Results A sportsman is more likely to perform in the future how he has performed in the past than he is to perform in any other way.

Ninety per cent of what happens on the

football field can be explained by the ability of the players, as revealed in the results they have achieved.

I do not clutch this figure out of the air, by the way, as I shall explain in a moment.

The all-important question, of course, is how we interpret these past performances and convert them into odds that express what is likely to happen in the next contest.

I will explain how I evaluate past performances in my ratings, which are published every day in the *Racing Post*. I will also tell you a couple of ways in which you can develop your own sets of match odds intuitively, without a computer – or even, for that matter, a paper and pen.

I could go into great detail discussing algorithms, computer software programmes and so on – and long before I reached the end of this chapter, most of you would have flicked on to the next one.

I will try to give you ideas on how you do things yourself, in your own way.

The ratings I compile are used to produce estimates of the likelihood of different results occurring in games from more than 20 countries across Europe, not only in England and Scotland but also Spain, Italy and Germany and elsewhere from Turkey to Denmark and Portugal to the Ukraine.

I constantly compare my pre-match forecasts with post-match results, using standard statistical tests to check how accurate they are. And what these tests tell me is that around 90 per cent of the post-match results are explained by the pre-match forecasts.

I do not say this so that you will think my ratings are wonderful. They are not, really. All they do is offer an estimate of how well a team are likely to perform today, given how well they have performed in the past.

I say this to convince you that the single most important influence on the result of a football match is the ability of the players.

In my computer ratings process I assess past performances according to the score, the quality of the opposition, the venue and the date.

I do not think you will be surprised by this. On the contrary, I am sure almost everyone will agree that these are the variables which matter.

The bigger the margin of victory, the more creditable the performance. The better the opposition, the more creditable the performance. A home win is less notable than an away win, because nearly all teams record superior results on their own ground. The last performance is more significant than the one before, and so on.

Do not get too hung up, though, on individual performances in isolation, or even small numbers of performances in isolation.

In Euro 2004, Italy and Spain were knocked out at the group stage. I do not accept that Italy were a worse team than Sweden and Denmark, and I am speaking here as someone who advised a sell of Italy on the group indices. Nor do I accept that Spain were a worse team than Portugal and Greece.

In a low-scoring game like football, the best team win less often than in other sports. In a three-match mini-league, it is comparatively easy for a good team to finish behind inferior opponents. In snooker, the best player wins less often over a first-to-five-frames format than he does over the first to 17.

In my ratings for club football I include the last 32 performances. I have found this to be the optimum number, having tested lots of others. Thirty-two games is almost a whole season in the Premiership and Scottish Premier League, and more than two-thirds of a season in the Football League.

The last performance, as I mentioned, is more significant than the one before, but it is not that much more significant. In my ratings, the most recent performance is given only three times as much weight as the one that occurred 32 games ago.

In general, large samples of results are more revealing than small ones.

I promised earlier that I would describe a couple of ways in which you can assess teams intuitively.

The first involves trying to relate teams to others in their division. If they played for a whole season how you think they are playing now, where do you think they would finish? Would it be in the middle? Higher or lower? How much higher or lower? At the top? At the bottom?

Now look the chart on the facing page, entitled 'How good are the teams?' It gives the statistics usually associated with different sorts of teams in a division, from good ones through middling ones to bad ones.

What you are trying to do is to decide which lines on the chart best describe the teams you want to assess.

Is one team, for example, like those on line M? In other words, a mid-table team. In most divisions, mid-table teams score roughly as many goals as they concede. In other words, their average goal difference per game (the first, or left-hand, column in the chart) is approximately zero.

In both the Premiership and the Football League, teams who finish a quarter of the way down a table – fifth in the Premiership, eighth in any division of the Football League – usually have an average goal difference per game of +0.3. That is to say, if you subtract the number of goals they concede from the number of goals they score, and divide the result by the number of games they play, you will usually end up with a figure of around +0.3. They are like the teams on line J.

Teams who finish three-quarters of the way

HOW GOOD ARE THE TEAMS?

Ave gl diff per game	Ave gls total per game	Gls ratio for:against	win %	draw %	loss %	Ave pts per game	
+1.2	2.8	71:29	65	22	14	2.16	**A**
+1.1	2.8	70:30	62	23	15	2.10	**B**
+1.0	2.7	68:32	60	23	16	2.04	**C**
+0.9	2.7	67:33	58	24	18	1.98	**D**
+0.8	2.7	65:35	55	25	20	1.91	**E**
+0.7	2.6	63:37	53	26	21	1.85	**F**
+0.6	2.6	62:38	51	26	23	1.78	**G**
+0.5	2.6	60:40	48	27	25	1.71	**H**
+0.4	2.6	58:42	46	27	27	1.64	**I**
+0.3	2.5	56:44	43	28	29	1.57	**J**
+0.2	2.5	54:46	41	28	31	1.50	**K**
+0.1	2.5	52:48	38	28	34	1.43	**L**
0.0	2.5	50:50	36	28	36	1.36	**M**
-0.1	2.5	48:52	34	28	38	1.29	**N**
-0.2	2.5	46:54	31	28	41	1.22	**O**
-0.3	2.5	44:56	29	28	43	1.15	**P**
-0.4	2.6	42:58	27	27	46	1.08	**Q**
-0.5	2.6	40:60	25	27	48	1.02	**R**
-0.6	2.6	38:62	23	26	51	0.96	**S**
-0.7	2.6	37:63	21	26	53	0.90	**T**
-0.8	2.7	35:65	20	25	55	0.84	**U**
-0.9	2.7	33:67	18	24	58	0.78	**V**
-1.0	2.7	32:68	16	23	60	0.73	**W**
-1.1	2.8	30:70	15	23	62	0.68	**X**
-1.2	2.8	29:71	14	22	65	0.63	**Y**

down a table – 15th in the Premiership, 18th in the Football League – usually have an average goal difference per game of -0.3. They are like the teams on line P.

In the Football League, teams who finish at the top normally have an average goal difference per game of +0.8 (line E), those at the bottom -0.8 (line U). In the Premiership, the extremes are even further from the centre – teams who win the Premiership usually have

WHAT ARE THE APPROPRIATE MATCH ODDS?

HOME	DRAW	AWAY	FIXTURES										
1.12	12.46	41.36	AY										
1.13	11.54	36.69	AX	BY									
1.14	10.70	32.59	AW	BX	CY								
1.16	9.94	28.99	AV	BW	CX	DY							
1.17	9.25	25.82	AU	BV	CW	DX	EY						
1.19	8.63	23.03	AT	BU	CV	DW	EX	FY					
1.21	8.06	20.58	AS	BT	CU	DV	EW	FX	GY				
1.23	7.54	18.41	AR	BS	CT	DU	EV	FW	GX	HY			
1.25	7.08	16.50	AQ	BR	CS	DT	EU	FV	GW	HX	IY		
1.28	6.65	14.81	AP	BQ	CR	DS	ET	FU	GV	HW	IX	JY	
1.31	6.27	13.32	AO	BP	CQ	DR	ES	FT	GU	HV	IW	JX	KY
1.34	5.92	11.99	AN	BO	CP	DQ	ER	FS	GT	HU	IV	JW	KX
1.37	5.61	10.82	AM	BN	CO	DP	EQ	FR	GS	HT	IU	JV	KW
1.41	5.32	9.78	AL	BM	CN	DO	EP	FQ	GR	HS	IT	JU	KV
1.45	5.07	8.86	AK	BL	CM	DN	EO	FP	GQ	HR	IS	JT	KU
1.50	4.83	8.04	AJ	BK	CL	DM	EN	FO	GP	HQ	IR	JS	KT
1.55	4.63	7.31	AI	BJ	CK	DL	EM	FN	GO	HP	IQ	JR	KS
1.60	4.44	6.66	AH	BI	CJ	DK	EL	FM	GN	HO	IP	JQ	KR
1.66	4.28	6.09	AG	BH	CI	DJ	EK	FL	GM	HN	IO	JP	KQ
1.73	4.13	5.57	AF	BG	CH	DI	EJ	FK	GL	HM	IN	JO	KP
1.80	4.00	5.11	AE	BF	CG	DH	EI	FJ	GK	HL	IM	JN	KO
1.89	3.89	4.70	AD	BE	CF	DG	EH	FI	GJ	HK	IL	JM	KN
1.98	3.79	4.33	AC	BD	CE	DF	EG	FH	GI	HJ	IK	JL	KM
2.08	3.71	4.00	AB	BC	CD	DE	EF	FG	GH	HI	IJ	JK	KL
2.19	3.65	3.70	AA	BB	CC	DD	EE	FF	GG	HH	II	JJ	KK
2.32	3.60	3.44		BA	CB	DC	ED	FE	GF	HG	IH	JI	KJ
2.46	3.56	3.20			CA	DB	EC	FD	GE	HF	IG	JH	KI
2.62	3.54	2.98				DA	EB	FC	GD	HE	IF	JG	KH
2.79	3.53	2.79					EA	FB	GC	HD	IE	JF	KG
2.98	3.54	2.62						FA	GB	HC	ID	JE	KF
3.20	3.56	2.46							GA	HB	IC	JD	KE
3.44	3.60	2.32								HA	IB	JC	KD
3.70	3.65	2.19									IA	JB	KC
4.00	3.71	2.08										JA	KB
4.33	3.79	1.98											KA
4.70	3.89	1.89											
5.11	4.00	1.80											
5.57	4.13	1.73											
6.09	4.28	1.66											
6.66	4.44	1.60											
7.31	4.63	1.55											
8.04	4.83	1.50											
8.86	5.07	1.45											
9.78	5.32	1.41											
10.82	5.61	1.37											
11.99	5.92	1.34											
13.32	6.27	1.31											
14.81	6.65	1.28											
16.50	7.08	1.25											

L	M	N	O	P	Q	R	S	T	U	V	W	X	Y
LY													
LX	MY												
LW	MX	NY											
LV	MW	NX	OY										
LU	MV	NW	OX	PY									
LT	MU	NV	OW	PX	QY								
LS	MT	NU	OV	PW	QX	RY							
LR	MS	NT	OU	PV	QW	RX	SY						
LQ	MR	NS	OT	PU	QV	RW	SX	TY					
LP	MQ	NR	OS	PT	QU	RV	SW	TX	UY				
LO	MP	NQ	OR	PS	QT	RU	SV	TW	UX	VY			
LN	MO	NP	OQ	PR	QS	RT	SU	TV	UW	VX	WY		
LM	MN	NO	OP	PQ	QR	RS	ST	TU	UV	VW	WX	XY	
LL	MM	NN	OO	PP	QQ	RR	SS	TT	UU	VV	WW	XX	YY
LK	ML	NM	ON	PO	QP	RQ	SR	TS	UT	VU	WV	XW	YX
LJ	MK	NL	OM	PN	QO	RP	SQ	TR	US	VT	WU	XV	YW
LI	MJ	NK	OL	PM	QN	RO	SP	TQ	UR	VS	WT	XU	YV
LH	MI	NJ	OK	PL	QM	RN	SO	TP	UQ	VR	WS	XT	YU
LG	MH	NI	OJ	PK	QL	RM	SN	TO	UP	VQ	WR	XS	YT
LF	MG	NH	OI	PJ	QK	RL	SM	TN	UO	VP	WQ	XR	YS
LE	MF	NG	OH	PI	QJ	RK	SL	TM	UN	VO	WP	XQ	YR
LD	ME	NF	OG	PH	QI	RJ	SK	TL	UM	VN	WO	XP	YQ
LC	MD	NE	OF	PG	QH	RI	SJ	TK	UL	VM	WN	XO	YP
LB	MC	ND	OE	PF	QG	RH	SI	TJ	UK	VL	WM	XN	YO
LA	MB	NC	OD	PE	QF	RG	SH	TI	UJ	VK	WL	XM	YN
	MA	NB	OC	PD	QE	RF	SG	TH	UI	VJ	WK	XL	YM
		NA	OB	PC	QD	RE	SF	TG	UH	VI	WJ	XK	YL
			OA	PB	QC	RD	SE	TF	UG	VH	WI	XJ	YK
				PA	QB	RC	SD	TE	UF	VG	WH	XI	YJ
					QA	RB	SC	TD	UE	VF	WG	XH	YI
						RA	SB	TC	UD	VE	WF	XG	YH
							SA	TB	UC	VD	WE	XF	YG
								TA	UB	VC	WD	XE	YF
									UA	VB	WC	XD	YE
										VA	WB	XC	YD
											WA	XB	YC
												XA	YB
													YA

an average goal difference per game of around
+1.1 (line B), those who finish last around
-1.1 (line X).

The statistics in the table, I should add, are
idealised ones. In theory, a team with an
average goal difference per game of +1.1 will
win 62 per cent of their games, draw 23
per cent and lose 15 per cent, gaining an
average of 2.1 points per game (80 over a
38-game Premiership season). The total
number of goals in their games will average
2.8. In practice, these figures will often
vary a bit.

So, which lines on the chart do you think
best describe the teams you want to assess?
Let's suppose you think one team are like
those on line G, the other like those on line I.
Let's suppose, too, that the team you think
are like those on line G are playing at home
to the team you think are like those on line I.

Okay – now turn to the chart on pages 150-
151 entitled 'What are the appropriate match
odds?' It might look complicated but, believe
me, it's not.

We want the match odds appropriate for
fixture GI. Run your finger across the fixtures
columns until you get to the one beginning,
in descending order, GY, GX, GW, etc. Run
your finger down this column until you get to
GI. Now run your finger back across this line
until you reach the appropriate match odds.

They are, in decimal format, 1.98 for a home
win, 3.79 for a draw and 4.33 for an away
win. In fractional odds, those become just
short of evens for the home win, slightly more
than 11-4 for the draw and 10-3 for the away
win (on the page opposite is a chart that
converts decimal odds into fractional odds).

If a team like those we have called G
were playing away to a team like those we
have called I, the appropriate match odds
would be those for fixture IG – 2.46 for a home
win (somewhere between 7-5 and 6-4), 3.56

FRACTIONAL ODDS INTO DECIMAL ODDS

Fractional	Decimal	Fractional	Decimal	Fractional	Decimal
1-10	1.10	5-9	1.56	15-8	2.88
1-9	1.11	4-7	1.57	2-1	3.00
1-8	1.13	8-13	1.62	11-5	3.20
1-7	1.14	5-8	1.63	9-4	3.25
2-13	1.15	4-6	1.67	12-5	3.40
1-6	1.17	5-7	1.71	5-2	3.50
2-11	1.18	8-11	1.73	13-5	3.60
1-5	1.20	4-5	1.80	11-4	3.75
2-9	1.22	5-6	1.83	3-1	4.00
1-4	1.25	10-11	1.91	10-3	4.33
2-7	1.29	Evens	2.00	7-2	4.50
3-10	1.30	11-10	2.10	4-1	5.00
1-3	1.33	6-5	2.20	9-2	5.50
4-11	1.36	5-4	2.25	5-1	6.00
5-13	1.38	11-8	2.38	11-2	6.50
2-5	1.40	7-5	2.40	6-1	7.00
5-12	1.42	6-4	2.50	13-2	7.50
4-9	1.44	8-5	2.60	7-1	8.00
5-11	1.45	13-8	2.63	8-1	9.00
1-2	1.50	7-4	2.75	9-1	10.00
8-15	1.53	9-5	2.80	10-1	11.00

for a draw (somewhere between 5-2 and 13-5) and 3.2 for an away win (11-5).

The other way of assessing teams intuitively involves trying to estimate what proportion of goals in a match each would score.

Imagine a series of games between the two teams at a neutral venue. How many goals would the first team score in those games and how many goals would the second team score? What would be the ratio of first team goals to second team goals? Would it be 50:50? Higher? 70:30? Too high? 60:40? Hmm, still not sure?

Don't be too embarrassed to get a pile of coins and spread them out on a table in front of you. Put five on one side and five on the other. Does this seem right? Not enough over there? How about seven and three? Too many now? Try six and four. I do this myself sometimes when I am not convinced, for one reason or another, that my computer-generated assessment of the balance between two teams is plausible.

Suppose you settle on a split of 60:40. You think that in a series of games between these teams at a neutral venue the first team would score 60 per cent of the goals and the second team 40 per cent.

Now go back to the first chart, 'How good are the teams?' You will see from the third column that the teams on line H normally score 60 per cent of the goals in their games and concede 40 per cent. On average, their opponents are like the teams on line M. We know this because, on average, most teams' opponents are like those on line M – ie, mid-table.

We can conclude, therefore, that you think this fixture will be like one between a team from line H and a team from line M. Let's say the former are at home, the latter away.

The second chart tells us that the match odds appropriate for fixture HM would be 1.73 for a home win (8-11), 4.13 for a draw (somewhere between 10-3 and 3-1) and 5.57 for an away win (almost 9-2).

You will have noticed that so far I have discussed only games between teams from the same division. What, you might ask, about the FA Cup or the League Cup?

I say: assess a team first within the context of their own division, then allow for the differences between divisions. A Premiership team would normally have an average goal difference per game 1.0 higher if they played in the Championship, 1.7 higher if they played in League One and 2.4 higher if they played in League Two.

2. Goals The number of goals in a game is

WHAT IS THE TYPICAL RELATIONSHIP BETWEEN SUPREMACY AND GOALS?

Supremacy expectation	Goals expectation
0.0	2.5
0.1	2.5
0.2	2.5
0.3	2.5
0.4	2.6
0.5	2.6
0.6	2.6
0.7	2.6
0.8	2.7
0.9	2.7
1.0	2.7
1.1	2.8
1.2	2.8
1.3	2.8
1.4	2.9
1.5	2.9
1.6	3.0
1.7	3.0
1.8	3.1
1.9	3.1
2.0	3.2
2.1	3.2
2.2	3.3
2.3	3.3
2.4	3.4
2.5	3.5
2.6	3.5
2.7	3.6
2.8	3.7
2.9	3.7
3.0	3.8

uncommon knowledge

 Expectation explained

the importance of being aware of probability

A mathematical term that occurs often in this chapter is expectation.

In technical language, the expectation in any event is the sum of each possible outcome multiplied by the probability of it occurring. I know: this sounds like gobbledygook. Don't worry: it will become clearer when we consider an example.

Imagine you walk into a casino, buy a pile of chips, sit down at a roulette table and proceed to bet one chip at a time on black.

Each time the croupier spins the wheel and drops the ball, you can either win or lose. If you win, you will be paid out at even money – you will get your chip back plus one more. If you lose, you will sacrifice your chip. What is your expectation of each bet? On a European roulette wheel there are 37 slots, numbered nought to 36. Eighteen are coloured black, 18 red. The zero is neither black nor red.

Each time the game is played, you have an 18/37 chance of winning one chip and a 19/37 chance of losing one chip. Your expectation is (18/37 x 1) + (19/37 x -1), which equals 0.4865 - 0.5135 or -0.027.

You have a negative expectation. If you play the game repeatedly, you can expect to lose 0.027 (or 2.7 per cent) of your total stake.

This is an important point to grasp. If we say the goals expectation in a football match is 2.6, we do not mean that there will be 2.6 goals. There can't be. There must be nought, one, two, three or some other whole number.

What we mean is that if you could reproduce these precise circumstances a great number of times, the average of all the goal totals – assuming we have got our expectations right – would be 2.6.

influenced by two factors – the relative strength of the teams and the goals records of the teams.

The first, in my opinion, is very much more important than the second. According to my research, it is roughly three times as important.

As a general rule, the greater the goal difference between two teams, the greater the goals total. It stands to reason, really.

In spread betting, the difference between the number of goals each team score is called supremacy. In a chart alongside, I have illustrated how the goals expectation in a match varies, in typical circumstances, with the supremacy expectation.

Expectation, by the way, is a mathematical term that I have tried to explain in the panel on the previous page.

Even if you bet only on fixed-odds, you will still want to know what the goals expectation should be – or, at least, you will if you want to bet on goals totals or correct scores.

As you can probably deduce from the chart, goals expectations are normally at their lowest when supremacy expectations are zero – when two teams are evenly matched and each is as likely to win as the other.

As supremacy expectations go up so, usually, do goals expectations.

Let's imagine a game between two teams we will call City and United. Let's imagine City have an average goal difference per game of +0.5 and United have an average goal difference per game of +0.1.

If they met at a neutral venue – say in a cup final – the supremacy expectation would be 0.4 City/United (0.5 - 0.1 = 0.4).

If they played at a non-neutral venue, the team playing at home would enjoy a slight advantage and the team playing away would suffer from a slight disadvantage. Exactly how much varies from competition to competition and season to season, but you will not go far wrong if you assume that it all adds up to about four-tenths of a goal – certainly, not if the teams are from the Premiership and Football League or one of the top European divisions like La Liga or Serie A.

If City were playing at home to United, therefore, the supremacy expectation would be 0.8 City/United (0.5 - 0.1 + 0.4 = 0.8).

In matches with a supremacy expectation of 0.8, the typical goals expectation is 2.7.

Let's assume, however, that United's games have been unusually high-scoring. We said earlier that they have been scoring an average

WILL THERE BE MANY GOALS?

Goals expectation	% chance of under 2.5gls	over
2.0	68	32
2.1	65	35
2.2	63	37
2.3	60	40
2.4	57	43
2.5	55	45
2.6	52	48
2.7	50	50
2.8	47	53
2.9	45	55
3.0	43	57
3.1	40	60
3.2	38	62
3.3	36	64
3.4	34	66
3.5	32	68
3.6	31	69
3.7	29	71
3.8	27	73

of 0.1 goals per game more than they concede. Normally, the total number of goals in the games of such a team would average 2.5. Let's assume that goals in United's games have been averaging 3.0 – or 20 per cent more.

When City play at home to United, the goals expectation should be higher than 2.7 – but not 20 per cent higher.

According to my studies, teams who have been involved in high-scoring games in the past tend to carry on being involved in high-scoring games in the future – only, their next games are not as high-scoring as the previous ones.

Similarly, teams who have been involved in low-scoring games in the past tend to carry on being involved in low-scoring games in the future – only, their next games are not as low-scoring as the previous ones.

I said before that, when evaluating goals expectations, the relative strength of the teams is three times as important as the goals records of the teams. Or, to put it another way, the second factor has only one quarter of the overall importance.

When City play at home to United, the goals expectation should probably be 2.8, perhaps 2.9 – about five per cent more than 2.7 (because 20 per cent multiplied by a quarter is five per cent).

Actually, it's not quite that simple, but don't worry too much about the complications. What I have given you here is a quick, rough calculation which most of the time will produce a figure that is about right.

Now look at the chart on this page 'Will there be many goals?' It tells you the percentage chance of there being fewer or more than 2.5 goals in games across a range of different goals expectations. In a fixture with a pre-match goals expectation of 2.8, for example, there is a 47 per cent chance of the final scores adding up to nought, one or

WHAT IS THE USUAL RELATIONSHIP BETWEEN MATCH ODDS AND CORRECT SCORE ODDS?

	MATCH ODDS			CORRECT SCORE ODDS: HOME			
HOME	*DRAW*	*AWAY*	*1-0*	*2-0*	*2-1*	*3-0*	*3-1*
1.12	12.46	41.36	12.24	7.50	17.38	6.95	16.10
1.13	11.54	36.69	11.76	7.40	16.50	7.03	15.69
1.14	10.70	32.59	11.32	7.31	15.70	7.14	15.33
1.16	9.94	28.99	10.92	7.24	14.97	7.27	15.02
1.17	9.25	25.82	10.55	7.19	14.32	7.42	14.76
1.19	8.63	23.03	10.22	7.16	13.72	7.59	14.55
1.21	8.06	20.58	9.91	7.15	13.19	7.80	14.39
1.23	7.54	18.41	9.64	7.16	12.71	8.04	14.27
1.25	7.08	16.50	9.39	7.18	12.28	8.31	14.21
1.28	6.65	14.81	9.17	7.23	11.91	8.62	14.19
1.31	6.27	13.32	8.98	7.30	11.57	8.97	14.23
1.34	5.92	11.99	8.81	7.39	11.28	9.38	14.31
1.37	5.61	10.82	8.67	7.51	11.04	9.84	14.45
1.41	5.32	9.78	8.55	7.65	10.83	10.36	14.65
1.45	5.07	8.86	8.46	7.83	10.66	10.95	14.91
1.50	4.83	8.04	8.39	8.03	10.53	11.62	15.23
1.55	4.63	7.31	8.35	8.27	10.44	12.38	15.63
1.60	4.44	6.66	8.33	8.55	10.39	13.25	16.11
1.66	4.28	6.09	8.34	8.87	10.37	14.25	16.67
1.73	4.13	5.57	8.37	9.23	10.40	15.38	17.32
1.80	4.00	5.11	8.43	9.65	10.46	16.68	18.09
1.89	3.89	4.70	8.52	10.13	10.57	18.18	18.97
1.98	3.79	4.33	8.63	10.67	10.72	19.90	19.99
2.08	3.71	4.00	8.78	11.29	10.92	21.89	21.16
2.19	3.65	3.70	8.97	12.00	11.17	24.19	22.51
2.32	3.60	3.44	9.19	12.80	11.46	26.86	24.05
2.46	3.56	3.20	9.46	13.72	11.82	29.96	25.82
2.62	3.54	2.98	9.76	14.76	12.24	33.58	27.84
2.79	3.53	2.79	10.12	15.95	12.73	37.81	30.16
2.98	3.54	2.62	10.58	17.34	13.26	42.68	32.65
3.20	3.56	2.46	11.10	18.91	13.88	48.35	35.49
3.44	3.60	2.32	11.68	20.69	14.58	54.96	38.72
3.70	3.65	2.19	12.34	22.71	15.36	62.69	42.40
4.00	3.71	2.08	13.07	25.01	16.25	71.72	46.60
4.33	3.79	1.98	13.89	27.63	17.25	82.32	51.39
4.70	3.89	1.89	14.81	30.62	18.38	94.76	56.88
5.11	4.00	1.80	15.82	34.02	19.64	109.39	63.16
5.57	4.13	1.73	16.96	37.90	21.06	126.62	70.37
6.09	4.28	1.66	18.22	42.33	22.66	146.97	78.65
6.66	4.44	1.60	19.63	47.41	24.44	171.01	88.18
7.31	4.63	1.55	21.20	53.22	26.45	199.48	99.16
8.04	4.83	1.50	22.95	59.88	28.71	233.23	111.84
8.86	5.07	1.45	24.91	67.52	31.25	273.32	126.49
9.78	5.32	1.41	27.08	76.31	34.10	321.01	143.45
10.82	5.61	1.37	29.52	86.43	37.31	377.81	163.12
11.99	5.92	1.34	32.23	98.08	40.93	445.57	185.97
13.32	6.27	1.31	35.27	111.53	45.02	526.52	212.54
14.81	6.65	1.28	38.67	127.05	49.63	623.35	243.49
16.50	7.08	1.25	42.47	145.00	54.83	739.34	279.60

CORRECT SCORE ODDS

	DRAW				AWAY		
0-0	*1-1*	*2-2*	*0-1*	*0-2*	*1-2*	*0-3*	*1-3*
37.05	26.47	75.66	95.53	442.76	131.37	3070.36	910.98
34.68	24.48	69.11	85.86	383.08	116.99	2556.46	780.72
32.49	22.67	63.28	77.29	331.91	104.37	2131.52	670.28
30.49	21.04	58.07	69.67	287.99	93.29	1779.77	576.52
28.65	19.56	53.42	62.90	250.26	83.54	1488.27	496.81
26.96	18.22	49.27	56.87	217.81	74.96	1246.42	428.97
25.41	17.01	45.56	51.51	189.87	67.40	1045.53	371.14
23.98	15.91	42.24	46.73	165.78	60.73	878.46	321.78
22.67	14.92	39.27	42.47	145.00	54.83	739.34	279.60
21.47	14.02	36.61	38.67	127.05	49.63	623.35	243.49
20.38	13.21	34.24	35.27	111.53	45.02	526.52	212.54
19.37	12.47	32.11	32.23	98.08	40.93	445.57	185.97
18.45	11.80	30.21	29.52	86.43	37.31	377.81	163.12
17.60	11.20	28.52	27.08	76.31	34.10	321.01	143.45
16.83	10.66	27.01	24.91	67.52	31.25	273.32	126.49
16.13	10.17	25.66	22.95	59.88	28.71	233.23	111.84
15.49	9.73	24.47	21.20	53.22	26.45	199.48	99.16
14.91	9.34	23.42	19.63	47.41	24.44	171.01	88.18
14.39	9.00	22.49	18.22	42.33	22.66	146.97	78.65
13.92	8.69	21.69	16.96	37.90	21.06	126.62	70.37
13.50	8.42	20.99	15.82	34.02	19.64	109.39	63.16
13.13	8.18	20.40	14.81	30.62	18.38	94.76	56.88
12.81	7.98	19.90	13.89	27.63	17.25	82.32	51.39
12.53	7.81	19.49	13.07	25.01	16.25	71.72	46.60
12.29	7.67	19.17	12.34	22.71	15.36	62.69	42.40
12.10	7.57	18.94	11.68	20.69	14.58	54.96	38.72
11.94	7.49	18.78	11.10	18.91	13.88	48.35	35.49
11.83	7.44	18.71	10.58	17.34	13.26	42.68	32.65
11.76	7.42	18.71	10.12	15.95	12.73	37.81	30.16
11.83	7.44	18.71	9.76	14.76	12.24	33.58	27.84
11.94	7.49	18.78	9.46	13.72	11.82	29.96	25.82
12.10	7.57	18.94	9.19	12.80	11.46	26.86	24.05
12.29	7.67	19.17	8.97	12.00	11.17	24.19	22.51
12.53	7.81	19.49	8.78	11.29	10.92	21.89	21.16
12.81	7.98	19.90	8.63	10.67	10.72	19.90	19.99
13.13	8.18	20.40	8.52	10.13	10.57	18.18	18.97
13.50	8.42	20.99	8.43	9.65	10.46	16.68	18.09
13.92	8.69	21.69	8.37	9.23	10.40	15.38	17.32
14.39	9.00	22.49	8.34	8.87	10.37	14.25	16.67
14.91	9.34	23.42	8.33	8.55	10.39	13.25	16.11
15.49	9.73	24.47	8.35	8.27	10.44	12.38	15.63
16.13	10.17	25.66	8.39	8.03	10.53	11.62	15.23
16.83	10.66	27.01	8.46	7.83	10.66	10.95	14.91
17.60	11.20	28.52	8.55	7.65	10.83	10.36	14.65
18.45	11.80	30.21	8.67	7.51	11.04	9.84	14.45
19.37	12.47	32.11	8.81	7.39	11.28	9.38	14.31
20.38	13.21	34.24	8.98	7.30	11.57	8.97	14.23
21.47	14.02	36.61	9.17	7.23	11.91	8.62	14.19
22.67	14.92	39.27	9.39	7.18	12.28	8.31	14.21

two, and a 53 per cent chance of them adding up to three or more.

The last chart in this section, on the preceding two pages, investigates the relationship between match odds and correct score odds.

It is, I think, fairly self-explanatory. It can be used in conjunction with one of the earlier charts, 'What are the appropriate match odds?' because the same sets of match odds appear in both. The goals expectation for each match has been assumed to be typical, nothing out of the ordinary.

WHICH PRICE REPRESENTS THE BEST VALUE FOR MONEY? You should

always bet at the best available price. Sometimes, it is not immediately apparent what this is. While you are comparing odds on an identical event, it is.

If one bookmaker is quoting 11-8 about a football team winning a match and another bookmaker down the road is quoting 6-4, you should take the trouble to go down the road and get the 6-4.

If you accept only good bets – still easier said than done, not only after reading this book but even after a lifetime of study and application – you will win more money than you lose.

If you always bet at the most advantageous price, you will maximise your winnings.

And it's not just the odd halfpenny we're talking about here. If you could get 6-4 on every bet you would otherwise have accepted at 11-8, your profit on winning bets would go up by almost ten per cent.

There are professional punters who say that, for them, the difference between profit and loss over a season amounts, in practice, to nothing more than their insistence on always betting at the best available price.

All punters, from the most successful to the

WHICH BET REPRESENTS THE BEST VALUE FOR MONEY?

Supr	Total Goals	25:10:0 indices		Match odds			Asian handicaps			
		Fav	Outsiders	Fav	Draw	Outsiders	Favourites		Outsiders	
0.0	2.5	11.8	11.8	2.79	3.53	2.79	0	2.00	0	2.00
0.1	2.5	12.4	11.2	2.62	3.54	2.98	0	1.88	0	2.14
0.2	2.5	13.0	10.6	2.46	3.56	3.20	-0.25	2.12	+0.25	1.90
0.3	2.5	13.6	10.1	2.32	3.60	3.44	-0.25	2.00	+0.25	2.00
0.4	2.6	14.1	9.5	2.19	3.65	3.70	-0.25	1.89	+0.25	2.12
0.5	2.6	14.7	8.9	2.08	3.71	4.00	-0.5	2.08	+0.5	1.93
0.6	2.6	15.3	8.4	1.98	3.79	4.33	-0.5	1.98	+0.5	2.02
0.7	2.6	15.8	7.9	1.89	3.89	4.70	-0.5	1.89	+0.5	2.13
0.8	2.7	16.4	7.4	1.80	4.00	5.11	-0.75	2.03	+0.75	1.97
0.9	2.7	16.9	6.9	1.73	4.13	5.57	-0.75	1.93	+0.75	2.08
1.0	2.7	17.4	6.4	1.66	4.28	6.09	-1	2.12	+1	1.89
1.1	2.8	17.9	6.0	1.60	4.44	6.66	-1	1.99	+1	2.01
1.2	2.8	18.3	5.6	1.55	4.63	7.31	-1	1.88	+1	2.14
1.3	2.8	18.8	5.2	1.50	4.83	8.04	-1.25	2.06	+1.25	1.94
1.4	2.9	19.2	4.8	1.45	5.07	8.86	-1.25	1.96	+1.25	2.04
1.5	2.9	19.6	4.4	1.41	5.32	9.78	-1.5	2.11	+1.5	1.90
1.6	3.0	20.0	4.1	1.37	5.61	10.82	-1.5	2.02	+1.5	1.99
1.7	3.0	20.4	3.8	1.34	5.92	11.99	-1.5	1.93	+1.5	2.08
1.8	3.1	20.7	3.5	1.31	6.27	13.32	-1.75	2.06	+1.75	1.94
1.9	3.1	21.0	3.2	1.28	6.65	14.81	-1.75	1.96	+1.75	2.04
2.0	3.2	21.4	2.9	1.25	7.08	16.50	-2	2.14	+2	1.88
2.1	3.2	21.6	2.7	1.23	7.54	18.41	-2	2.02	+2	1.98
2.2	3.3	21.9	2.5	1.21	8.06	20.58	-2	1.92	+2	2.09
2.3	3.3	22.2	2.2	1.19	8.63	23.03	-2.25	2.08	+2.25	1.92
2.4	3.4	22.4	2.0	1.17	9.25	25.82	-2.25	1.98	+2.25	2.02
2.5	3.5	22.6	1.9	1.16	9.94	28.99	-2.25	1.90	+2.25	2.12
2.6	3.5	22.8	1.7	1.14	10.70	32.59	-2.5	2.04	+2.5	1.97
2.7	3.6	23.0	1.5	1.13	11.54	36.69	-2.5	1.95	+2.5	2.05
2.8	3.7	23.1	1.4	1.12	12.46	41.36	-2.75	2.08	+2.75	1.93

least successful, could improve their profit and loss account by doing the same.

Okay, so much for the simple stuff. Nowadays, it's not so simple. Nowadays, there are many different ways of betting on a football match. Let's consider only the most common of the result-related ones.

You could back a team to win a match with a fixed-odds bookmaker. You could buy their supremacy with a spread firm – or, alternatively, buy their 25:10:0 index, which makes up 25 if they win, ten if they draw and zero if they lose. You could back the team on an Asian handicap with another fixed-odds bookmaker.

Which represents the best value for money?

Let's suppose you can back a team to win a match at 6-4, buy their supremacy for 0.15, buy their 25:10:0 index for 12.5 or back them at 1.95 off scratch on an Asian handicap (with your stake returned if the match is drawn).

In this example – which does occur – the best bet is actually the Asian handicap, followed by the 25:10:0 index, supremacy and, lastly, the straightforward win wager.

In other real life examples, however, the order would be different.

In the chart on the preceding page I have attempted to illustrate how various fixed-odds and spread bets relate to each other.

You will see, for example, that if you can buy a team's supremacy for 0.8 you will have an exactly comparable price if you can buy their 25:10:0 index at 16.4, back them to win the game at 1.80 (4-5) or back them on an Asian handicap giving up three-quarters of a goal at 2.03 (slightly better than evens). If you could get, say, 1.83 (or 5-6) about the win, you would have a better bet than the buy of supremacy at 0.8.

You can use this chart to get an idea, in any given real life situation, of which medium represents the best value for money (if you are comparing prices from a person-to-person betting exchange, remember to allow for the commission you would have to pay on any winnings. It makes a difference).

The best policy is always to bet at the most advantageous price, irrespective of the medium. You should, however, familiarise yourself with the characteristics of each of those mediums. If you find you are uncomfortable with any of them, stay away from them. There is no shame in this.

With a fixed-odds bet you can, depending on the odds, win many times your stake. You can only lose your stake.

With a spread bet you can either win or lose many times your stake. In the football supremacy market, for example, the average make-up is 1.3 goals away from the midpoint of the original quotes. But in some games it will be many more. You should remember this when deciding on the level of your stakes.

Some people love the volatility of spread betting. Others do not. If you are one of them, don't worry – don't spread bet.

With Asian handicaps you have a fixed-odds bet which is always pretty close to even money. If, say, you back an outsider getting a one-and-a-half-goal start, you will lose your stake if they go down by two goals. But you will still only lose your stake if they are beaten by three goals – or four, or five, or any other number.

With an Asian handicap bet, however, you will never a win a sum much bigger than your stake. With fixed-odds bets and spread bets, sometimes you will.

WHY ARE YOU BEING OFFERED A SEEMINGLY GOOD PRICE? You now know how to estimate what the odds should be on a variety of different events in a football match. You also know how to compare the odds you are being offered across a range of betting mediums and identify which ones represent the best value for money to you.

The last thing you need to know before placing a bet is why the odds you are being offered are different from what you think they should be.

It is essential that you do know. Your computations could be wrong. The bookmaker's assessment of the teams might be superior to your own.

If so, it is better to realise this now, before you have stumped up any cash, rather than after the bet has gone down.

If you follow my ideas on assessing football teams – or any others that are remotely similar – and you believe that the odds you are being offered are wrong, it will almost certainly be because the odds you are being offered imply that one or both of the teams will perform differently today from how they have performed in the past.

It does happen. Ten per cent of what happens on the football field cannot be explained by the ability of the players, as revealed in the results they have achieved.

The odds you are being offered express not only how likely a bookmaker thinks something is to happen but also how much money his customers are betting on that something happening.

So, why does the bookmaker think one or both teams will perform uncharacteristically today? Or why do his customers think they will? Are they right to do so? And if not, why not?

In football, there is a large body of received wisdom – ideas which sound so plausible that almost everyone accepts them as being true. Some of this received wisdom is right. Some is not. The only way to find out which bit is which is by examining the facts.

When the odds express a belief that the result will be influenced by an extraneous factor that actually has no influence on the result at all, those odds may represent value for money to you.

To give you a flavour of the sort of things I am talking about, here are five commonly-held misconceptions about the beautiful game. You can call them football fallacies.

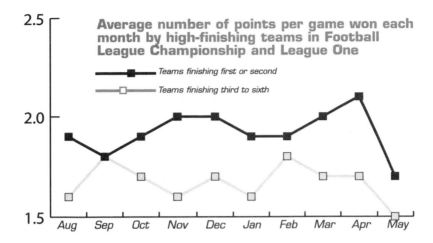

Average number of points per game won each month by high-finishing teams in Football League Championship and League One

■— Teams finishing first or second

□— Teams finishing third to sixth

FALLACY ONE – THEY NEED TO WIN, SO THEY ARE MORE LIKELY TO It isn't true. It sounds plausible – perfectly plausible – but it isn't true. The reason why it isn't true I will hazard a guess at in a moment.

We hear the 'need to win' argument every year in the final few weeks of a season, when teams who have everything to play for come up against opponents who have nothing to play for. We are talking here about teams going for a championship, promotion, the play-offs or an escape from relegation in games against opponents who are safely ensconced in mid-table.

The bookmakers' odds on these games are completely different from what they would be at any other time, because the bookmakers know that nearly all of the money bet on these games will go on the team with the greater need of the three points.

Yet there is no evidence that they are more likely to get them.

In the graph above I have shown the average number of points per game won each month by promotion-hunting teams in what we now call the Football League Championship and League One. The graph covers ten seasons. The upper line is for teams who eventually finished first or second, in the automatic promotion places. The lower line is for teams who eventually finished between third and sixth, in the play-off places.

I chose the Championship and League One because those were the only divisions in England with an identical promotion regime throughout the ten seasons.

You will see that, if anything, these promotion-hunting teams did worse in May, when they played their last few games, than they did in any other month of the season.

Over the years in the *Racing Post*, I have produced a number of similar graphs, each one depicting the results achieved by a different group of teams who were either chasing promotion or running away from relegation. And they all pointed to exactly the same conclusion – that teams who need to win in the final few weeks of a season are no more likely to do so than they are at any other time.

Why should we expect, say, a relegation-threatened team to play better this Saturday than they did last Saturday? The belief that they will presupposes two things. That they weren't trying last Saturday, when they also needed to win. And that they could play better if they did try.

Let's think about this in a different way. Because, actually, there may be a good reason why, overall, teams who need to win perform no better than usual and teams who don't need to win perform no worse than usual.

Why does someone become a professional footballer? Among other things, it's because they like playing football.

Top coaches will tell you that there are lots of players who can impress in training but not in matches. And lots of others who can impress in ordinary matches but not in important ones.

Sven-Goran Eriksson says: "I have had

players in training put away 99 per cent of their penalties, but in matches could only make 60 per cent of them. Others are active, attacking and constantly winning the ball – but only in training."

His excellent book *Eriksson On Football* is really an extended discussion of the ways in which coaches can try to help players perform without feeling pressure. Because pressure can wreak havoc on performance.

In a vital end-of-season fixture, you might have one team playing under greater pressure than they have experienced before in their lives and another suddenly released from all pressure, playing only for the joy of doing so, just like they do every day on the training ground.

Do you still want to back the team who need to win?

FALLACY TWO – THEY'RE ON A GOOD RUN, SO THEY'RE GETTING BETTER / THEY'RE ON A BAD RUN, SO THEY'RE GETTING WORSE It isn't always true – certainly, not as often as many people think.

What would you make of a team who had had not lost any of their last eight games? You would probably think they were pretty good.

What would you make of a team who had not won any of their last eight games? You would probably think they were pretty bad.

Actually, a perfectly ordinary mid-table team are likely to run up both of these sequences at least once in a season.

A mid-table team will usually win 36 per cent of their games, draw 28 per cent and lose 36 per cent. In other words, they will avoid defeat in 64 per cent of the games they play. The chance of them avoiding defeat in eight consecutive games is one in 36. Likewise, the chance of them failing to secure a single victory in eight consecutive games is also one in 36.

You might not be convinced. I wasn't, either, when I first did the calculations. So I got out some old Rothmans annuals and flicked through the pages of teams who had finished halfway down their divisions. And what I found was that each team I checked did indeed run up at least one sequence of eight or so games without a defeat and another of eight or so games without a victory.

You can be sure that toward the end of each of these good runs bookmakers and punters were beginning to think that the team had got better, and toward the end of each of these bad runs they were beginning to think that the team had got worse.

In fact, neither conclusion was true.

On average, the team who finish top of the Premiership fail to win 37 per cent of the games they play. Even Arsenal, when they went unbeaten throughout season 2003-04, failed to win 32 per cent of the games they played.

In other words, the best team in England will usually fail to win approximately one out of every three games they play. Yet when these draws and defeats occur, the betting markets, just like the sillier newspapers, can overreact.

There is rarely a value-for-money bet on the Premiership before it begins. Sometimes there is once the season has got under way – and when there is, it is almost always on the challenger who has just failed to win one or two games.

As a sequence of good results gets longer, we should progressively upgrade our assessment of the team. And as a sequence of bad results gets longer, we should progressively downgrade our assessment of the team.

But not as dramatically as most people do.

In the graphs on the facing page I have shown the results recorded by Premiership and Football League teams during the last

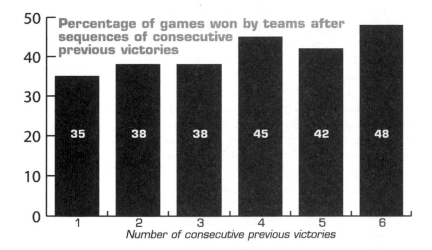

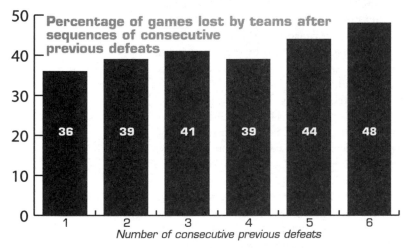

Both graphs: Premiership and Football League 1994-95 to 2003-04

ten completed seasons after different numbers of consecutive victories or defeats.

You will see that of all the teams who won six games in a row – many of whom would have been genuinely good teams if assessed on their record over a longer period of time – fewer than half won the next game.

And similarly, of all the teams who lost six games in a row – many of whom would have been genuinely bad teams if assessed on their record over a longer period of time – fewer than half lost the next game.

Obviously, some teams do change significantly during a season. I suggest that if a team start to register results that appear uncharacteristically good or bad you ask yourself whether anything has changed at the club. Have they, for example, changed the manager – and if so, is there any reason for thinking the new one will be any better or worse than the old one? (See, also, Fallacy Five).

Have they brought in some new players or shipped out some old ones – and if so, is there any reason for thinking the team will now be any better or worse than it was before? Was there any reason for thinking the team were under-performing or over-performing in the past – and if so, why is that reason no longer valid?

After three games without a win – two against Manchester United, who went on to finish third in the Premiership, and one against Chelsea, who went on to finish second – Arsenal were quoted at evens to win at home to Liverpool.

This was Good Friday 2004. Arsenal were still top of the league and unbeaten in the Premiership. All you needed for that price to represent value for money was for Arsenal to turn in what, for them, had been a typical performance during that season. And they did.

FALLACY THREE – THE CUP IS A GREAT LEVELLER Wrong. In fact, it is arguable that in recent years the betting markets have failed to recognise how comprehensively the FA Cup is now dominated by the big clubs.

It used to be said that the best team won the Premiership and the luckiest team won

FA CUP RESULTS 1994-95 to 2003-04				
Divisions	*W%*	*D%*	*L%*	*Average GD*
Premiership v Championship	58	26	16	+0.9
League One v League Two	48	31	21	+0.6

the FA Cup. Now the best team, or one of the very best teams, usually win the FA Cup as well.

During the nine years from 1996 to 2004, the FA Cup was won three times by Arsenal, three times by Manchester United, twice by Chelsea and once by Liverpool.

During that time, Arsenal and Manchester United were the best two teams in England, Liverpool and Chelsea usually one of the next two. Okay, so one of the best teams usually lift the trophy, but are the others – along with lots of good teams – ambushed on the road to Cardiff or Wembley? Do the corpses of football's giants litter the verges of the M4 and M40?

No more often than they should.

In any game, anything can happen. Inferior teams will sometimes beat superior opponents. But in the FA Cup it doesn't happen any more often than it should.

We remember Third Division Bristol Rovers' 2002 victory at Premiership Derby, with a hat-trick from Nathan Ellington. We forget all the other bottom-division teams who did not beat Premiership opponents. In fact, during the last ten seasons, no other team from the lowliest section of the Football League have won away to Premiership opponents.

We fail to notice the unspectacular results, just as, in a different context, we fail to notice all the planes that do not crash and all the ships that do not sink.

In the chart above, I have given the FA Cup results recorded during the last ten seasons by Premiership teams against what we would now call Championship opponents and by what we would now call League One teams against League Two opponents. You will see that Premiership teams scored an average of 0.9 goals per game more than Championship opponents, League One teams scored an average of 0.6 goals per game more than League Two opponents.

We can gauge the relative strength of these divisions from the results of clubs promoted and relegated between them. In the same ten seasons, the average goal difference per game of clubs relegated from the Premiership to the Championship improved by 1.0, while the average goal difference per game of clubs promoted from the Championship to the Premiership deteriorated by 1.0.

The average goal difference per game of clubs relegated from League One to League Two improved by 0.7, while the average goal difference per game of teams promoted from League Two to League One deteriorated by 0.7.

The gap between the Premiership and Championship in one-off FA Cup ties was very similar, though not identical, to what it was in ordinary league fixtures. Likewise, the gap between League One and League Two.

I have correspondents who argue persuasively that in knockout competitions tiddlers can be offered at value prices against the big fish. You will have to judge each match on its merits, using techniques like the ones I described earlier. All I can say is that there is no evidence for the almost universally accepted belief that the FA Cup is a great leveller.

FALLACY FOUR – THEY WILL BE TIRED AFTER PLAYING IN EUROPE

I beg your pardon? This excuse is trotted out even though sometimes four or even five days can elapse between a midweek European tie

DO MIDWEEK EUROPEAN TIES ADVERSELY AFFECT WEEKEND PREMIERSHIP PERFORMANCES?

	W%	D%	L%	Average GD
Results all season	48	27	25	0.6
Results after European tie	49	26	25	0.6

Note: seven seasons from 1994-95 to 2000-01

and the next Premiership fixture. Half of all European games, of course, are played at home.

And even the furthest-flung away game rarely involves a flight of more than three hours. And we are asked to believe that highly-paid, highly-trained athletes, in the peak of physical fitness, are still feeling groggy half a week or so later? I don't buy it.

The chart above shows the results recorded by English Champions League, Uefa Cup and Cup Winners' Cup participants in the seven seasons from 1994-95 to 2000-01. On one line you will find the results they recorded in Premiership games after European ties. On the other, you will find the results they recorded in all Premiership games, whenever they were played. You will notice that the two sets of figures are effectively the same. If anything, post-European results were fractionally better.

FALLACY FIVE – THEY'VE CHANGED MANAGER, SO RESULTS WILL IMPROVE Again, it isn't true – at least, not as a generally applicable rule.

It is often said that you should back a team who have just changed manager because the players will be eager to impress their new boss. The argument presupposes that they are capable of impressing their new boss.

The odds, in any case, will often have been adjusted to reflect the widely held belief that the team who have just changed manager will now get better. I have conducted a number of studies which suggest this simply does not happen.

One, on the Premiership between seasons 1998-99 and 2003-04, found that clubs who changed manager actually did worse in their next game than might have been anticipated. We remember the clubs who changed manager and promptly won. We forget all those who changed manager and promptly lost again.

In the longer run, the outlook is still grim. A 35-year study of the Bundesliga by University of Munster researcher Alexandra Tippenhauer – whose father, Hans-Dieter, was sacked by Arminia Bielefeld in 1980 – found that clubs who sacked a manager did no better in the next 12 games than they had done in the previous 12. A study in Holland by Dutch academics reached similar conclusions.

Ultimately, the net effect of all managerial changes must be zero. All clubs change their manager at one time or another. For every club that goes up in the standings, another must go down.

Which ones go up will depend on many factors, among them the quality of the new manager, the calibre of the players already at his disposal and the funds available to buy new players. The belief that changing a manager, in itself, improves results, if only in the short term, is false.

SPREAD BETTING In my opinion, spread betting is the most fascinating of all football betting mediums. It has a variety, and a volatility, you will not find anywhere else.

It is also, in my opinion, the most difficult medium on which to win money. The price-makers and price-takers are both among the most sophisticated you will encounter – matched only, perhaps, by those who specialise

RELATIONSHIP BETWEEN GOALS AND GOAL TIMES

Goals expectation	First goal time expectation	Second goal time expectation	Last goal time expectation	Total goal minutes expectation
0.5	73	87	21	25
0.6	70	86	25	30
0.7	67	85	28	35
0.8	65	84	31	40
0.9	62	83	34	45
1.0	60	82	36	50
1.1	58	80	39	55
1.2	56	79	41	60
1.3	54	78	43	65
1.4	52	76	45	70
1.5	50	75	47	75
1.6	49	73	49	80
1.7	47	72	51	85
1.8	46	71	52	90
1.9	44	69	54	95
2.0	43	68	55	100
2.1	42	67	56	105
2.2	41	65	58	110
2.3	39	64	59	115
2.4	38	63	60	120
2.5	37	62	61	125
2.6	36	60	62	130
2.7	35	59	63	135
2.8	34	58	64	140
2.9	34	57	65	145
3.0	33	56	66	150
3.1	32	55	66	155
3.2	31	54	67	160
3.3	31	53	68	165
3.4	30	52	69	170
3.5	29	51	69	175
3.6	29	50	70	180
3.7	28	49	70	185
3.8	27	48	71	190
3.9	27	47	72	195
4.0	26	46	72	200

in Asian handicaps.

Although you can spread bet on a sometimes bewildering number of events in a football match, many are related to each other. For example, goal times are related to goal totals – the times at which goals are scored are related to the total number of goals that are scored.

If you can estimate the supremacy expectation and the match goals expectation (we have discussed ways of doing this), you can estimate the team goals expectations. And with all of these, you can predicate expectations for the time of the first, second and last match goal, first and second team goals and also total goal minutes.

If the supremacy expectation is, say, 0.4, and the goals expectation is, say, 2.6, the favourites' goals expectation is (2.6 + 0.4)/2 = 1.5 and the outsiders' goals expectation is (2.6 - 0.4)/2 = 1.1. Put another way: 1.5 - 1.1 = 0.4, which is supremacy; and 1.5 + 1.1 = 2.6, which is total match goals.

In the table on the preceding page I have described the general relationship in the Premiership and Football League between goals expectations and goal time expectations.

So where are the individual firms weak? Probably a better way of phrasing this question would be to ask: where are the individual firms less strong?

Spread firms examine their trading records to identify markets in which they are doing less well, and where they need to improve. Anything I say here, therefore, may become obsolete with the passage of time – perhaps a quite short passage of time.

But in the summer of 2004, what I can tell you is this: Sporting Index habitually quote the time of the first match goal higher than other firms. Because the spread is three minutes wide, most of the time it still does not represent value for money to sellers. But sometimes it does. Presumably Sporting have adopted this practice because they have learnt from experience that most of their customers who play in this market want to buy.

From Sporting's point of view, why should they allow customers to buy at, say, 39, if you can get them to buy at 40 or 41, perhaps even 42?

IG Index, I think, sometimes give too much weight in their goals spreads to the past goals records of the participating teams. As I have argued before, these are comparatively unimportant.

Overall, IG must still be making money in the goals markets, otherwise they would have changed their pricing policy before now. But I still feel that sometimes they offer value for money prices to those who are able to recognise them.

Neither Cantor nor Spreadex, so far as I am aware, have a specific market of which the same can be said – though in every market they will from time to time quote a price that is wrong, just as IG and Sporting will.

CONCLUSION One of the privileges of writing for the *Racing Post* is that from time to time you get the opportunity to speak to people who are very successful at betting. I always try to identify what it is that makes them successful. One thing, it seems to me, they all have in common is this: that they all work very hard. I never met anyone who earned a significant sum of money from betting who thought that what they did was easy. On the contrary.

In practice, the more time and effort you are able to put in the better your sports betting will become. Perhaps it's appropriate that in America the bookmaker's overround, his built-in profit margin, is called the vig. Because, as someone once said (unless I misheard): "The price of free dough is eternal vigilance."

step outside the premiership

BASEMENT BETTING

EVERYONE LOVES AN ANTE-POST football wager and there is usually better value to be had in the lower divisions than in the Premiership due to the amount of teams who come from supposed obscurity to take the title at big odds.

With betting on football going through the roof, it is now possible to bet on top divisional goalscorer, promotion and relegation as well as the popular, if hard to predict, handicap betting and seasonal match bets.

I believe match betting is where the true nuggets lie. Bookmakers used to impose a minimum-trebles stipulation on lower-league season-long matches but serious money can be made now there are no such restrictions.

Find a team you fancy to do well (or badly) and one layer or another will usually put them in with a side who are similarly priced on the outright market but whom you consider to be under or overrated. Bingo. No worries about another team coming along and messing up your bet. It's one of the few areas where bookies can sometimes be accused of taking their eye off the ball and it is always worth scanning through all the seasonal match bets for outstanding value.

The first piece of advice to anyone looking to have a punt on a team to win any of the

By MARK LANGDON

Football League divisions is don't be scared to take on the teams at the top of the market. Every man and his dog knows there are only five teams who can possibly win the Premiership but things are much tighter the further down you go.

For instance, the 2003-04 league winners were Norwich (25-1), Plymouth (20-1) and Doncaster (33-1). Favourites in general in the lower leagues tend to represent bad value, particularly in what is now known as League One.

Just one favourite (Birmingham, who were 4-1, in 1994-95) in the 11 years between 1993-04 and 2003-04 managed to reward their backers, while a host of hotpots, including Manchester City (2-1), Cardiff (13-5) and Carlisle (10-1 shots who eventually finished 21st in 1995-96), flopped. It is a section littered with surprises and shooting for the stars is often the best policy with 50-1 and 66-1 pokes consistently making the frame.

Teams dropping down from the Premiership used to be able to bounce straight back up to the top flight but the financial crisis which has hit so many clubs means life away from the glamour and glitz is invariably a sad existence and it takes some time to recover. You must be wary of teams who have had to sell off their prized assets, particularly if they are a big-name outfit still being priced up on reputation.

In the 2003-04 season, West Ham, who were as short 8-13 to win back promotion and just 3-1 for the title, were never in the running for the championship and lost in the play-off final to Crystal Palace after a slow start caused mainly by the exodus of players from Upton Park. It will continue to happen to other teams and punters should be very wary of taking short prices about teams relegated from the Premiership.

The basement division is tough to weigh up.

A high turnover of players can often transform a team from also-rans to championship contenders, and League Two is arguably the toughest to predict.

One of the golden rules, no matter what division, must be to bet each-way, particularly if you are doing a yankee or other seasonal multiple. The place money is usually good enough for a fair return and it also protects against the agony of backing a team who have already gained promotion easing off in the final weeks rather than pushing for the added bonus of the trophy.

The play-offs are usually referred to as a lottery but one eye-catching fact comes out of the League Two end-of-season shenanigans. Since the play-offs began, in 1988-89, through to 2003-04, the team that finished in the highest regular-season position were promoted 11 times out of 16.

MATCH BETTING The best way of sussing out value on a football coupon is to price up the matches yourself, a principle that applies

basement betting

Dodge the desperados

Another golden rule is don't back teams who need to get three points. These outfits are always shorter than the odds suggest they should be and offer poor value for money, even if they do triumph every so often.

THE STORY OF THE PLAY-OFFS

1988-89 TO 2003-04

Won competition

	Ch'ship	Lge 1	Lge 2	All	%
1st	4	5	11	20	41.67
2nd	4	4	1	9	18.75
3rd	5	1	3	9	18.75
4th	3	6	11	10	20.83

Semi-finals

	Ch'ship	Lge 1	Lge 2	All	%
1st bt 4th	8/16	10/16	13/16	31/48	64.58
2nd bt 3rd	8/16	12/16	9/16	29/48	60.42

Finals

	All	%
Higher bt lower	27/48	56.25

basement betting

Keep tabs on team news

Team news, no matter what stage of the season, is important the further down the leagues you go and it's always worth looking on the club websites, as well as teamtalk.com and ananova.com for the latest injuries and suspension updates. However, remember sometimes a bookmaker could have over-compensated for a particular player being missing. One man does not make a team.

from the Champions League right down to the Football League.

When you have so many fixtures to assess it is impossible to be able to work your way through the congestion without doing your own prices. At first it could take a couple of hours but eventually it will become second nature and it is a method used by most professionals to make money.

Don't go flying into bets whenever your prices differ from the bookies. Give it a test run for as long as it takes you to feel comfortable with your strategy and even then keep asking yourself why your prices are different.

Only then, when all possible avenues have been explored, should a bet be considered. If you make a mistake, learn from it. Analysing where you went wrong is just as important (if not more so) as patting yourself on the back for putting one over the bookies.

As far as backing favourites goes, a senior odds-compiler once told me after a round of weekend fixtures: "Yet again we did it in big time on the Premiership where all the good things won but we got it back and some more on the Football League games.

"Time and time again these short-priced favourites get turned over and still the punters, particularly those in our betting shops, stick them in accas. Thank God for those results."

It all comes down to the fact that Football League divisions are more competitive than the Premiership and backing these odds-on favourites on a regular basis is a quick way to the poor house.

An example of this comes in the form of Wimbledon, who are now known as Milton Keynes Dons. They finished bottom of Division One in the 2003-04 season with just 29 points (eight wins), yet if you backed them each week to a £1 stake you would have been in profit to the tune of ten pence.

the world of non-league footy

OUTER LIMITS

A 3-1 WINNER IN A CONFERENCE game pays exactly the same as a 3-1 winner in the World Cup final and there is money to be made for those who take the time to acquaint themselves with life below the top four divisions.

In many ways, punters have a larger edge over the oddsmakers at non-league level because, while a smaller proportion of the betting public will take an interest in the outcome of, say, Morecambe against Canvey Island, in the same way, your bookmaker will have far fewer staff with enough knowledge of the subject to set prices on the contest as accurately as they would if Manchester United were playing Arsenal.

Some firms put their trust in just one compiler to generate prices for the week's non-league programme and if you can be selective and research well, there is every chance you will have put more thought into a fixture than the person setting the prices. That is a recipe for success.

ANTE-POST BETTING The typical Conference winner is a team who finished in contention the season before. From 1998-99 to 2003-04, four of the six champions (Cheltenham, Rushden, Yeovil and Chester)

By PHIL AGIUS

Low profile, larger edge: profit from teams such as Halifax and Hereford

had finished second, third or fourth in the previous campaign.

To identify a likely winner, try to find clubs on a sound financial footing, preferably well-supported (as salary-cap restrictions mean teams cannot overspend on wages if they do not have the income) and with a well-regarded manager.

Sides relegated from the Football League are inevitably among the favourites to bounce straight back but only Shrewsbury in the last five seasons have managed to regain their status at the first attempt. And even that was via the play-offs after they finished third. The previous four relegated sides – Scarborough, Chester, Barnet and Halifax – finished fourth, eighth, fifth and eighth in their first year.

In lower divisions, teams have a better chance of making faster improvement, but none of the champions of the Conference's three feeder leagues in 2002-03 or 2003-04 (Conference North and South began in 2004-05) finished lower than eighth the season before they won the title.

Keep an eye on the outright markets

outer limits

 Keeping informed

internet an invaluable tool

The Non-League Paper provides a multitudes of match reports and news which can be invaluable to punters, although you should be aware that many of the reports are submitted by the home club and may be biased. Their Friday edition offers in-depth team news and previews for the weekend action.

Here are some of the best online resources:

www.nonleaguedaily.com
Constantly updated with news items from throughout the pyramid

www.confguide.com
The ultimate online guide to the Conference boasts a plethora of stats and a lively forum

www.footballwebpages.co.uk
The best place for up-to-date form tables

www.footballconference.co.uk
New for 2004-05, the official site for the non-league's top flight

www.bbc.co.uk
A great source of Conference team news

www.tonykempster.co.uk
Brilliant independent site for lower-level teams' results and tables

www.fchd.btinternet.co.uk
Football Club History Database contains full statistical records (and cup progress) for all English teams

in-running. Hucknall were unconsidered 33-1 shots at the start of the Unibond League campaign in 2003-04. By the end of September they were top of the table and it was becoming clear that with a number of experienced League players in their line-up they were no flash in the pan. Yet the Nottinghamshire side were still on offer at 9-1. They won the league by nine points.

DON'T SHY AWAY FROM AWAY TEAMS One of the biggest opportunities to profit on non-league games stems from the oddsmakers placing too much emphasis on home advantage when setting their prices.

Ability and form matter far more in matches at this level than the location of the game.

The advantage to Manchester United of playing in front of a packed Old Trafford is obvious. The benefit a Ryman League team gains from playing in front of 180-odd folk is less easy to see. If you begin to assess matches with a view to backing the away team unless anything you learn persuades you otherwise, you should identify some big-priced winners.

THE HERE AND NOW Current form is critical to non-league bets as with clubs operating such small squads, injuries and suspensions can make a huge difference to the quality of the team you are betting on.

Teams can swing in and out of form throughout the campaign and catching them on the up is a great route to profit. Signing a centre-back who sorts out defensive problems, getting a striker back from injury or simply getting one lucky win which sparks a bit of confidence in the squad can all see form turn around sharply. Confidence is crucial in the lower leagues. Many of the players are those who were jettisoned by league clubs because they had talent but were unable to display it consistently, so when they strike a rich vein of form, get on them.

You'll find that match markets are priced up largely on league positions and spotting a fast riser, or just as usefully, a team in a slump, can produce some great bets. A great resource for this is the footballwebpages site, which provides four-, six- and eight-match form for the Conference and its feeder leagues. If, for example, you spot a team in the lower reaches with three wins out of their last four, take their chances seriously.

WHAT THE BOOKMAKER SAYS Skybet compiler Mike Triffitt admits that informed punters could gain an edge over bookmakers in the lower reaches.

"Things change so fast in the non-league and we really have to keep on our toes to avoid being caught out. Punters do best on big singles and we have some shrewd customers who do very well. Often you see a result they have won on and can't work out how they predicted it, then you read the match report and realise you'd missed some important team news. In the cups, we can only do our best to assess the relative strengths of the leagues. We are happy to lay the big teams in the FA Trophy as they increasingly don't seem to take it seriously."

IT'S A KNOCKOUT Cup betting involving non-league teams falls into two categories, non-league teams against League clubs in the FA Cup and all-non-league competitions.

While greater knowledge of clubs at this level can assist you in finding big-priced cup giantkillers, the real money is to be made in the national knockout competitions for the minnows – the FA Trophy and FA Vase.

Bet365 and Skybet have pioneered betting on these competitions and this is an area where hard work can really pay off. Use the lower-league tables available on the internet or in the Non-League Paper to find out the strengths of teams. Using Tony Kempster's excellent site (www.tonykempster.co.uk) enables you to see how the various lower-level leagues compare. For example, Fisher Athletic in the Dr Martens East Division are a Step Four club in the Pyramid (Conference is Step One, Conference North and South are Step Two, and so on), while Ramsgate in the Go Travel Kent League are a Step Six club (ie, they would need to win two promotions to play at the same standard as Fisher).

Many people may presume the difference in standard between two teams they have never heard of is negligible. In reality it can be vast. Changes in the relative strengths of the lower leagues can evolve over time, so assess the performances of one league's clubs against others in earlier rounds for

outer limits

 Heed the fans' voice

check out form on forums

Team news is vital and spending time familiarising yourself with who teams' key players are can help immensely when they are unavailable and, of course, when they return. If you have time, trawling through the websites and message boards for facts and opinions is also worthwhile.

Don't believe everything you read on the forums, but if there is a general view that a team will struggle without a certain player, they are probably right. And it's very likely that every extra nugget of information you obtain will be one the oddsmaker didn't have when he set his prices. If Thierry Henry has twisted his ankle, everyone knows; if Havant and Waterlooville's star midfielder is called away due to business commitments, you may be one of a select band to know.

use later on in the competition. An example of this came in the FA Vase fourth round in 2003-04. AFC Wimbledon, spurred on by the hype surrounding the spin-off of the league club, were massively odds-on at home to Colne of the North West Counties League Division Two.

Colne were 9-1 despite their league being at the same level in the pyramid (Step Six) as that from which the Dons came.

The price was huge for two teams of similar standing and Colne duly won 2-1 away on their way to reaching the semi-finals. But don't assume the biggest value bets will all be at fancy prices. These competitions often serve up a host of 10-11 shots who should really be 2-9.

As regards outright betting on non-league's FA Cup – the FA Trophy – outsiders have prospered in recent seasons as Conference clubs have begun to see the competition as secondary to either gaining a place in the Conference play-offs or avoiding relegation. Look for a solid mid-table team aiming to liven up their season or an ambitious club from Step Two.

it's not all about the old firm

SCOTTISH SENSE

TO MANY PEOPLE THERE ARE ONLY
two teams in Scotland. I probably don't need
to tell you that the pair are Celtic and Rangers.
Yet, while it is true that they have dominated
the top division and the two cups for most
of the last century, from a betting perspective
there are 40 other clubs to consider.

To start, though, we'll look at the Old Firm.
They attract most of the money and provide
the majority of the live TV action. Backing
them regularly is not an easy road to riches,
which will surprise few people despite their
stranglehold. Although you would have made
a very small profit supporting them religiously
to the same stake during seasons 2002-03 and
2003-04, it is a high-risk strategy for little
reward and is not recommended.

Unless you fancy their opponents at a
nice price, the best way to bet in games
involving the Glasgow giants is to look for a
correct-score bet. In Alex McLeish's first
18 months in charge of the Gers they won 14
of their 25 matches at Ibrox 2-0 or 3-0.
This sequence broke down in 2003-04 when
their defence was leaking goals, but it goes to
show that it is possible to detect trends that
can bear fruit, albeit not forever.

Overall, punters tend to lose less money
backing away sides than home sides. This

By STUART
CARRUTHERS

Old enemies: but there's more to life in Scotland than Celtic and Rangers

is in no small part down to the fact that home advantage is worth far less in Scotland than in England and other major European leagues, and decreases as you go down the divisions. Figures for home advantage are about 0.35 goals in the SPL, 0.25 in Division One, 0.2 in Division Two and 0.15 in Division Three.

Data analysis shows that in the first four seasons of the new millennium only in the SPL would you have lost less money backing homes than aways, suggesting that while home advantage is overestimated in the lower leagues, the reverse is true in the top division. Due to the margin added to the bookmakers' prices, just backing home teams in the SPL or away sides in the lower leagues makes no long-term profit. There is a useful way to use this information, though.

BACKING THE HOTPOTS Many people consider backing teams at long odds-on an easy route to financial ruin, but they may be tempted to reconsider when they learn that of the teams starting at 1-5 or shorter in the first four seasons of the 21st century, 97 of 99 won (many in the form of Celtic or Rangers), giving a profit of £13.57 to a £1 stake.

Overall, backing favourites is preferable to backing outsiders as a clear favourite-longshot bias exists in Scottish football. This indicates that the favourite wins more often than the market suggests, hence there is value to be had by backing the shorter-priced side.

One of the possible reasons given for this is that due to a difficulty in ascertaining team news, bookmakers are more wary of outsiders in lower-league Scottish football than they are of the favourites. It is not unheard of for a team to be weakened by the fact that one of the players is getting married on a particular Saturday and that some of his team-mates are missing the match to attend the ceremony. Layers would sooner that happened to a team that is 8-1 than a supposed 2-9 good thing.

In the five seasons between 1999 and 2004 you would have made a profit from blindly backing all away sides who started favourite. Given that away sides offer better value and that a favourite-longshot bias exists, it comes as no surprise that these teams do very well. When you find an in-form side you want to follow, you are likely to increase your profit margin by waiting until they are away to a lower-placed side.

OUTRIGHT BETTING We all know that Celtic and Rangers dominate the SPL. You have to go back to 1985 to find the last time one of the pair didn't win the league. The gap between the Old Firm and the rest has gradually increased since the mid-1990s and dramatically so during the period when financial problems blighted the rest of Scotland's elite sides at the start of the 21st century. Celtic and Rangers have each tended to run up sequences of domination and the monopoly of the title usually continues until major team changes happen.

scottish sense

 The cup strategy

look for a knockout shock

The Old Firm also dominates the betting on the Scottish Cup and League Cup and they both usually go off around the 6-4 mark. They are best left alone unless you have a particularly strong belief that one of the pair is stronger than the other, and it is worth looking for an outsider for an each-way bet.

What you are hoping for is the luck of the draw and for your team to avoid the Old Firm until the final; this usually involves Celtic being drawn against Rangers in an earlier round. In the ten seasons from 1994-95 to 2003-04 Celtic and Rangers met twice in the Scottish Cup final and once in the League Cup final. There is a 57.5 per cent chance of the two Glasgow giants squaring up to each other before the Scottish Cup final (assuming neither is knocked out by another team), and a 54.3 per cent chance of a pre-final encounter in the League Cup.

Assuming the team you like is a big enough price – most other SPL sides are priced between 20-1 and 40-1 – it's often a risk worth taking. In the ten seasons from 1994-95 to 2003-04 two teams other than Celtic and Rangers won each of the two knockout tournaments. That's a 20 per cent success rate for non-Old Firm teams, which is in itself an incentive to sniff around for a longshot to back.

So apart from choosing which of the sworn enemies wins the title, the only option is to back a team to win the league without the Old Firm. Look for a team that finished in the top six in the previous season and has kept most of its playing staff during the close-season.

Bookies don't go up with outright odds for the lower leagues until shortly before the season starts. This is largely due to the fact that a few thousand pounds and a couple of quality players can make a big difference at this level. Most clubs only sign players on season-long contracts so every summer there is a high turnover. When looking for the right bet, start with last term's league table and then pay close attention to each club's arrivals and departures. Most Division Three sides have one or two stars who hold them together. It is crucial to see if the club you fancy has held on to them before parting with your money.

beware the big names

ON THE CONTINENT

CONTRARY TO WHAT SOME PEOPLE might think, you don't need to buy a satellite system that turns your back garden into something resembling Jodrell Bank to become a winning European football punter.

By IAN COYNE

Obviously, it doesn't do any harm to take in as much of the action from the continental championships as possible. But Sky Sports gives Spain's La Liga brilliant coverage with live games on Saturdays, Sundays and occasionally in midweek, as the transfers of David Beckham, Michael Owen and Jonathan Woodgate to Real Madrid and Henrik Larsson to Barcelona increased interest in Spanish football among British followers.

And while Sky seldom shows German league games as they happen, its Bundesliga Review show is comprehensive enough to keep you up to date with the goings-on in that country.

Eurosport's coverage of Italian and French football is less polished than Sky's, but as punters we are more interested in the action than features on which ice-cream parlour Roma striker Francesco Totti likes to hang out in on his day off, so that needn't bother us too much.

If you adhere to the universal rules of sports betting outlined elsewhere in this book, such

Beckham and Owen at Real: interest in Spanish football is on the up

as being selective, not only betting because you are going to watch a game, doing research into team news, and having a half-decent grasp of the laws of probability, you have the basic tools at your disposal to either take on the layers or other punters on the betting exchanges.

Doing your homework does not guarantee that you will make money. It is how you apply what you discover that is the vital factor. Here are some of the most important points to consider when backing a team in a fixture on the continent.

ABILITY OR REPUTATION? Odds-compilers tend to quote teams according to their reputation as a big club rather than how good they actually are. It was once said that often they price up teams who have long since retired.

They do so, of course, because the majority of people who are betting on their prices are unduly influenced by reputation rather than form.

It happens in England but it happens even

more starkly on the continent and it is well worth making a list of the teams in each league that even the most casual football watcher would be able to name, as these sides will always attract more money than they should and will consequently be artificially short for many of their fixtures.

This list is by no means comprehensive, and you have to reassess how you rate a team each season. But as a rough guide these are the teams to always think extra long and hard about before supporting:

Spain Barcelona, Real Madrid.

Germany Bayern Munich, Borussia Dortmund.

France Paris Saint-Germain, Marseille, Monaco, Lyon.

Italy Juventus, Milan, Inter, Lazio, Roma.

That is not to say that any of these are bad sides. Barcelona were transformed after signing Edgar Davids on loan from Juve in January 2004 and finished second in La Liga that season, while Milan were worthy Italian champions that year.

But the point is that they are at skinny odds even when they aren't playing well. The 2003-04 season gave a clear example of how hard it was to profit on the best-known teams. The only pre-season favourites to take the title were Lyon, who earned their third consecutive French championship.

Bayern ended up second in the Bundesliga despite being best at 4-7 at the outset to win it, while Real were left in the unusual position of needing to qualify for the Champions League the following year from the preliminary round after losing each of their last five games.

In Real's case, they were shown so often on Sky that it was clear to all viewers that selling holding midfielder Claude Makelele to Chelsea had left them lacking a defensively-minded influence in the centre of their team, yet they

194

on the continent

 Less glamour – more value

why the long price?

There have been plenty of examples in recent years of the layers being slow to react to the better-than-expected performances of some lesser-known European club sides, and more often than not the generous odds on offer about these clubs were well worth taking.

Osasuna enjoyed an excellent start to the Spanish season in 2003-04, and even though they trailed away towards the end, the Pamplonans' 12th-place finish was still decent for a team who were fancied for relegation by many.

Sevilla finished above several more celebrated names in sixth in La Liga, while Sochaux narrowly missed out on a place in the Champions League, finishing a highly creditable fifth in the French League. But perhaps the best examples of teams that consistently represented good value were seen in Germany, where Werder Bremen stormed to the title and little-fancied Bochum finished fifth.

All the above teams enjoyed famous wins over some of the more illustrious clubs. And even though the league table suggested they had a fair chance of victory, they were still big prices to do so.

Osasuna beat Atletico Madrid and Deportivo La Coruna at home, but their most notable win came at champions Valencia on January 25, 2004. Sochaux beat Marseille on January 31, Werder could still be backed at 11-10 to beat Dortmund, who were having a shocking season, at home on February 28, and at 16-5 to defeat Bayern at the Olympiastadion on May 8 – though they were six points clear of them and on the cusp of winning the title. Werder won both. Bochum enjoyed big-odds victories over Bayern (home) and Leverkusen (away) in consecutive weeks in February.

It isn't always possible to see these lower-profile teams live, but if you do some research you can find out whether they are genuinely improved, or whether their results are merely a flash in the pan.

were usually a shade of odds-on to win away, even against teams above halfway in the table. Even in their title triumph the previous season Real failed to win ten of their 19 away games. That figure rose to 11 in 2003-04, the difference being that they lost six matches, rather than just three, so it was more profitable to back their opponents than lay Real.

You can't go against these teams every week, yet you should always be prepared to do so selectively – and this brings us on to the next subject . . .

HOW DO I GET THE INFORMATION I NEED?

Most punters will, quite rightly, want to make sure a team they are considering backing isn't missing the striker whose goals have fired them into an unusually high position in the standings, or members of a defence that has conceded an impressively low number of goals.

Getting team news isn't always easy, especially if you don't read the language of the country that that side comes from and therefore can't make use of a foreign newspaper or its website. However, many club's websites (especially the Bundesliga outfits) have an English version button.

www.germansoccer.net, which gives team news and lists the probable formations of the sides, is highly useful. The site also gives its own tips on the forthcoming games.

But beware – in contrast to the otherwise excellent info available, the betting advice given leaves plenty to be desired! If you want tips, stick with the *Racing Post*.

A general search using the club's name will generally direct you to sites that provide team news and visiting these is recommended.

Other useful reference tools are monthly magazines *World Soccer* and *Football Italia*, both of which you should be able to find at larger newsagents. *World Soccer* gives a brief report on the goings-on in each country and often focuses on a player in form from that league.

For latest scores, www.livescore.com will give you up-to-the-minute info on how your bet is going. For stats, www.soccerway.com, which contains information on just about every league on the planet, is unmissable.

This site archives results going back many seasons, and breaks teams' records down into home and away league tables enabling

on the continent

 Suspicious stalemates

In the Italian league, it's not unusual to see the draw far shorter than 2-1 in games where, on paper, a point apiece serves both sides well. The draw can only represent value at that price if the match is fixed. There is a long history of teams playing out comfortable draws near the end of the season, and recently some teams have been brought before the Italian league authorities accused of pre-arranging results. However, while most punters will prefer to leave these games alone, there are knowledgeable punters who are prepared to lay the draw in these Italian matches on the exchanges. They argue that the draw price can go so low as so-called money-buyers pile in (odds-on in some instances!) that they can afford to lose on the occasions when such gambles are landed, because there are enough times when they aren't to make it a profitable strategy.

you to form ratings for the sides.

Soccerway really comes into its own around the end of the season, when punters should be asking . . .

THIS TEAM NEEDS TO WIN – BUT CAN THEY? Some punters don't like to bet on European matches near the end of the season, as they can't be sure whether teams who are sitting in mid-table, neither able to earn promotion nor threatened by relegation, will be trying to win.

However, it is at this time of year that some of the best bets can be had.

When else would you get the chance to back a mid-table team at odds-against at home to a team who are near the foot of the table? When else would exchange layers be able to get matched at odds-on when opposing a struggling club to beat a better team on their own patch?

These prices get offered only because many punters attach far too much importance to a team's desire for points, rather than their ability to get them.

There were plenty of examples of this in 2003-04. One of the most profitable sides to oppose were Celta Vigo, who were surprisingly relegated from the top flight in Spain after qualifying for the Champions League the season before.

Coral actually made their Galician neighbours Deportivo 9-5 outsiders to win a home derby with Celta on May 15, as defeat would have edged Celta closer to the drop. Depor had little to play for except regional pride, but earned a comfortable 3-0 victory nevertheless.

And Celta had already lost a remarkable ten home league games that term when Mallorca visited on the last day of the campaign, yet they were just 8-15 to beat the 7-1 islanders. Celta lost 2-1. ■

inside international football

TAKING ON THE WORLD

THERE ARE FOUR BIG INTERNATIONAL tournaments that bookmakers bet on – the World Cup, European Championship, African Nations Cup and Copa America – but only two really catch the imagination of the betting public. Huge volumes are traded on the World Cup and European Championship from high-rollers and small-stakers alike.

By MARK LANGDON

But how easy is it to make money on these high-profile events?

WORLD CUP The quality of the most important sporting event outside the Olympic Games has been slightly diluted in recent years as Fifa bow to political pressure by allocating more qualifying spots to countries from Asia and Africa, but the cream usually rises to the top eventually.

Since sports betting took off at the start of Italia 90, the longest-priced winner has been 7-1, while Germany at 20-1 were the biggest-priced team to make the final. In a tournament of shocks in 2002, Rudi Voller's nondescript outfit took advantage of numerous countries being taken out in the group and last-16 stages.

But Greece's 100-1 Euro 2004 victory means it would be dangerous to assume we need not look too far down the lists to find the

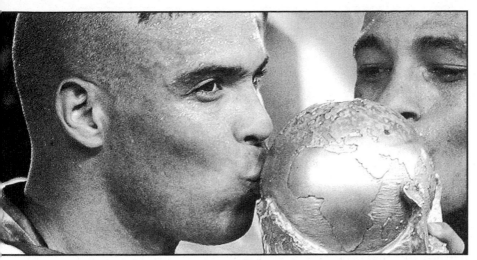

Brazil's 2002 World Cup: they are the only country to win outside their continent

winner, although one should never overlook the well-known fact that, up to and including the 2002 finals, only Brazil (in the 2002 World Cup and in Sweden in 1958) were successful outside their own continent.

Obviously, the climate and pitch conditions can have a huge significance, particularly in the baking heat, and you should always be looking at a team who are well suited to the weather. And even though the favourites usually thrive in the World Cup, the pre-tournament betting is never unfailingly accurate and a smattering of outsiders usually get into the knockout stages.

So in this new world, in which trading positions on the exchanges are so popular with clued-up punters, don't be afraid to back sides who are outsiders with a view to laying them back at shorter prices.

In the modern era, Sweden (50-1) and Bulgaria (80-1) both made the semi-finals in USA 94, Croatia (66-1) reached the last four at France 98 and co-hosts South Korea also fell only at the last hurdle having been available to back at 300-1 in 2002.

taking on **the world**

**Bookmakers'
chart-break**

scoreline loophole exposed

They say there are no easy games in international football any more and UK bookmakers found this out to their cost in the early years of the 21st century.

Their correct-score prices for international matches are generated from a chart and are based on the home team's win price. Thus, if the hosts are 4-6 to win, they may be 7-1 to win 1-0, 8-1 to win 2-0 and so on.

But these charts were hastily revised in 2003 after a group of shrewd punters spotted that a disproportionately large group of World Cup and European Championship qualifying matches involving a giant of European football against a minnow were finishing 2-0.

The prices were still reflecting the situation of a bygone age when sides like Germany, Italy and Spain could usually be relied upon to stuff the likes of Luxembourg, the Faroe Islands and Andorra by at least five goals.

Instead, the minnows started to be better coached and better organised and were able to defend more professionally even if they still lacked a cutting edge in attack. And the superpowers were quite happy to go a couple of goals ahead, bring off their star names and coast to victory.

Consequently, bookmakers were seeing an influx of 2-0 correct-score multiples on international nights and were often stung as that scoreline occurred far more frequently than the odds implied they should.

Eventually, the 2-0 scoreline was slashed and the loophole closed.

South Korea had ideal climatic conditions as well as some favourable refereeing decisions in their favour but the common factor in those other big-priced semi-finalists was an ability to score goals.

Croatia's Davor Suker triumphed in the Golden Boot, while Hristo Stoichkov, the Bulgaria talisman in 1994, was joint top-scorer with six goals. So if you are attracted to an underdog with a lethal hitman, the chances are they could do some serious damage.

Talking of the Golden Boot, it generally all comes down to which strikers' teams are drawn in an easy group.

Ronaldo in 2002 faced 1,000-1 pokes China, Suker managed to play against both Japan and Jamaica, while Stoichkov made hay against Greece, who had just three teams below them in the outright betting in 1994 and were a shambolic outfit compared to the side that went on to conquer Europe ten years later.

Another move to consider is to lay all the group favourites. In 1990 and 1998 you would have won a negligible amount by backing all the group favourites to a level stake, but the market leaders blew up in 1994 and 2002, when punters staking £10 on each would have lost £15.67 and £31.94 respectively.

EUROPEAN CHAMPIONSHIP Greece
provided one of the biggest shocks in international football when they won the 2004 event as 100-1 shots, beating hosts Portugal 1-0 in the final, but they were not the first and will undoubtedly not be the last underdog nation to spring a surprise in the European Championship.

Many observers believe this 16-team competition is stronger and harder to win than the World Cup and because of the quality of every outfit, including the perceived rags, it is terribly difficult to predict. Suffice to say that steering well clear of short prices is advised.

Germany (7-2) justified favouritism at Euro 96, but 18-1 shots Denmark, who were told they were competing only a matter of weeks before the finals after Yugoslavia had been expelled from the competition, took the honours at Euro 92 when seventh of eight teams in the betting.

The Czech Republic reached the 1996 final before losing at 80-1, and then eight years later the Greeks became gods in the bookmakers' eyes when providing the layers with one of their greatest ever tournament results.

There is nothing to link the success of

Denmark, Greece and the Czechs, but don't be afraid to back a team once they show their class. For instance, Greece were still rank outsiders despite beating favourite after favourite and it's important to be open-minded about a team's ability as a competition progresses.

The lesson to be heeded from Greece's triumph is that the market can be slow to react to the fact that a team representing a nation with little heritage on the international stage is infinitely better than its predecessors. While the Greeks were conquering Europe, they were still being priced up as if their dismal failures of two, four, six and more years ago were of significance.

An international football team can change drastically in two years, both in terms of the players available and the quality of the coach. Current form is everything. What a country achieved or failed to achieve in previous years is irrelevant.

Because the European Championship tends to be competitive, the draw becomes a big factor, particularly in the opening group matches and knockout stages. Hills spokesman Graham Sharpe once said: "Casual punters don't like to back draws. It's usually only the shrewdies."

Be a shrewdie. Don't be afraid to punt the draw. In the four European Championships between 1992 and 2004, having a £10 bet on the draw in every opening group game would have yielded a profit of £115, while, when the pressure rises in the knockout arena, so does the chance of a match being level after 90 minutes.

Six of the eight semi-finals in that timespan ended all-square after regular time and it makes sense to keep the draw on your side, either by having an Asian handicap bet or by laying one of the teams you don't fancy.

Another decent punting strategy is to back under 2.5 goals in the final, with no showpiece having produced three goals since 1980 up to and including the 2004 championship.

Finding a Golden Boot bet is pretty much the same for the Euros as the World Cup. Milan Baros, 66-1, scored five goals for the Czechs in 2004, who had 500-1 shots Latvia in their opening section, while Alan Shearer notched five times for England at Euro 96 thanks largely to the Three Lions' easy start against Switzerland and Scotland – two of the four worst teams in the competition.

AFRICAN NATIONS CHAMPIONSHIP

The timing of the tournament – January – is a real killer for the competing teams as players are put under increasing pressure by their clubs to fulfil their commitments to their league teams rather than their countries and until the competition is moved to the end of the European season, it is impossible to give long-term advice.

Keep a close eye on team news, with bbc.co.uk and fifa.com providing punters with an excellent service. But whatever happens keep stakes small as erratic results spring up all over the place.

COPA AMERICA
This used to be the South American equivalent of the European Championship. However, since the continent went to one huge qualifying pool for the World Cup, the Copa America has struggled to live up to its billing.

Brazil and Argentina usually send experimental squads to the competition, and, while they both made it to the final in 2004, which Brazil won on penalties, it can pay to follow guest teams from North and Central America, who usually take the tournament more seriously. Mexico always look to go well as they prepare for their World Cup qualifiers in the Concacaf section. But, as with the African Nations, don't go crazy.

a compiler opens his mind

SETTING THE ODDS

SUN-TZU, THE ANCIENT CHINESE warrior, said in his epic work *The Art Of War*: "If you know the enemy and know yourself, you need not fear the result of a hundred battles."

For punters, the enemy are the odds-compilers, so to avoid fearing your next hundred wagers, it is useful to know who you are up against.

Do these men know more than we do? Do they eat, breathe and sleep football? Are they armed with ultra-sophisticated computer programmes that help them to generate faultless prices that give punters no edge? Or do they just pick up a fixture list, spend a minute or two on each game and hope they have got their prices accurate enough to avoid a complete disaster for the firms that employ them?

Sorry to disappoint anyone who might hope the odds are hastily thrown together and that anyone out there with a few hours to spare can spot scores of mistakes on a single coupon, but, yes, sports odds-compilers are indeed a diligent and conscientious breed who leave no stone unturned in their efforts to make life as hard as possible for those who punt on their prices.

Ask people whose opinion on British

By BRUCE
MILLINGTON

204

**John Wright: view
from the coalface**

football counts for most and the majority will probably reply Alan Hansen or Andy Gray. But with all due respect to those shrewd and erudite Scotsmen, their views are less important than those of the average odds-compiler.

A TV pundit can get something hopelessly wrong – didn't Hansen once say that you win nothing with kids just as the Manchester United team of the youthful Giggs, Scholes, Butt, Beckham and Nevilles embarked on a successful Championship campaign? – and the only consequence is that he might lose a bit of face.

If a compiler gets something hopelessly wrong, ruthless punters pounce and the guilty man's employers are liable to get irate.

When it comes to putting your money where your mouth is, nobody does it with a greater degree of risk than a compiler, especially a football compiler.

Given the enormous volume of matches that the leading bookmakers price up every week, the scope for errors is obvious. Punters can choose whether or not to bet on a match. Oddsmakers, 99 per cent of the time, do not have that luxury.

One of the foremost practitioners of the art is John Wright, who is senior sports odds-compiler for Coral.

He has been with the firm at their Barking, Essex, headquarters since 1985 and has witnessed at first hand the spectacular growth of the sports betting sector of the business.

In my capacity as sports editor of the *Racing Post* I have found Wright to be one of the best people in the betting industry for a quote.

Capable though the PR men are who act as the public face of their companies, they cannot provide the same view from the coalface as Wright and his fellow compilers.

Some oddsmakers prefer to operate in complete anonymity, but Wright, while in no way a publicity-seeker, is always available to give the bookmakers' side of things. And now, with the following account of a week in his life, he offers a fascinating insight into how football prices are compiled and traded, where he feels his company is most vulnerable and what makes a successful oddsmaker.

THURSDAY The week effectively begins today, when I start the preparatory work for the following week's matches. To begin with I will collate a definitive fixture list for the period covering next Tuesday to the following Monday. That involves checking various websites to ensure I have all the fixtures right as well as the kick-off times and I also try to find out if there have been any changes of venue. It has happened in the past that I have priced up a particular Uefa Cup game unaware that it has been switched to a neutral venue.

Obviously, this is a major problem for a company like us, which produces coupons for our betting shops. We are extremely reluctant to change prices once they have been printed and distributed so it is crucial to try to get them right before they go to press.

At busy times I can be pricing up in excess of 200 matches and to an extent you live and die by your worst price, so the importance of checking absolutely every detail is obvious.

Once I have finalised the fixtures and worked out how many coupons we need to produce, I then get my suspensions list up to date. This is a vital task.

There are certain teams whose price can alter significantly depending on whether a player is suspended or not, and the easiest thing to miss is if a lower-league player has had an automatic red card reduced on appeal to a yellow, thus meaning his ban is shortened or rescinded. I might be 5-4 a team on the understanding that a player is banned, but if he plays they are a 10-11 chance. And then it

setting the odds

 Rising from obscurity

how football betting took off

Getting started is probably the hardest part of becoming an odds-maker. Certainly when Wright left school and decided he wanted to pursue a career in the world of bookmaking there was no such job as sports odds-compiler.

'Back in 1985 you had to have an interest in horseracing just to get a foothold in the industry,' he recalled. 'Sports betting was almost non-existent in those days.

'I started with Coral on the day Steve Cauthen won the 1,000 Guineas on Oh So Sharp.'

Back then that would have been the day's main event. Now, it competes with a vast array of events for punters' attention.

'When I first joined Coral football betting consisted almost entirely of the basic weekend longlist. The midweek prices were only ever published in our advert in *The Sporting Life* – there was no printed midweek coupon,' Wright said.

'I remember the guys at The Life used to phone us at the pub to tell us to get back to the office to proof-read the black and white advert.'

The differences between then and now are enormous.

'Football has gone from providing a tiny percentage of our turnover to being a key element of the business and it is growing all the time.'

is just a case of checking on team news after the midweek games just played. I would say 85 per cent of my research is done via the net with the rest being daily newspapers and magazines like World Soccer. We are lucky that one of our compiling team is fluent in Spanish and Italian so he can trawl websites like Marca for up-to-the-minute news. Finally I am ready to start pricing up the matches, a process that takes me right through until Friday.

FRIDAY The whole point with odds-compiling is that when you price up a football match you are taking three main factors into account: what prices you think the three outcomes should be based on form, what prices you think they should be based on how the market will react, and what prices you think the other bookmakers will be.

In other words, it is not as simple as just going up with prices derived entirely on how the teams are playing, what their head-to-head records are, etc. I might rate a particular home team a 4-6 chance but I know that if I go 4-6 everyone will stick them in their coupon bet and we might end up with liabilities we don't want. Often I can go 8-13, knowing we will still see money for them.

And then there is the issue of what the other compilers will do. I might fancy Manchester United to beat Liverpool for my life and be desperate to make sure I am top price about Liverpool. The skill is to work out how big I need to go to make sure that when the prices of all the bookmakers are published in the *Racing Post* the following Friday my Liverpool price appears in black type [to indicate it is the biggest or joint-biggest price on offer]. There are times when I will put up a price about a team I want to lay fully expecting to be best-offer and find that other compilers have gone even bigger.

Some games can be priced up in next to no time. If Tottenham are at home to Arsenal I know what I am going to be within 30 seconds. I might do some research to query the prices, but more often than not I will stick with my original feel price. After a while an experienced compiler should be able to price up matches virtually on instinct without making too many ricks.

Other matches are far harder to deal with, and that is when having a team of compilers like we do is so important. Four of us price up every match, but the final call is with me. There are times when I am, say, 8-11 a team and the other three guys are 10-11. The final call is with me but I will discuss the price with the rest of the guys and sometimes it will turn out I have missed something and will go 10-11 whereas on other occasions I will stick to my guns.

There is a particular type of team that I am always happy to lay. I am talking about those mid-table Premiership sides who look so impressive when playing on the counter-attack away from home but who cannot assert any superiority when at home to the division's weaker teams and do not have the game to break them down. In 2003-04 it was a very successful policy of ours to be top-price about the likes of Blackburn and Southampton when they were odds-on at home to the strugglers.

By the end of Friday I aim to have all the next week's prices as complete as possible with just the Saturday results to factor in.

SATURDAY The midweek prices must go to the printers by 6.30pm so Saturday is all about trying to make sure every little late detail is factored into the prices before they are signed off. In other words, Coral's prices on the midweek coupon do not reflect events that happen beyond Saturday evening.

If the Monday papers reveal that a player has gone for a scan the day before and is out for a month, that team's midweek price will effectively be wrong.

This is where the punters have an advantage over us, but we do all we can to avoid changing coupon prices because it does not go down well with our regulars, who like the price on the coupon to be the price they get.

I get into the office in time to watch the lunchtime match on Sky, during which I will always be on the lookout for any information that might mean I should consider a price change.

My PC has a facility that automatically flicks up any mention of Coral on the Betfair chatroom, where punters might be discussing what they consider to be a rick price or whatever, and I have newsnow.co.uk constantly updating me with latest information.

And while the main task is to get next week's

setting the odds

Being right a delight

The real job satisfaction comes when a team I really want to lay is unsuccessful. You get a real thrill from being a standout price about them and then they fail to win.

Sometimes you get to know how the compilers from the other firms will go with certain teams. I remember a few seasons ago that Ladbrokes would always seem to be right about Bury – shortest when they won and biggest when they didn't.

prices spot on, I am also keeping an eye on how we might do on the games taking place today. The traders will keep me updated with which teams have been best backed so by the time I leave the office to make the short tube journey to West Ham if they are playing at home I will know who we want to win and who we want to lose.

During the match, I will receive a constant stream of text messages from the office keeping me updated with how our bogey teams are getting on.

I am out of my seat the moment the final whistle goes and back at my desk by 5.15 to make the final alterations to the tissue. Prices can change quite a bit depending on the Saturday results. Take a midweek match between Leicester and Tottenham for instance. I might originally be 5-4 Leicester, 7-4 Tottenham and 11-5 the draw. But if that afternoon Leicester have gone and won 2-0 at Arsenal and Spurs have lost 3-0 at Bolton, I will go something like 10-11 Leicester, 5-2 Tottenham, 11-5 the draw.

It is important not to get too carried away by one result, though. With most teams, punters will place a lot more importance in their latest performance than perhaps they should. It's another thing to bear in mind when making the last-minute changes.

The final prices go off to the printers at 6.30pm and between then and the final proofs coming back a couple of hours later I concentrate on updating the ante-post prices. This is an increasingly important task as the ante-post markets become ever more popular. The key points to take into account when deciding how to revise a team's long-term price are how they played that afternoon, how well backed they have been during the week and what their next few fixtures are like. I often like to avoid reducing a team's price too much on the strength of one win. They might have

setting the odds

 **Watching
the teams**

the value of being there

I go to West Ham because it is extremely useful to take the opportunity to watch teams live. I am a Millwall fan and am completely dispassionate about the Hammers. Generally I am more interested in their opponents.

In the 2003-04 season, for instance, I watched Norwich play superbly at Upton Park. They looked solid at the back and lethal on the counter-attack, and while they only drew 1-1 I made sure I kept them on my side as far as the Division

One title betting went. They won the championship and we ended up with an excellent book on the market.

Then again, you have to be careful not to get too carried away about a team just on the basis of seeing them once in the flesh. I remember watching QPR absolutely murder Plymouth at Loftus Road. Plymouth were terrible, yet they ended up running away with the division and finished well clear of Rangers.

beaten an inferior team 2-0 at home, but where is the surprise in that? Plus, if they have three tough fixtures up next you can keep them unchanged, knowing you will lay them to people who are unaware that their prospects of adding significantly to their points total in the coming weeks are not especially bright.

Likewise, a team that has nicked a draw against a decent outfit and have easy games ahead of them are often worth having on your side so their price will invariably be cut.

Depending on how busy the midweek programme is, I can be away by anything from eight o'clock to midnight.

SUNDAY Each of the compilers does one Sunday in four and the day's main task is to update the long-term markets after the day's action. Even if I am off, I might ring up and have some input into the Premiership betting if there have been some key fixtures.

Otherwise, I will go through all the Sunday

papers, starting with *Football First*, which I read from cover to cover because it has reports and stats from all matches.

MONDAY In by 7.30am because there is a lot to do in a short space of time. I have until 1pm to finalise the prices for next weekend. I read The Game, the football supplement in *The Times*, plus as many other papers as I have time to get through and am back on the net, searching for meaningful news updates.

Apart from the main coupon, we have the handicaps, corners, half-time prices and first scorers to deal with. We price up 13 players from every team in the four divisions to score the first goal, which is quite an under-taking.

Once all the prices are finalised, it is all about checking, checking and checking again. A mistake on the coupon can be very costly. It happens about once a season that we have to do a reprint but that is expensive and can delay distribution into the shops so it is to be avoided unless absolutely necessary.

I often think how much easier the job would be if, like many online and telebet firms, we did not have coupons and could just our change prices as and when we felt it necessary.

I remember being in Australia to watch England in the cricket World Cup in 1992 and walking into a betting shop. I asked for some rugby league prices and the manager just pressed a button and printed me out the latest show.

In a sense it would be great to be able to do the same, but you can't just go changing things like that because the shop regulars would not like it. These guys are our bread and butter and if they are able to back a team at 7-4 on the coupon when I would love us to have cut them to 11-8 because their centre-forward and goalkeeper have been crocked we just have to live with it.

setting the odds

Forward defensive

We have a guy in Sheffield who generates all the lower league first scorer prices and he is brilliant. The obvious danger in this market is that we will be unaware that a centre-half has been moved into attack. It happens quite regularly.

Fortunately we have some excellent shop managers based near many football grounds and they will usually let us know if we are vulnerable from a positional switch. I remember being 33-1 about a Darlington defender who played up front. You can build up huge liabilities when the true price should be closer to 6-1.

Most first-scorer prices are derived from a benchmark price which we have for all Premiership players. If, for instance, Thierry Henry's benchmark price is 7-2 and we key in Arsenal's price for the match in question – say 4-9 – that might give us a first-scorer price of 11-4.

setting the odds

 Digging for clues

the joys of cup week

The early rounds of the FA Cup are always interesting from a compiling point of view. You really need to know all you can about some of the more obscure non-league sides that get through the preliminary stages and that means scores of phone calls to local journalists and team managers. Most of them are great. They will gladly let you know all their latest injury news and give you a clue how they will line up and are far more approachable than the arrogant people who exist at the so-called elite end of English football.

TUESDAY This is a less intensive day and, as far as I am concerned, the last day of the working week. It is a big European day as we sign off all the weekend Euro coupons on a Tuesday. We bet on eight divisions across Europe and will have all the tissues prepared in advance so we can just revise them according to the latest news and get them away.

European football is difficult to price up because we are up against people who know as much about, say, Dutch football as the average Englishman knows about the Premiership. But our European specialist is extremely good and we do well out of it. In fact, we do well out of football as a whole over the course of a season.

On a good weekend we can win 60 per cent of the total amount bet on football with us. On a bad weekend we can lose up to ten times our turnover, although hopefully that will remain a once-a-season occurrence.

WEDNESDAY A day off, although there is almost always at least one evening match to be watched. Then it's back into the office on Thursday morning to start the process all over again.

golf guru's guide to glory

FAIRWAY TO HEAVEN

IT'S NO NEW PHENOMENON – since time immemorial, golf and betting have gone together like fish and chips. What Sunday morning fourball would be complete without its sidestake, whether it be for a golf ball, a fiver or the four-figure sums that were regularly wagered at the great gambling clubs like Sunningdale?

Great hustlers like Titanic Thompson made a handsome living out of the game before World War II, mostly in Florida, by tricking millionaire tourists into big-money golf matches they had no chance of winning, and Lee Trevino and Raymond Floyd, both Major champions, cut their teeth as young pros by playing matches for a hundred bucks when they had only ten in their pocket.

In 1991 two opportunist punters from Essex, Paul Simons and John Carter, went round the country plundering odds of up to 100-1 from one-shop bookmakers, unaware the correct price was no more than 5-4, about holes-in-one at five televised tournaments and would have cleaned up £500,000 but for being knocked for part of their winnings.

Known as the Hole-in-One Gang, they knew exactly what the correct odds were as they had all the European Tour media guides listing the aces from previous years. There was no

By JEREMY CHAPMAN

You can pick up more than just your ball punting successfully on golf

betting on golf

 A matter of course

Keep stakes to a minimum when a course new to a tour is being played for the first time. All sorts of strange things happen when players are not familiar with a layout.

big secret about it, but they knew that the man in the street, and little bookmakers without a golf adviser, thought holes in one were almost as rare as a sighting of the dodo.

Simons and Carter were fully aware they had no chance with the major bookmaking chains, who knew the time of day; they also knew that the little man in one-horse towns might very well not.

Armed with Yellow Pages for the length and breadth of England, a great line in bluff, Cockney charm and unlimited patience, they drove thousands of miles taking odds from 3-1 to 100-1 on aces at the US Open, Open, Benson & Hedges, Volvo PGA and European Open. There was nothing illegal about it and they all came up.

But many bookmakers thought that *The Sporting Life*'s Green Seal Service, the great arbitrator of betting disputes at the time, would rule in their favour, forcing Simons and Carter to accept the 'correct' odds instead of the inflated ones.

The biggest whinger of all was Arthur

Whittaker from Derby, whose shop manager had laid three £50 bets at 100-1. But The Life would have none of it, ruling that there was a world of difference between palpable error (which would have given the layers a get-out) and errors of judgement.

In fairness, most bookies did stump up, but some shamed the industry, especially one firm, Spectrum Racing of Brighton, whose owner fled and sold up rather than fork out £43,000. In all there were £80,000-worth of non-payers but still enough left for the boys to buy Mercedes and have riotous gambling trips around the world. Sadly, Simons died a few years later but not before he had enjoyed himself.

Fast-forward to 1995 and without doubt the biggest coup in golf, perhaps on any sport. The clever fellow was Graham Hill, a computer wizard from Oxfordshire, who left the bookies dazed and distraught with a series of accumulators on Doral Open three-balls in Florida that netted just a few coppers short of £815,000 for the relatively minor outlay of £109, including tax.

He made ten selections, nine of them being outright winners. Billy Mayfair was the sole "villain" of the piece. He was only the joint-winner of his match.

The plan was take each of the Big Three, Ladbrokes, William Hill and Coral, for their then maximum sports payout of £500,000. Unfortunately for Graham, thanks to Mayfair cutting stakes in half, Hills had 'only' to shell out £274,903, Ladbrokes £271,630 and Coral £267,724. There's no pleasing some people, and Hill, who had won £39,000 on a football bet four years earlier, was heard to mutter: "If only Mayfair had done his stuff . . ."

With so much money wagered on golf, tens of millions of pounds by the time the new millennium came round, and it being just

betting on golf

 Aoki ace so expensive

Another hole-in-one that pained the bookies was the one by Isao Aoki at the second hole in the 1979 World Match Play Championship at Wentworth. Bovis, who had built some holiday homes in Scotland, were offering one to any of the 12 competitors who aced the second and asked Ladbrokes to "insure" it for them. Aoki's ace came at 8.40am and Ron Pollard, then Ladbrokes' PR director, recalled: "It was being televised and it was my misfortune to turn the set on just as Aoki played the shot. Peter George, then MD of the racing division, passed by and said brightly: 'Good morning!' to which I could only reply: 'Not really. We've already lost 40 grand'."

about the only sport where players and spectators share the same arena, there has always been a serious concern that punters could change the course of an event by shouting at the top of someone's backswing or by treading balls down in the rough.

The Royal & Ancient, which controls the Open Championship, still do not permit bookmakers on-course, though the European Tour brought that barrier down in the 1970s when first Ladbrokes, then Coral, Hills, Victor Chandler and Paddy Power hoisted marquees at main-tour events, Hills and Chandler getting the 1993 and 2004 Ryder Cups.

HOW YOU CAN WIN The chaps I have already mentioned were either very clever or simply struck it lucky, and the one who won the most, Graham Hill, was not even a regular golf punter. Football was his game. He claimed no expert knowledge of golf, but in order to beat the enemy on a regular basis you certainly need to know your golfing onions.

Apart from my own knowledge of the game accumulated over 40 years, my office at home is overrun with reference books, I watch dozens of hours of golf on TV every week, and when I go out for an evening to do something else, the golf is taped for late-night or early-next-morning viewing. It is vital to see how people are swinging and putting.

Some players score well but you can see they do not have confidence in one or two areas of their game and cannot replicate a good score for three more days.

To win at golf, you have to be up with the pace at least; better still, ahead of it. Just like football, you need to be in-the-know about players who are carrying injuries, players who have poor/great records on certain courses, players who go well at certain times of year, players who target certain objectives and use minor tournaments to experiment or build up to the Majors and other lucrative weeks. Hunches play a part too; sometimes you just sense that a player is coming up to a victory.

Is there a secret to backing regular golf winners? If I knew it, I'd probably keep it to myself. To reveal it would render my job redundant, and I'm not that daft! But there is no secret. As Gary Player once said: "The more I practise, the luckier I get." So it is with golf punting, or any sort of punting: the more you put into it, generally the more you get out of it.

The principal requirement is judgement. You have to know when a bookmaker has made a mistake. It happens a lot less rarely now than it did in the 'good old days' when golf was very small beer indeed.

Now it is the second-biggest betting sport after football but when I started writing about it, the only tournaments people wanted to bet on were the Open, what was then the Piccadilly World Match Play and, maybe, the Masters and the few tournaments the BBC showed, many of them 'delayed' coverage so that you did not know whether you were watching live or canned golf. There was no Sky Sports and there was certainly no betting in-running.

To know a mistake when you see one, you have to make your own tissue for each event. That requires getting 'the runners' from the requisite website and doing your homework: current performance, course form, length of course, likely weather conditions, plus any other ingredient you think is important.

Put them all together and come up with a price. That's what the odds-compilers do. To beat them, you have to know as much, maybe more. Then you have to get up very early as prices that stick out have been known to vanish as quickly as David Duval.

Over more than 30 years of golf tipping, first

betting on golf

 A sport that can shock

crucial to remain patient

There are times when you believe you can justify a hefty bet on a certain golfer and he promptly goes and misses the cut. Much about golf is totally incomprehensible. How can you explain Ben Curtis winning the Open Championship at 750-1 in his rookie year and on the first occasion he had ever seen a British links?

How can you explain Scott Drummond, an unknown Brit who had missed eight of his previous 11 cuts and never finished higher than 15th in Europe, winning such a high-profile tournament as the 2004 Volvo PGA Championship, beating players of the world pedigree of Ernie Els and Vijay Singh almost out of sight – and doing it without apparently a care in the world, going out in the final pairing for the first time in his career and shooting a last-round 64 that contained neither a bogey nor a five?

And how can you explain Todd Hamilton twisting the knife into Open punters, following Curtis's triumph with a 750-1 stunner of his own?

You can't. You just have to ride the bad weeks – and in golf these can last a long time. You can go seven or eight tournaments without a draw of any kind, even a place, and you simply have to take it on the chin. That is, so long as you have a proven record of winning in the long-term. Keep a record of all your bets, don't kid yourself. If you made a profit last year and the year before, the likelihood is that you will make a profit this year. No guarantee, but a very good chance.

in *The Sporting Life* and latterly for the *Racing Post*, I have managed to keep my head above water with a staking plan that has evolved down the years. Punters who have followed me religiously have made a good profit. There have been losing years but many more winning ones.

A profit of more than 1,000 points to recommended stakes has been achieved on outright selections in the period from 1997-2004 alone.

Many of the tips I fully expected to win did not, but thankfully a goodly number of 50-1, 66-1 and 100-1 shots have redressed the balance. What has kept me going is that I have been able to justify all my selections, at least to myself.

There always has to be a reason for backing a golfer; despite the huge number of players in a tournament, as many as 180 on occasions, it is not like roulette or doing the Lottery.

The successes of players such as Curtis and Drummond prove conclusively that almost any one of any given field can win a golf tournament these days. As 2001 Open champion Duval once said: "The public think there is a big gap between the world No. 1 and the world No. 24, but over the course of a season, it's only a putt here or there. There's very little to choose between all of us."

WHAT AIDS DO YOU NEED? I don't believe you can make it pay these days without a PC or laptop. Without one, you are slow out of the stalls as regards runners, comparative prices and Betfair, which has revolutionised golf prices, particularly regarding outsiders where 80-1 and 100-1 shots with bookmakers are frequently available at two, three or even five times those odds.

The brilliance of Betfair is that it is a hedging medium backers never had before. If their pre-tournament fancies get into position, they can now lay them back to guarantee a good profit come what may. And the in-running odds knock spots off those put up by bookmakers, some of which are tighter than an Aberdonian when the bill arrives for his round of drinks.

But tread warily with the outright place markets on Betfair, which are only occasionally good value, and steer well clear of the minority markets such as the LPGA (US women) and Champions Tour as these are usually a joke, aimed at catching out the ill-informed. Odds of 1-2 for world No 1 woman Annika Sorenstam when she's a 7-4 chance, and 15 or so runners at 20-1 or less in the over-50s markets await some mug to take them up.

betting on golf

 Give yourself cutting edge

It's often worth waiting until the halfway cut before having your main bet. This turns a 156-runner race into, at most, a 20-runner handicap. You miss the big prices but at least you have a serious runner going into Sunday night on Sky.

betting on golf

 Interpreting the stats

Use the official stats wisely and often but don't take everything you read there as gospel. For example, with the flag at the back, a player a foot short of the green putts an inch or two off the green on the other side. He putts again a yard past and misses the one back. In my book, that's four putts. But the tours don't count putts made from off the green because they say the player has the option of putting or chipping. That four-putt goes down as a two-putt in the record books.

Sadly, there are a fair few mugs about. Who can forget the poor chap who lost his entire life savings, some £10,000, after laying 2003 Madeira Open favourite Bradley Dredge at immense odds on Betfair because he had seen on the European Tour website that the Welshman had taken 30 shots on his first hole. It turned out that somebody at HQ had inadvertently pressed an extra button. In reality, Dredge had recorded a birdie three, a slight difference of 27 strokes, and went on to win the tournament by eight.

Anyone in golf knows that no professional shoots a 30 however difficult a hole is – and the first in Madeira is pretty easy. So it pays to know at least something about your subject before you venture into betting on it.

That's where the *Racing Post*, the most important weapon in your war against the enemy, comes in. It's all there – informed comment, form (course and current), price charts, tour statistics, course descriptions, weather forecasts, spread betting, threeballs, twoballs, matches, group betting, and any special offers going that week. The first-round stroke averages are especially useful for three-ball punters. And all for less than a half of lager. Why ring up tipping lines? If you don't agree with our opinion, work out your own winner.

You will also need accounts with as many bookmakers as you can find. That's vital if you're going to get the best prices. Look out, too, for any special offers knocking around during big events.

In the 2004 Open for instance, two firms were offering to refund losing bets if Tiger Woods won while another did likewise if a British or Irish player was successful.

And three layers gave an extra sparkle to each-way betting by offering a quarter the odds for the first six players. It is pleasing to report that during that tournament, the

betting on golf

 Required reading

best to go buy the book

The *Racing Post* apart, there is various good reading matter for golf punters. Keith Elliott's *Golf Form*, a hardy annual for more than a decade, is full of ideas, not all of them watertight, but unmissable for anyone who bets on the game.

It is a remarkable work of reference with short essays about every player who matters on the two main tours and full betting records of every tournament, plus the gospel according to Elliott, always good for an argument at the 19th hole. It just seems to grow and grow and is now about to crash the 1,000-page barrier.

The Timeform of golf is Tiger-Tees, a weekly ratings guide that comes out on Mondays based on players' performance in relation to the Standard Scratch Score of each course. A subscription service, it can be very useful for sussing out 72-hole match-bet material.

And you won't be fully tooled up without the official tour player-profile and tournament-record guides: for the European Tour, it's Pro-Golf; the American guides (PGA Tour Media Guide, Champions Tour Media Guide and LPGA Guide) can be ordered from Sportspages, the London sports bookshop (as can Elliott). Most of the information contained can be unearthed on the respective websites, but it is easier bedtime reading to have the facts in softback form. Besides, not everyone has a PC . . . yet.

major bookmakers finally did the decent thing and relented on their horrendous standard each-way rule which saw them pay out only on the first four placed players. A quarter the odds the first five is now, thankfully, a universal offer.

WHAT WEBSITES? The big websites for golf are www.pgatour.com for the American scene and www.europeantour.com. Both sites have multiple dropdowns where you can find out the fields, tee-times, course description, player-form, tour calendars, prize money, plus all the tour stats (driving distance, accuracy, greens-in-regulation, putting) for the current year – in fact, pretty well all the nitty-gritty you need to get the 'feel' of an event before working out your selections.

Both sites have in-running scoreboards for

every tournament and the American even has a newish toy, Tourcast, where you see live graphics of where every shot your player has hit has finished up. There are no pictures on scorecards, so the saying goes, but it does help the punter know what sort of form that player is in when he can see whether his man is making his score out of the deep rough thanks to a hot putter or achieving it the more conventional fairways-and-greens way. It is also a valuable tool for punters betting in-running on a tournament.

Many is the time that a player's price shortens without TV viewers knowing why. The answer, invariably, is that Tourcast has revealed that the player in question has just hit his approach to within two feet while television viewers are watching an ad break. These two sites also cover the other tours within its remit – in the States, the Champions Tour and the Nationwide Tour, the latter always interesting for spotting up-and-coming young talent before it hits the main tour; in Europe, the Challenge Tour, which serves the same purpose as the Nationwide, to give gainful employment to journeymen golfers who have fallen by the wayside and lost their main-tour cards and youngsters on their way up through the ranks.

For a good fallback, try www.golfonline.com, run by leading US magazine *Golf*, which often beats the official website on tee-times, a big plus for those who like to prepare early so they can be first up when Betfair open their three-ball markets.

The other sites you will want at one time or another are www.lpga.com and its European equivalent www.ladieseuropeantour.com.

When it's all quiet in Europe and the States, a period that grows ever shorter as the calendar of events gets bigger, you will need to get to know www.sunshinetour.com for the South African circuit, www.jpto.org for those

KJ Choi: keep an eye on the Asian Tour for emerging stars

big-money invitational events in Japan, www.pgatour.com.au for the Australasian Tour, and www.asiantour.com for all the background on those weird and wonderful Orientals like Kim Yong-Duck, Boonchu Ruangkit and Thaworn Wiratchant that pop up every time the European Tour holds tournaments in Hong Kong, Malaysia and Singapore. Well worth perusing, because some of these are the KJ Chois of the future. There are links to all these sites at www.europeantour.com.

There are also individual sites for the four Majors, WGC events (www.worldgolfchampionships.com) and the tournament with the world's biggest first prize, Sun City Challenge (www.nedbankgolfchallenge.com).

Don't forget www.racingpost.co.uk's Sports Betting section for website versions of my words of wisdom (sometimes!), odds checks and a handy player formguide, and for those of you seeking another opinion before parting with your hard-earned, you can turn to bettingzone.co.uk and readabet.com, who have their own golf experts.

THE BOOKMAKER'S VIEW "There's no other sport where you can back runners at 50-1 and 66-1 with a regular, realistic chance of winning – for a new punter coming into betting, golf is a great place to start." The man speaking is Tim Pickering, for the last 16 years the golf odds guru for Totesport. He is a player on golf and says: "I'd be very disappointed if I didn't make it pay. You can back a 66-1 chance every year for ten years at Wimbledon without a cat in hell's chance of winning but if you do your research, you need only a couple of 50-1 winners a year to make golf pay. It doesn't mean you have to bet every week; some weeks you don't really fancy anybody, other weeks, there are no prices that stand out.

"In golf, you sometimes get 20-1 the field; you can't get that in any other sport, and there's some terrific value if you put in the homework. Just look at Jeff Maggert, 100-1 for Top American in the 2004 US Open with Ladbrokes. An amazing price considering his record in that Major and his overall Majors record. You know he won't win the US Open, but you are not backing him to."

What about 72-hole match betting? "The problem with that is that you are betting odds-on virtually all the time. So you have to have at least a 60 per cent success rate to make any sort of profit. That used to be easier to achieve when bookmakers simply put two 50-1 chances together. These days we are much, much more careful with our match-ups. I spend more time on these than on anything else as punters are a whole lot cleverer these days, thanks largely to the *Racing Post*. All the work is done for them.

"But the punter has more chance with match betting than threeballs. That's the hardest of the lot. Lots of punters playing on threeballs are putting 4-1 and 5-1 chances in their multiples, players with no chance in my view, and, to be fair, they are having some success. And the amateur champions can be overpriced, particularly in the first round – they seem to have no fear of playing with Tiger & co.

"Remember, though, that for the Majors we bookmakers are pricing up 30 and 40 threeballs and twoballs. The punter only needs to bet on one or two. And the *Racing Post* table marks up the percentages – the punters never used to get that kind of help.

The best advice? "Don't bet for the sake of it. Don't bet every week, only bet when you believe it is value, do your homework, follow players in form. Simple, really."

Biggest lesson learned as an odds-compiler? "Don't ever think you know more than other people – there are a lot of clever ones around."

SPREADS There are five main spread markets: finishing positions, ten-man indices, 72-hole matches, 18-hole day-one matches and hotshots. The 18-holers are the most volatile because there's ten points for winning and three further points for each stroke you win by. Take Shaun Micheel v Nick Faldo, round one of the 2004 US Open. Micheel 71, Faldo 81. USA 40pts, GB 0. Nice if you are with Micheel, very nasty if you fancied Faldo.

Hotshots (four named golfers who have to finish in the top ten to make buyers smile) are rarely worth the trouble. Those clever-clogs at Sporting, IG, Cantor and Spreadex usually manage to slip in one with plenty of question marks against his name, or simply a player you don't really want. Only if you actively want all four players should you think of buying. Otherwise it's a sell or, more often, a pass.

Spread insiders often reveal that all sports markets are framed for punters to buy (or, in the case of finishing positions, to sell), and golf is no different. Conversely, they add, if you

betting on golf

Post delivers double blow

Totesport have bitter memories of the time the *Racing Post* cost them a packet. Tim Pickering recalls: "Our worst disaster? That would be July, 2003 and the 92-1 double on Ernie Els and Kenny Perry that the Post put up. It cost us more than any horseracing disasters that year, and there's plenty of them – in fact, it was our worst result of any sort that year. Never at any stage did it look as if we had a chance of getting out of it." And Tim's happiest moment? "Jean Van de Velde blowing the 1999 Open. I made him 10-11 when he took a five-shot lead into the last round. He was much shorter elsewhere. We didn't have him in the book, so I took a chance. I thought we'd blown it when he had still had a two-shot lead on the 72nd tee. His collapse was my biggest relief and that Open our biggest success story. We took virtually nothing on the winner, Paul Lawrie, laid well over six figures on the final day, and kept almost every penny."

betting on golf

 Take a rain-check

Always keep an eye on the weather forecast. Tournaments can get reduced to 54 or even 36 holes. If you have reason to believe that only one of the last two rounds will be played, there can be terrific value in backing the front two or three on the leaderboard. With only 18 holes to play, they have a much greater chance of staying at the front because there's less time for others to catch up. Remember that in tournaments where three different courses are used, as in the early-year pro-ams, no result can be declared over less than 54 holes because every member of the field must have played all three courses. Unplayable Californian courses in February meant that round three of the 1998 Pebble Beach Pro-Am had to be put back to the next available gap in August – six months later. All bets stood for the summer.

get short of every market (or long of those finishing positions), you will end up in front in the long-term. Of course, that often means betting long odds-on and requires balls.

Much of the play has been taken away from spread betting by Betfair. Before that came along, a spread bet was the only way punters could act as bookmakers. Now they can play bookmaker to their hearts' content on the exchange.

The least volatile bet, the 72-holer, has no hidden extras so stakes can be higher there, but my preferred betting medium is finishing positions. This is the purest form of spread betting: if your chosen golfer has an excellent week, you will win money selling his finishing position.

In every other form of spread bet, your man can have a great week but his opponent(s) on matches and indices can have better ones, and you can often end up doing your dough. But if your man shoots, say, ten under par on the week, it's all Lombard Street to a china orange that he will beat his finishing-position mark, which is rarely less than 20th and often in the high 20s and 30s.

On the spreads, always look for consistent players, rather than stars. A run of high finishes comes to an end some time, but if you can find some solid course form to set alongside current good play, you will be unlucky to come a cropper too often.

Finishing position sells are also a great way of supporting players of dubious courage when it comes to the business of actually winning a tournament. If you have sold a choker at 30 and he fluffs a three-footer on the final green, you win 28-times your stake instead of 29. Back him on fixed-odds and your dream payday turns to fresh air.

THE MAJORS The US Masters, at Augusta every April, is by far the most reliable Major for betting purposes because it is the only one of the four Grand Slam championships that's held at the same course every year. The same players do well year after year, even if they are out of form everywhere else. You only have to look at Jose Maria Olazabal's cracking Masters record over the past few years and compare it with his abysmal form elsewhere.

Players who fly the ball a long way through the air are favoured because of the undulations of the course, which is much hillier than it looks on TV. This has led to some false thinking that shorter hitters have little chance, especially now the course has been 'Tiger-proofed' and lengthened.

The facts do not back this up: shorter-than-average hitters such as Ben Crenshaw, Olazabal, Bernhard Langer, Nick Faldo and Mark O'Meara have won ten Masters between them. But long hitters at the top of their game are undoubtedly at an advantage; that's why Tiger has won three Masters and Phil Mickelson and Ernie Els fought out the finish in 2004.

The key to Augusta is getting iron shots to the right side of the flags so as to avoid three-putting and to give genuine birdie chances. There are plenty of birdies available, especially on the par fives.

So look for the players whose iron play is hot, rather than go for the massive hitters who may lack the finesse to deal with all the problems around the glassy greens.

Next best for form students is our Open which, despite some recent shocks (Paul Lawrie, Ben Curtis and Todd Hamilton), usually goes to one of the fancied runners. The 'British' is always played on a links (at or near the sea, a traditional course with no trees) and there are only a handful of those on the championship rota: St Andrews, Muirfield, Royal Troon, Turnberry, Carnoustie in Scotland; Royal Birkdale, Royal Lytham,

betting on golf

 Study how holes play

At Majors time, Sporting and IG come up with some specials such as European performance and disaster-hole indices. These need a lot of study and are not markets to rush into as they can be extremely volatile. Information about past years' scores at all holes is available on the golf sites. Success or otherwise usually hinges on the weather. If it blows a lot, the short 17th hole at Sawgrass, the signature hole of the Players Championship in the US, can be a golfing nightmare. So can the Postage Stamp at Troon. Double-figure scores have been recorded at both. Without wind, they can be frightening to look at if you're a hacker, either because of the endless water (at Sawgrass) or the sheer quantity and depth of the bunkers (Troon), but pretty much pussycats to play if you're a top pro.

Royal St George's and, returning to the fold soon, Royal Liverpool, which last hosted an Open back in 1967. Unlike the Masters and US Open, the Open has proved a hard one to win twice in recent times.

The last multiple winner was Greg Norman in 1993. Annual backers of Tiger Woods from his Open bow as a pro in 1997 up to and including 2004 are showing a loss as Woods's only victory came at St Andrews in 2000.

Because of the huge luck element in the Open, caused by the weather, many professional punters prefer to wait until the halfway stage before putting their money down. By that time the playing-field is much more level with the main cast names going out at approximately the same time.

With the field teeing off over a nine-hour stretch for the first two days and substantial variation in wind strengths on seaside links, your money can quickly be blown right off course if your man gets on the 'wrong' side of the draw.

This happened to Els in 2003. He opened with a 78 in the worst conditions and could never get in a blow. Generally speaking, an early-late pair of starting times beats a late-early one.

The US Open is played on mostly the great traditional courses, which are tricked up with narrowed fairways and heavy rough around the green to take finesse out of the game and generally reward boringly straight, medium-length players who hit green after green in regulation, hence victories for players like Tom Kite, Lee Janzen, Corey Pavin, Curtis Strange (twice) and Jim Furyk.

Occasionally, when the USGA doesn't tamper too much with a course, such as Bethpage Black in 2002, pure class prevails with Woods winning from Phil Mickelson. It is such a weird tournament that two of plodding Andy North's only three tour wins came in this second Major – and the lone victory of Orville Moody's main-tour career came in the 1969 US Open.

The policy with the USPGA Championship has been to take it to some interesting new venues – it was linksy and highly-praised Whistling Straits in 2004 – mixing them in with some of the magical older venues such as Oak Hill, Medinah and Winged Foot.

The courses are deliberately not made too hard because this Major is open to two dozen club professionals and as it is the club-professional arm of the tour that organises this one, they are not keen to make their own teaching pros look stupid.

Rich Beem and Shaun Micheel were recent big-priced winners but the vast majority of USPGA champions come from the game's greats.

The biggest surprise came when ninth reserve John Daly, then an unknown 500-1 chance, came in at the last moment to replace Nick Price, who had to duck out late in the day, and conquered Crooked Stick in 1991.

TEAM GOLF AND MATCHPLAY There are three main Cup contests that are bet on – the Ryder Cup (Europe v US), the President's Cup (US v The Internationals, ie. the rest of the world minus Europe) and the Solheim Cup (Europe v US women) and the big word of warning is: bet on the late singles in team golf at your peril!

In recent Ryder and Solheim Cups we have seen what can happen once an overall result has been achieved – players still out on the course concede their individual match or shake hands on a half, or play on to the bitter end for pride.

Anything can happen and usually does. That's why the price of the tie in matches at the bottom of the draw is much shorter.

betting on golf

 No-hopers should quit

Punters should heed the words of EV Lucas of the *New York Times*, who once wrote: "In betting, there are two elements that are never lacking: hope as hope and an incomplete recollection of the past."

In order words, don't fool yourself. If you can't make golf pay after giving it a fair trial, admit it and find something else to bet on.

Betting on team golf is fraught with danger. Remember that if you back a team in the Ryder Cup and the result is a tie – we've seen two of those, in 1969 and 1989 – you lose your money because the price for a tie is quoted.

But if you back a team in the President's Cup, where the rules say that, in the event of the match finishing up all square, one nominated player from each side will fight it out until a winner is declared, you get your money back if unforeseen circumstances occur, such as insufficient time or light which prevent an outright result being obtained. At least, that's what happened in South Africa in 2003, after which both teams had half a cup.

The two main matchplay events are entirely different. The one at La Costa, California, is 18-hole matchplay right up to the 36-hole final. That is a format which guarantees upsets every round. It is short-haul golf and once you get a couple behind, there is next to no time to get them back.

A couple of years ago Tiger Woods lost to reserve Peter O'Malley in the first round, and in 2004 he would again have made a first-round exit if opponent John Rollins's nerve had held. Instead, Woods staggered past the post... and went on to win the tournament.

The second, at Wentworth, is far longer established and is 36-hole knockout from start to finish.

Hence, more logical results and continuity, with local resident Ernie Els becoming a five-time winner in 2003, matching the feat of Gary Player and Seve Ballesteros. In both tournaments there is a grey area over what the actual winning score is, whether it is, say 2 and 1 or 3 and 1 when players shake hands without finishing a hole.

This is important on spread betting supremacy markets. What counts, whether you agree with it or not, is the winning score as announced by each match referee.

THREEBALLS, TWOBALLS AND GROUPS

Since the abolition of betting tax, bookmakers have taken every liberty possible with their percentages. Threeballs, once priced up to 109 per cent, are up to 112 with some firms and the groups are becoming unplayable. At 100-30 all five runners, that's now a 15 per cent profit margin; four-man groups at 5-2 each of four represents a 14 per cent edge.

So you have to be pretty sure of your ground before taking the enemy on. Betfair beats them to a pulp on these markets. Punters love threeballs but, apart from that Oxford man who picked up almost £815,000 for ten winners at Doral, I've never found anyone who can make them pay.

I certainly would never claim to be in front. As 18-hole short-haul events, they regularly defy form and logic.

Why? It may be because the players are not chiefly competing against each other but against the card of the course. In Thursday and Friday threeballs, the main aim is to jockey for position and make the cut for the weekend.

BOTTLERS, CHOKERS AND GOOD GUYS

The easiest thing for a punter to say when his man has lost from a winning position is: "He's a bottler." But everyone bottles tournaments to a greater or lesser degree.

No one would dare call Tiger Woods a choker but what would you call the way he played the last hole in Dubai in 2001 after four days of head-to-head golf with Thomas Bjorn?

The pair were dead level standing on the last green and Tiger slashed at the drive, carving the ball into trees.

Then he put his third shot into the stream guarding the green, and handed the title to

betting on golf

Cup matches problematic

Remember the 1997 Ryder Cup at Valderrama? Colin Montgomerie was ordered by non-playing captain Seve Ballesteros to call the final match out against Scott Hoch a half even though the American was standing over a 15ft putt to save it, simply because Europe had already won the contest.

A sporting gesture no doubt, but agony for any number of punters, those who had nominated a specific winning score and those who had backed against Hoch being top American points scorer among them.

It was much the same in the 2003 Solheim Cup; Europe won so early on that half a dozen individual matches had plenty of golf left in them. But all the European girls still on the course downed tools and walked in to celebrate victory, with one conceding victory when she wasn't even losing. Tread carefully on late singles matches.

betting on golf

 Respect the amateurs

A few threeball thoughts: Tiger Woods is not a great first-day player and always odds-on, often big odds-on. You need to be brave to take him on, but it will pay over the stretch. Top-class amateurs are often overpriced in major championships – Ricky Barnes, Matt Kuchar and Casey Wittenberg are three that come to mind. Unlike journeymen pros, they have no trepidation about being paired with the giants of the game. In fact, they relish it with the passion of youth. The Masters, with its wide fairways, shows them off to particular advantage, though Kuchar had a great US Open as an amateur too. Don't bet odds-on anybody. Twoballs are easier but a long-term profit is still hard to achieve.

Bjorn. If that wasn't bottling it, I don't know what is.

And when Vijay Singh finishes bogey, double-bogey as he did in one bread-and-butter tournament, they don't call him a choker either. Instead, they say he was gambling trying to make up ground.

Yet if that sort of finish is produced by Scott Verplank, Jay Haas, Fred Funk, Woody Austin, Angel Cabrera, Stewart Cink, Steve Flesch, Padraig Harrington or any of the dozens of serial under-achievers, they get labelled bottlers.

Why, I even recall former *Racing Post* sports editor Derek McGovern calling Nick Faldo and Ernie Els bottlers in print. And Faldo, in his pomp, used to have the best nerve in golf. But as Harrington says, the more times you get into contention, the more times you are going to lose tournaments, and it may not even be your fault. Sometimes, others simply outplay you.

Players who have gone many years without winning find it particularly difficult. You only had to watch Jay Haas in his first Champions Tour Major, the Senior PGA Championship, in mid-2004.

On his main-tour form he should have waltzed it. But because he had not won for 11 years, all the doubts crept in at the end, and Hale Irwin, a man used to that winning feeling as the most successful over-50s golfer of all time, worried him out of it.

Through experience, you will discover who are the golfers you can back with confidence to win tournaments and who are the ones you can only back in match bets or on finishing positions.

But as I said before, absolutely anyone can win on either tour these days, although many can only do so with a bit of help from their rivals. Just ask Ben Curtis, probably the poorest Open champion of modern times. ▪

cricket full of scope for profit

STUMPING THE LAYERS

CRICKET IS SYNONYMOUS WITH THE sound of leather on willow. But not just with bat hitting ball – a wallet landing on the bookmakers' cash desk, too, as betting on the game has grown into a massive global business.

By ED HAWKINS

The layers regularly report huge bets on international cricket, which is played all year round, while there is increasing interest in the county game in England, which can be a gold-mine for punters who do their research.

Whether it's Test matches, one-day internationals or the four county competitions there is a multitude of markets to get stuck into from top batsman to how may sixes will be scored.

Despite the ugly match-fixing scandals of the past there is no slowing of interest in betting on the game. It is an enormous industry on the Asian sub-continent with the Indian market often dictating prices in the UK.

And as for spread betting, cricket could have been invented for it. It is considered the most volatile of sports, with large sums of money being won and lost on every delivery.

TEST CRICKET Stereotyping is not the done things these days but when it comes to betting on five-day Test cricket it is nigh-on essential. While in other sports punters are discouraged

234

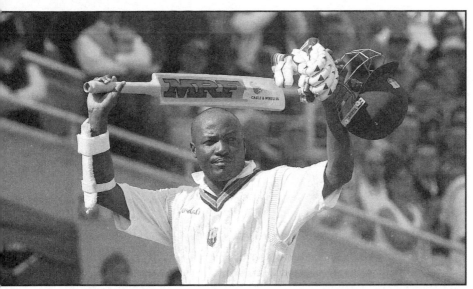

Lethal weapon: Brian Lara's batting has hit the spread firms for six

from forming a view about a side and religiously sticking to it, in cricket it generally does no harm.

As Test sides rarely change – a good crop of 15 or so players could stay together for ten years – their strengths and weaknesses stay the same, often because they are used to playing in conditions at home which are alien to the rest of the world.

And it is important to bear in mind these traits when betting. At the time of writing, Australia, the best in the world, are only really suspect against top-class spin, England struggle in non-bowler friendly conditions, India are poor travellers (their 2-1 series win in Pakistan in 2004 was their first over a fellow superpower since 1993), Pakistan and Sri Lanka slip up on fast, bouncy wickets and pitches that swing (they are used to playing on slow, low pitches) and West Indies batsmen are also dodgy against the moving ball (they lost 4-0 in England in 2004).

South Africa and New Zealand are pretty

betting on cricket

 Getting a result

always look to oppose draw

Often Tests don't last the allocated five days and the jibe aimed at the game – they play for five days and then it ends in a draw – couldn't be further from the truth.

It is possible to make a good profit by continually laying the draw on betting exchanges or backing both teams with fixed-odds firms.

Ladbrokes' odds-compiler Jonathan Smith says: 'The draw will always be short because the Indian market will back it whatever the weather or pitch is like. Then they'll lay it back at odds-on on the sub-continent.'

The draw price will plummet with the slightest hint of bad weather.

A good example was the Trent Bridge Test between England and New Zealand in 2004.

England were dominant, New Zealand were injury-hit and they were playing on a wicket renowned for a lack of durability. The draw was around 5-4, bookmakers saw plenty of interest and England won inside five days.

England, despite the largely mythical bad weather, is the second least likely country to host a draw. Australia, due to their aggressive cricket, had not had a stalemate in their last 25 before their two-Test series with Sri Lanka in June 2004.

◇ Draws in last 25 home matches (up to June 30, 2004): 0 Australia, 0 Bangladesh (played only 11 Tests), 4 England, 5 Sri Lanka, 6 South Africa, Zimbabwe, 7 Pakistan; 8 India, New Zealand, West Indies.

adaptable teams while Zimbabwe and new boys Bangladesh are the also-rans and not considered superpowers.

England will invariably find it hard work on the sub-continent, but on the flip side the Three Lions tend to have the upper hand when India, Pakistan and Sri Lanka visit.

Bookmakers are generally switched on to this, although they committed an error when making India favourites to win in New Zealand in 2003. The Kiwis won 2-0.

Sometimes it can go wrong, however. The West Indies were favourites to beat England in the Caribbean in 2004 but foolishly prepared pitches which would suit the English bowlers and lost 3-0.

Those characteristics are best remembered for betting on outright series, while for individual Tests it is important to look at ground records, paying particular attention to the coin toss. This is crucial and it is often advisable to wait until the toss before parting with your money.

As a rule it is always better for teams to bat first as pitches get worn over five days of cricket. A worn wicket can be exploited by the most average of bowlers.

SPREADS Spread betting on Tests is hugely volatile with batsmen capable of massive scores and bowlers able to take apart line-ups single-handedly. This is the appeal, however.

The most popular markets are individual batsmen's runs in a match or over a series.

Brian Lara scored a world record 400 not out against England at Antigua and you wouldn't want to have been short of his runs in that match – they were quoted at 60-65 before his incredible knock.

But Lara is one of three current players who you would need nerves of steel to sell in an individual innings or over a series.

India's Sachin Tendulkar and Australia's Matt Hayden are the others, forming a trio that are considered the best in the world.

Normally you will only be able to trade series runs if England are involved, or if it is a special series which is televised live in the UK.

Generally a batsman's series runs are pitched high because firms know punters want to buy. Mistakes are sometimes made, however. For example, Lara's record in series preceding that clash with England, and his record against the boys from Blighty, suggested quotes of 435 were too low.

That was a four-game series so the spread firms were not expecting Lara to score more than 108 runs per game. An above-average Test batsman will be down for around 65-70 runs a match, with the quote usually based on career form.

The trick is to do your research. Look at the player's most recent Test form, his record against the side and bowlers he is playing against and how he has been faring in county cricket or warm-up matches. You should find stats which encourage taking on the odd quote.

Spread firms also operate markets like highest team score, lowest team score, series runs and series ton-ups (the aggregate of individual scores over 100) for a series.

With these markets it is key to know the vagaries of the pitches that the games are being played on. There is no point in getting long of series runs if the first match is being played on a seaming and swinging Headingley wicket in Leeds. The quote after the opener will almost certainly be considerably lower than the one you bought at.

It is all about timing. Look to buy if game one is on a good batting wicket and look to sell if it is on a poor one. Then you will be able to close out for a profit if the subsequent Tests are taking place on wickets which do not suit your bet.

ONE-DAY INTERNATIONALS The most popular form of the game to bet on and better value than Test cricket. International sides' characteristics still apply but to a lesser extent as the better side has less time to impose its authority on the game, with each side batting for 50 overs. The favourites are far more likely to be upset in one-day internationals. For example Bangladesh had never won a Test at the time of writing but they had won four one-day matches, most notably when beating Pakistan in the 1999 World Cup.

The key thing for punters to bear in mind when backing teams is how the one-day squad differs from the Test outfit.

Australia and India, the two best one-day teams in the world, are considered the best two Test sides. Their one-day teams hardly

HOW THE TOSS MATTERS

Win % day-night games		Win% day-night games batting second after losing toss
64	Australia	55
63	South Africa	53
58	Pakistan	50
45	England	38
45	Sri Lanka	37
43	India	40
37	West Indies	37
33	Zimbabwe	26
32	New Zealand	30

Bangladesh have won one day-night game

change from their five-day line-ups and it was no coincidence that the pair contested the 2003 World Cup final in South Africa.

The argument is that the best players should be able to adapt to either form of the game and Australia and India have certainly backed that up. England have not been listening, however, and have persisted in picking so called one-day specialists instead of their Test players. If they continue to do so they should be opposed in the majority of one-day games.

The toss is just as important in one-day cricket, and it becomes absolutely crucial when games are being played under lights as the table alongside shows.

The reason for sides struggling when batting second under lights is that the ball swings more in the night air and is harder to see.

Understandably punters are put off betting on floodlit matches until they know the toss result, although it is considered an advantage to bat second in day games because sides know the total they require to win.

Aside from betting on the outcome, backing a batsman to be top scorer for his team can offer good value because bookmakers make the best batsman favourite rather than the one more likely to score most runs.

For example Brian Lara is always too short for the West Indies. He had not top-scored since June 2003 before he began the NatWest Series in England in 2004. Over that period opener Chris Gayle had been the most prolific run-maker, and backing openers is a sensible system as they have the chance to use the most overs.

SPREADS The same rules apply as Test matches. The firms offer a few more markets, notably all-rounder performances, with one point given per run, ten for each catch and 20 for every wicket taken.

Often it can pay dividends to sell three or

four men offered from the same team because in a game of 50 overs, it is unlikely that all of them will make a big enough impact to cost you money, especially when specialist batsmen and bowlers are expected to score the majority of runs and take the wickets.

COUNTY CRICKET The main competition is the County Championship, with 18 counties split into two divisions, playing each other home and away between April and September. The winners of Division One are considered the champions, the bottom three are relegated and the top three from Division Two are promoted.

Home sides tend to have a slight advantage. In 2003, 43 matches were won by the home side and 31 by the visitors.

You have a decent chance of making a profit on Championship matches because bookmakers bet to between 98 and 103 per cent between them. All operate on a draw-no-bet basis in order to take the unpredictability of the weather out of the equation.

The layers are not as clued up on championship games as other forms of the game and if you work hard on finding out team news early you can take advantage of wrong prices.

Look on the internet at local newspaper websites or even phone the club itself for injury news. Knowledge of the pitches is important. If a side is not performing with the bat you don't want to be backing them on a ground which historically favours the bowlers.

To pick a winner for either division you need to have a thorough study-up of the squads.

The men that make the difference are the overseas players because every county side has its fair share of decent batsmen and bowlers who can swing the ball in English conditions.

The best example of this was when Pakistan spinner Mushtaq Ahmed signed for Sussex

betting on cricket

 Understand d-l method

A key element you should be wary of is the weather forecast. Always check it before betting on a one-day game because if it rains the Duckworth-Lewis method is used if overs are lost.

The D-L method is a mathematical equation devised to work out what a team would have scored if it hadn't rained. It is used to set totals and alter them.

Often it can work in the favour of the team batting second, as they will know what they need after the end of each over if the rain comes.

Famously, South Africa got their maths wrong in the 2003 World Cup and it cost them qualification from their group.

in 2003. He was able to bamboozle English batsmen and Sussex duly romped to their first title. They were 40-1 at the start of the season.

If a team has a good spinner then they are invariably a good value betting proposition. Surrey were able to call on Saqlain Mushtaq for their period of domination while Northamptonshire were promoted in 2003 thanks to spinners Jason Brown and Graeme Swann.

The golden rule is to be wary of sides that have a lot of England players. Due to central contracts they very rarely play so although Steve Harmison is in the Durham squad, don't back them on the strength of that as he rarely turns out for them.

Another handy tip is to look at bonus points for the previous year. Teams are awarded points for the amount of runs and wickets they take so you can gauge strengths and weaknesses and then compare them to the players they have signed.

Otherwise it is important to read the broadsheet newspapers, which all have in-depth reports on Championship matches, and listen out for any rumours of dressing-room unrest, which can destroy a team.

NATIONAL LEAGUE The main one-day competition is the Totesport League with teams split into two divisions of nine and ten with the bottom three relegated into Division Two and the top three promoted.

Often sides that come up from Division Two do well in the top flight. Surrey and Gloucestershire were first and second in 2003 after finishing second and first respectively in the lower rung in 2002.

Essex came third in Division Two the same year and repeated the trick in the higher echelon. Warwickshire finished third in Division One in 2001 after being promoted in third spot. Get checking those tables.

There is little evidence of home advantage

being a factor. In 2003 games were split pretty much 50-50 between hosts and visitors.

TWENTY20 CUP **Format** 20-overs-a-side slog fest. Three regional groups with top two and two best losers advancing to quarter-finals. Semi-finals and final played on same day at same ground. **When** Starts July, ends early August. **Punting pros** Early indications show group games are dominated by home teams. Backing the hosts in 2003 to £10 level stake yielded more than £140 profit. **Cons** Tough to predict with some counties taking it more seriously than others and shorter format gives the better teams less time to impose superiority.

C&G TROPHY **Format** The one-day knock-out tournament and FA Cup of cricket with the county sides playing minnows in round three. **When** Starts in May, final at Lord's late August or early September. **Punting pros** If you can identify the strong one-day sides it is possible to work out the teams which will make the quarter-finals as the draw is projected. **Cons** England players return to their counties, rendering form book irrelevant.

AROUND THE GROUNDS English county grounds have a wide variety of characteristics. Some retain these traits virtually for centuries, others can change appreciably over the course of a couple of seasons. So it is important to keep analysing individual grounds to see which type of bowlers thrive on them. You also get a clue by looking at the sort of overseas player each county recruits. Here is what one could expect at each venue in the summer of 2004:

Derbyshire, Derby With two swing bowlers spearheading the home side's attack, a slow seamer is prepared, but the ground actually has a reputation for being more

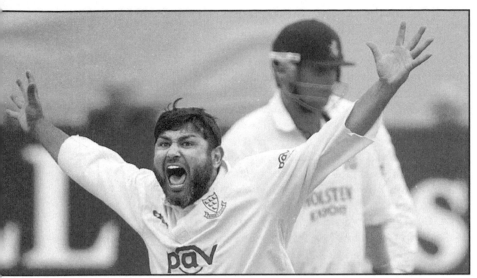

Imported attack: Mushtaq Ahmed helped Sussex to their first title

bowler-friendly than it is. It doesn't spin, either because the home side have not had such a bowler recently.

Durham, Riverside Considered to be one of the best for batting on with the bounce fast and true. If the river water-levels are high then the wicket will help the seam bowlers more. A definite advantage for sides batting second in one-day games.

Essex, Chelmsford One of the best batting strips in the country. Brad Hodge and James Foster both hit double centuries there in 2003. The wicket responds to turn, which probably explains the county's decision to recruit Pakistani spinner Danish Kaneria in 2004.

Glamorgan, Sophia Gardens A pitch which is fair on batsmen and bowlers. The tracks closest to the pavilion are slower than those in the middle of the square. A score of around 300 is thought to be competitive in the championship.

Gloucestershire, Bristol Gloucestershire's one-day success was built on an expertise of defending totals on slow, low Bristol pitches. If the wicket gets too dry then the pitch can crumble. The groundsman often waters the wicket as a result.

Hampshire, Rose Bowl Not good for batsmen. The Indian tourists were so disgusted with the pitch in 2002 that they complained. In 2004 Hampshire's early championship matches were all low-scoring but that probably had more to do with early-season swing and the fact that the hosts' batting was poor and the visiting outfits' even worse.

Kent, Canterbury A pleasant setting for batsmen to bed in and pile on the runs. It is no coincidence that David Fulton, Rob Key and Ed Smith scored heavily down the years batting on such a fast surface. Only bowlers who bend their back get anything out of it early on. It can deteriorate to the detriment of sides batting last.

Lancashire, Old Trafford Every county player will tell you that Lancashire do not shy away from preparing wickets that suit them. When Muttiah Muralitharan took 50 wickets in 2001 the wickets were prepared specifically for turn. They now spin more and more as the season goes on.

Leicestershire, Grace Road Good for batsmen, although not as excellent as some think because of the runs that Brad Hodge has scored in the past. He's just a top player. Efforts have been made to make it turn, but goodness knows why because they have not had a spinner of note for years.

Middlesex, Lord's The new ball will swing because of the high stands, enclosed atmosphere and heavy London air. However, as proved in recent Tests, the pitch appears to get better as it goes on.

Northants, Wantage Road In 2003 Northants deliberately prepared pitches that spun because of the presence of Jason Brown,

betting on cricket

 Dominating the game

One county side tends to dominate over a period of up to three or four years, be that in four-day Championship cricket or the one-day arena. Surrey won the Championship in 1999, 2000 and 2002 while Gloucestershire won eight one-day titles from 1999 to 2004.

To spot an emerging one-day team you will again have to look at the type of overseas player they are signing. If a side goes for one-day specialists you can be sure they will be putting all resources into success in the limited-overs sphere – Gloucestershire did this when they had Ian Harvey and, later, Jonty Rhodes.

Graeme Swann and emerging Monty Panesar in their squad. It's a good batting wicket, though, and one that batsmen can't wait to get in on. A result track in the championship in 2003.

Nottinghamshire, Trent Bridge Trent Bridge used to be infamous on the circuit for being impossible to bat on. Pitches were quick and seamed all over the place. That has changed, however and the track is better now. A definite advantage batting second in the championship and first in one-day games.

Somerset, Taunton An absolutely stonking batting track. In nine National League and C&G matches there in 2003 a ton was scored in each one. Another ground which gives advantage to sides batting first in the championship and second in one-dayers.

Surrey, The Oval Quick and bouncy and good to bat on with seamers finding it tough. With Ian Salisbury and Saqlain Mushtaq Surrey have made sure it is a turner, too.

Sussex, Hove It was a misconception that Sussex won the title in 2003 by winning the toss, batting first and bowling Mushtaq Ahmed all day at Hove. They batted first three times but won twice when batting second, too.

Warwickshire, Edgbaston A terrible Test pitch in recent years but the most startling fact about Edgbaston in county action is the record of sides batting second in one-day games. They won eight of 11 limited-overs clashes in 2003.

Worcestershire, New Road In 2003 the bowlers dominated – hardly surprising as New Road was renowned for its difficulty to bat on. That has all changed however, and 2004 saw the nature of the wicket change into one that was terrific to bat on.

Yorkshire, Headingley Yorkshiremen don't like change, so Headingley doesn't. Seam and swing all day long for the bowlers.

patience key to good strike-rate

BE A UNION LEADER

BETTING ON RUGBY UNION REQUIRES all the skills and disciplines needed in any other sport, plus one extra – infinite patience. Good bets don't come along as often as you might want, and there are often long, frustrating spells when hours of research lead nowhere. The key is to be ever-ready, to recognise a value bet early and jump in.

By GRAHAM WOODS

There are two reasons why bets can be thin on the ground. The first is that there aren't that many fixtures. Even at the busiest period in spring, when the Premiership, Celtic League and Super 12 league seasons are in full swing and the Six Nations is up and running, most bookmakers will price up a maximum of 18 domestic matches each weekend, with the possibility of three international fixtures thrown in. Compare that with football, where you will find around 150 matches across the UK and Europe on various coupons every weekend.

The other thorn in the side is that the staple diet of rugby wagers is the handicap bet. Match betting is becoming increasingly popular, but for the most part we will be backing a team at 5-6 or 10-11 with a start of, say ten points, or giving up five. That means you are taking on an odds-compiler who has spent his week researching and analysing

Watch and wait: patient punters who persevere can prosper at union

to find the exact margin at which the two teams become, in his view, inseparable.

Bookmakers know that the most successful rugby punters are the ones who have learned to wait. Paddy Power's compiler Brian Cusack, a former pro with Bath and Richmond, summed it up perfectly when he told me: "If the handicap is right, we don't see any money. If it's wrong we get filled in."

If it sounds off-putting, don't give up. There are aspects of the sport which favour the punter, and if you learn to be patient and research your market, there is money to be made.

Rugby union falls into two categories, with the majority of betting action focusing on the international game while domestic rugby has tended to be a niche market.

There are three sections to the international calendar – springtime in Europe is Six Nations time, in the summer the action moves to the other side of the world with European teams on tour plus the Tri-Nations, then in the autumn it's the northern hemisphere's turn to play host.

With games few and far between there is often little continuity of form to help us and line-ups can change dramatically. And in addition, apart from the Six Nations and Tri-Nations, the matches pit teams at different stages of their season against each other. In contrast, the domestic scene has teams in action week after week and running parallel in terms of preparation.

Individual tastes will dictate which part of the game you will focus on – and as ever you do need to specialise – but my own preference is for the club game ahead of internationals precisely because there is more regular action and form is easier to follow and more reliable. The main betting events are the English Premiership, the Celtic League, the Heineken European Cup and the southern hemisphere's Super 12.

Each competition has its own format and it is important to understand the set-up when placing ante-post bets. Most firms bet on who will top the table at the end of the regular season in the Premiership and Super 12, and then open a book on post-season play-offs, but others bet only on the Grand Final, so make sure of the terms when you place a bet. And bear in mind that teams approach the season differently when there are play-offs to be won. In the Super 12 the team finishing top of the table won the final every year from 2000 to 2003. In England, where the final is played at a neutral venue, that has only been the case once in the four years since the Grand Final was introduced. The play-off concept has encouraged some of the best teams not to expend their energy on finishing top of the league but rather to focus on timing their run and hit form at the end of the season.

STRENGTHS AND WEAKNESSES

Teams often change personnel significantly in the close season, especially in England, and

betting on rugby union

 Who plays in what?

the leagues

◇ Premiership

Format 12 teams play each other home and away. Top finisher goes straight to Grand Final, second plays third for right to face them.
When Starts early to mid-September, Grand Final in May.
Who bets on it All major bookmakers.
Punting pros Long season means there are plenty of matches and long-term form.
Cons Frequent interruptions for domestic knockout cup, Heineken Cup and internationals.

◇ Celtic League

Format 12 teams play each other home and away.
When Starts early to mid-September to end of April.
Who bets on it Bet365, Chandler, Paddy Power, Skybet, Betfair.
Punting pros Less high-profile so clued-up punters can have an edge on bookies. Plenty of live coverage.
Cons Same disruptions as for Premiership but with fewer teams from each country, international absences are more keenly felt.

◇ Heineken Cup

Format 24 European teams in six pools of four play each other home and away. Six pool winners plus two best runners-up are seeded into quarter-finals.
When Starts November, group stage at intervals through to February, knockout stages in April and May.
Who bets on it All major bookmakers.
Punting pros High standard of competition, five live games a week on Sky.
Cons Long gaps between group stage fixtures, teams often left with nothing to play for after three games.

◇ Super 12

Format 12 teams (five from New Zealand, four South Africa, three Australia), play each other once, top four go into semi-finals.
When Starts February, final in May.
Who bets on it All major bookmakers.
Punting pros Short, focused campaign with no distractions so teams generally at their best. Skill levels generally higher.
Cons Very different style from northern hemisphere, games tend to be open and high-scoring, scrums and line-outs not so fiercely contested, defence less of a priority.

◇ Parker Pen Cup and Shield

Secondary European competitions, knockout format. Firms may bet on selected matches but early rounds are often too uncompetitive with weak teams from Italy, Spain and elsewhere.

◇ All-Ireland League

Paddy Power and Betfair.

◇ NPC

New Zealand domestic league, occasional live matches. Skybet, Betfair.

◇ Currie Cup

South African domestic league, occasional live matches. Skybet, Betfair.

with coaches coming and going too, a club's fortunes can change dramatically. Bath escaped relegation on points difference in 2002-03, then topped the league by six points the following season under a new coach and with a reinforced pack.

Whether betting over the course of a season or on a match-to-match basis, the key is an ability to assess teams' strengths. It is the core knowledge you need, and this is where the nature of the sport favours the punter. Unlike football, where formations and line-ups are fluid, every rugby union team lines up in the same way and every playing position has a specific job to do. A basic understanding of the dynamics of the game is enough to realise that each team and every match can be broken down into sections, and the team that wins the battles will ultimately win the war.

The battle starts up front with the big guys, the pack. If the forwards don't do their job and secure possession, the game is up, and scrums and line-outs are the areas to look at. If a team is vulnerable in either area, they will struggle.

Next, defence, a facet of the game that is emphasised more and more, with most teams employing specialist coaches, often brought in from rugby league. In the seven seasons of the English Premiership up to 2003-04 it was the team which has conceded the fewest, rather than scored the most, points that finished top of the table on all but one occasion.

A solid kicking game is another requirement, not just in terms of going for goal but kicking from hand for territory, and then an incisive backline who can capitalise on possession and territory and turn that advantage into points.

Those are the areas to concentrate on when assessing a team's strength, but bear in mind too that balance is all important, and one-dimensional teams are soon found out. Be

PREMIERSHIP HANDICAP TABLES

2001-02	Home			Away			Total		
	W	L	D	W	L	D	W	L	D
Gloucester	9	2	0	6	5	0	15	7	0
Leicester	7	3	1	7	4	0	14	7	1
London Irish	6	4	1	7	3	1	13	7	2
Newcastle	6	4	1	7	4	0	13	8	1
Northampton	6	5	0	7	4	0	13	9	0
Sale	5	6	0	8	3	0	13	9	0
Wasps	8	3	0	4	7	0	12	10	0
Leeds	7	4	0	4	7	0	11	11	0
Bristol	5	6	0	5	4	2	10	10	2
Harlequins	5	6	0	5	6	0	10	12	0
Saracens	4	7	0	4	7	0	8	14	0
Bath	6	4	1	1	10	0	7	14	1

2002-03	Home			Away			Total		
	W	L	D	W	L	D	W	L	D
Northampton	8	3	0	9	1	1	17	4	1
Leeds	8	3	0	7	4	0	15	7	0
Wasps	6	5	0	8	3	0	14	8	0
Harlequins	7	4	0	6	5	0	13	9	0
London Irish	6	5	0	7	4	0	13	9	0
Sale	9	2	0	4	7	0	13	9	0
Gloucester	6	4	1	5	4	2	11	8	3
Bath	7	3	1	4	7	0	11	10	1
Saracens	5	5	1	6	5	0	11	10	1
Newcastle	7	4	0	4	7	0	11	11	0
Bristol	5	5	1	4	7	0	9	12	1
Leicester	5	6	0	3	8	0	8	14	0

2003-04	Home			Away			Total		
	W	L	D	W	L	D	W	L	D
Harlequins	7	4	0	10	0	1	17	4	1
Northampton	8	3	0	6	5	0	14	8	0
London Irish	5	6	0	9	0	2	14	6	2
Gloucester	7	4	0	5	6	0	12	10	0
Saracens	8	2	1	4	7	0	12	9	1
Leeds	7	4	0	5	6	0	12	10	0
Rotherham	7	3	1	4	6	1	11	9	2
Bath	5	6	0	6	4	1	11	10	1
Wasps	6	5	0	5	6	0	11	11	0
Newcastle	6	5	0	4	7	0	10	12	0
Sale	5	6	0	5	6	0	10	12	0
Leicester	4	5	2	4	5	2	8	10	4

*Results based on best available handicap for each team regardless of price. Games may produce two winners if the winning margin falls between the highest and lowest available handicap – eg Sale v Northampton: Sale could be backed at -2, Northampton at +4. Sale won 24-21.

betting on rugby union

 Web watching

it's on a different planet

www.planet-rugby.com
The guv'nor. This is THE website for results, fixtures, stats, news, player profiles, the lot, covering the international and domestic game right around the world. www.planeterugby.net is the French equivalent with good coverage of the French league.

www.scrum.com
Less comprehensive than planet-rugby but presentation of some areas is a little clearer and has different columnists.

www.zurichrugby.com
Main source of news for the Zurich Premiership in England, also has a good results archive.

www.celticleague.com
Does a similar job for the Celtic League. Team news for weekend matches is prominent and detailed. www.celtic-rugby.co.uk is a poor second.

www.ercrugby.com
Excellent source of statistics and news for the Heineken Cup and two Parker Pen competitions.

www.maillot-rugby.com/mag
Excellent statistical package for all major competitions with complete breakdowns of every team. Two

drawbacks are that there appears to be no archive relating to previous seasons, and it's in French.

www.superrugby.co.za
First port of call for information on the game in South Africa. Especially good in the Super 12 season as the preview section collates all the weekend team line-ups as they are announced.

www.rugby.com.au
Short on stats but good for news from Australia and Super 12 match reports.

www.nzrugby.co.nz
Similar to the Australian site, worth checking for news but light on detail.

www.centrebet.com
Australian bookmaker, Super 12 handicaps available on Tuesday morning UK time, well in advance of English bookmakers.

For ratings, try **www.eurorugby.com** or **www.footyforecaster.com** in Australia. Most clubs have their own websites (ercrugby.com has links to many of them), and local newspapers in rugby towns such as Leicester or Bath will give more news from inside the camp.

prepared to revise your assessment of a team too. Styles and playing and coaching personnel change, and it is all too easy to label a side and then stick with it blindly.

When it comes to betting on matches, you also need to find out the starting line-ups. Coaches have to name their side for international matches 48 hours in advance and clubs tend to observe the same principle.

HOW HANDICAPS RELATE TO MATCH ODDS

Handicap	Fixed-odds equivalent
0	5-6 • 5-6
1	4-5 • 10-11
2	4-6 • 11-10
3	8-13 • 6-5
4	4-7 • 5-4
5	8-15 • 11-8
6	1-6 • 6-4
7	2-5 • 7-4
8	1-3 • 9-4
9	2-7 • 5-2
10	1-4 • 11-4
11	2-9 • 3
12	1-5 • 7-2

The internet is the place to look, and the first port of call should be each individual club's website, but there are also good sites that will collate the data for you.

You will then need to dig through the form, and the best way by far is to keep your own records. Match reports in the Sunday and Monday broadsheets provide detailed analysis, and at the very least you should keep a note of the score and handicap of each match plus a couple of lines on how the game was won and lost, and each team's areas of strength and weakness. Don't disregard quotes from players and coaches as they can be very telling.

Many punters consider past form and head-to-head stats in tandem but it may be misleading to attach too much importance to the outcome of previous meetings between two sides.

Rugby union is a fast-evolving sport, particularly in the professional era and what happened five years ago has precious little bearing on what will happen at three o'clock on Saturday afternoon. If Team A have not beaten Team B since Elvis was alive then obviously that counts for something, but if your other research tells you that Team A are a solid bet and the only thing putting you off is past history, the best advice is to ignore it.

GETTING THE MOST OUT OF YOUR FANCY Once you have decided which team to back the next consideration is how to back them. On the fixed-odds you have a choice of match betting or going with the handicap, and you also have the option of a spread supremacy trade.

The table on this page gives a broad indication of how handicaps relate to match odds, and it illustrates quite starkly how just a few points make a huge dent in a team's price. Off scratch, you'd get 5-6 or 10-11, but just three points on the handicap sends that down to 8-13. Taking such cramped odds when the bookmakers reckon there is a single penalty score between the teams seems poor value, but by the same token, the underdogs are more generously priced.

So it is important to weigh up both options when betting on narrow handicaps. Is it worth accepting reduced odds of 5-6 from 6-5 for the insurance policy of a three-point start? Think back to the reasoning behind your bet. If you are anticipating a close, hard-fought battle, the answer may be yes. If your analysis tells you the team receiving a start are actually stronger, then the bigger price is the one to take.

Once the handicap moves into double-figures it is much more difficult to give an equivalent match-betting price as bookmakers tend to play around with their prices. One firm may equate a 13-point handicap to match odds of 2-9 and 3-1, while another goes 1-12 and 11-2. Often they simply don't want to lay a solid favourite and will slash their price accordingly.

Many people are put off backing a team giving up double-figure handicaps, believing favourites are too often overrated. There may be some truth in that belief. The tables alongside show which Premiership teams have been most successful against the handicap over the three seasons from 2001-02 to 2003-04, and there are a lot of unfancied teams up there. And the records show that the team who have rewarded Six Nations backers most over the four seasons from 2001 to 2004 are Italy, despite their record of just three wins in 20.

However, there are times when a large handicap is perfectly acceptable. At the start we said that the odds-compiler sets a handicap at the point where he believed the two teams to be inseparable. That is not strictly true.

betting on rugby union

 Weather a major factor

The effects of the weather have been covered extensively in the chapter on rugby league, and much the same applies in the 15-man game.

Wet conditions make handling difficult and frequent errors often lead to a stop-start game and few scoring chances, so be wary of backing teams to cover big handicaps and look for value in the points market.

It is worth adding that rugby union matches can be affected even more by strong winds as the game sees more kicking than the 13-man code, and less play with the ball safely in hand. It is also important to bear in mind local conditions around the world. South Africa is the best example, and the national side are notorious for forcing visiting teams to play their first match at altitude in Pretoria or Johannesburg, where the air is thinner, the ball travels further and players' stamina is tested.

He aims to come up with a figure where he believes he can see two-way action. English bookmakers will see plenty of money for the home side against Italy at Twickenham whatever the handicap, so they are happy to add a few points on.

And throughout the domestic leagues there are teams that are generally fancied and teams that are not. At the start of the 2004 Super 12, the champion Auckland Blues played the ACT Brumbies in Australia. The Blues were unbeaten the previous season and red-hot favourites to retain their crown. They went to Canberra giving up ten points, and were well beaten 44-27. The handicap did not reflect the relative strength of the two sides, merely that the bookmakers were confident punters would steam into the Blues.

Bookmakers are also unable set their handicaps too high, partly because they want to encourage two-way action, partly because they work on long-term statistical models that iron out lop-sided results. In one-sided internationals you can see figures up in the 70s or 80s, but in a league match it is rare for the handicap to go above 30 points, yet winning scores regularly top that. When winless Rotherham visited form side Leicester in the penultimate round of the 2003-04 Premiership, they had a start of 25 points. It was not nearly enough as they were trounced 75-13.

In that case, a buy of the favourites' supremacy on the spreads could have yielded big profits, and it is worth considering the merits of handicap and supremacy betting side by side as they are both associated with the winning margin. The big difference, of course, is that if your handicap pick squeaks home, you get paid out in full, whereas your return on a spread bet may be minimal.

One strategy is to support underdogs with a big start on the fixed odds, where your potential loss is known and cannot be affected by a landslide defeat, and support strong favourites on the spreads, so that barring a catastrophic reverse, your downside is likely to be small.

Another popular bet where the spread and fixed-odds worlds collide is total match points. This is a hugely popular market and can be an extremely profitable one. You don't need to pick a winner, just to know how the match will pan out. Take into account the conditions and the shape of the two teams lining up against each other. Two big heavy packs slugging it out on a wet windy evening in February makes for a scarcity of points.

Two lightweight teams who favour an open game playing on a sunny spring afternoon are more likely to rack up big scores. In both those scenarios finding a winner can be tricky, and the points bet may offer more value.

Many fixed-odds firms now bet on total points, going, for example, 5-6 above or below 39.5. However, a better option may be to bet with firms who offer three or four prices – for example, Skybet might go 5-2 under 30 points, 31 to 40, 41 to 50 and over 50. The key is that you are most likely to get involved in this market when you fancy an extreme scoreline, and at the prices it is well worth sticking your neck out at the under 30 or over 50.

Other popular match bets on the fixed-odds include winning margin wagers, where the winning score for each team is broken up into five-point, or occasionally ten-point bands. The best bets here are on narrow wins. Backing a team to win by 25 to 30 points might pay double-figure odds but with a game as open as that, who's to say the margin won't end up in the 30s or 40s? But if you fancy a team to edge a close-fought game, taking the 5-1 about a win by one to five points is far more appealing than 8-13 to win the match.

In most matches it is odds-on that a penalty will be the first scoring play. However, the

betting on rugby union

 Wait for the mistakes

First tryscorer betting is as much of a lottery as first goalscorer in football, and the only sensible approach is to root out wrong prices. In the 2004 Six Nations, France No. 8 Imanol Harinordoquy crossed the line first in two of his team's first four matches, and it was clearly part of the French gameplan that he should take up wide positions to act as an extra man in attack. Ladbrokes cut his price to be first tryscorer in the final match against England from the usual 20-1 or more about a back-row forward to 14-1, the kind of price you would expect for a winger. However, Skybet still offered 25-1 and got filled in when Harinordoquy delivered.

value can be found in backing a try to come first when you believe one team has a clear attacking edge – even with handicaps up in the 20s you can get 3-1 or better about the favourites opening the scoring with a try.

On the spreads, after supremacy and points the most popular market is probably try-scorers' aggregate shirt numbers. If you fancy a low-scoring match getting short of shirts can be more profitable than selling points as a stream of penalties won't erode your winnings. However, it is a more volatile market, and sellers can often be hit by scores from high-numbered substitutes towards the end. This is a market where you must be prepared to trade in-running. Buyers, particularly in games where the teams are quite equally-matched, often find better value by waiting for the game to open up.

Other spread markets widen out the options, as you can trade each team's tries, shirts and points, the time of their first try, and all manner of performance and mini-performance indices. It can seem bewildering, and it is not uncommon for punters to miss out on the best value by playing the wrong market.

IG's rugby union supremo Adrian Watts points out that all prices are derived from the supremacy and total points quotes. He said: "If you are one or two points out with those, it filters through to the other markets and the difference there can be bigger. With the performance indices, where you have to factor in a big chunk of points for the win, it makes a huge difference."

Watts claims the most popular markets for punters are those with a known downside, but he added: "People like backing action, buying points or shirts. There's still an inclination to back what they want to see. But really, punters have never had it so good. With all the tools they have in the different markets there is so much value if you shop around."

summer slot has boosted game

BIG LEAGUE PROFITS

SKY TV AND SPORTS BETTING HAVE gone hand in hand since the satellite channel's launch, and nowhere is this more evident than in rugby league.

By MARK LANGDON

Since the advent of summer rugby league, betting on the sport has gone through the roof with bookmakers offering a variety of markets on a number of different competitions.

The biggest and most popular from a betting point of view is Super League, where the teams play 28 regular-season games before the play-offs, which determine the Grand Final winner.

With live Sky matches most Friday and Saturday evenings and the sport emerging from football's shadow thanks to its summer slot, it's easy to see why there has been a boom in rugby league betting, and the number of choices for punters is not far behind football, though turnover is obviously still well beneath the kind of levels that the Premiership and Champions League attract.

Most bookmakers offer match betting, winning margins and first tryscorer options, as well as under/over points on live matches, but by far the most popular form of rugby league betting is the handicap because the uncompetitive nature of many Super League match-ups often leads to one team being

Rugby league is emerging from football's shadow thanks to Sky's support

excessively odds-on to win in 80 minutes for most punters' liking.

So what's the best way to make money from betting on Super League? Obviously, the ability of the teams must be taken into consideration, but it is imperative to check the weather before getting stuck in.

Former Great Britain international Mike Stephenson, who now works as an analyst for Sky Sports, once told me: "You have got to get with the outsiders when they get big starts in the rain. I know from experience. Once the heavens open, the ball is like a bar of soap and scoring tries becomes increasingly difficult."

It makes sense to go with those who get a start in the wet and betting on a low points total, either on the spreads or with traditional bookmakers, but the precipitation factor is often overlooked by the more casual punter, who is just desperate to have a bet.

Living close to the ground is an advantage but don't worry if you cannot gain a first-hand weather report from Widnes just by sticking your hand out of the window. Numerous websites such as the Met Office's meto.gov.uk provide a valuable service, although it must be remembered that there is nothing as unreliable as the great British weather.

The best way of using the weather to your advantage is to know your teams. Ask yourself these questions – do Team A like to play an open, expansive style of rugby? Do they continually try to offload in the tackle? Is their gameplan all about attempting to outscore the opposition?

If the answer to those three is yes, then the likelihood is they are a side best suited to playing in dry conditions where points are easier to come by and passing and inventive rugby is much easier to pull off. On the other hand, teams who go through the forwards and rely on territorial advantage to squeeze the life out of the opposition usually have more joy in the rain.

These teams are often big, powerful outfits who play low-risk rugby. Maybe they don't provide the best spectacle and will suffer in hot conditions but they are happy as a pig in muck when the pitch is soggy and handling is impossible.

However, it is still important to be up to date with the latest news and it's always good to visit Sportinglife.com for the breaking stories as well as making sure you order the trade paper Rugby League and Leaguer Express, which is published on Mondays. It's a must for serious punters, with match previews, reports and news from all the clubs in Britain and Australia. The paper's website, totalrl.com is also worth bookmarking.

Favourites tend to get disproportionately backed to overcome the handicap, but the statistics from the 2003 Super League season shows the opposite course of action pays dividends. Backing the handicap underdog in the 168 regular-season matches would have

betting on rugby league

Team news conundrum

Team news is another important factor but be careful of stories that claim one side is supposedly struggling with loads of injuries or there is an illness in the camp. More often than not, these rumours tend to be just that and it's amazing how often a player is listed as doubtful yet makes a miraculous recovery to line up in the team.

Some managers are prone to playing mind games with the opposition, which means lumping on a team whose rivals are reportedly down to the bare bones has been a costly business down the years, especially as the odds are usually cramped because the first people to hear about team-news stories and rumours are the bookies.

been successful 55.9 per cent of the time, which is not a terrific sum considering you have to bet at 10-11 (52.4 per cent), but it does go to show the favourites are probably slightly overrated in general.

Using any rigid system usually has flaws and it now seems commonplace for the supposed underdogs to rest players for games they are seen as having no chance of winning, to keep players fresh for matches in which they have a more realistic hope of victory.

That can often lead to handicaps in the range of -24 or -26 for teams such as Bradford, Leeds and St Helens to overcome and these matches are best treated with maximum caution. On paper, the big clubs would be expected to score points at will, yet you must remember players and coaches are totally uninterested in covering handicaps and will often ease off in the latter stages.

Take Leeds v Salford in round 12 of Super League 2004 as an example. Leeds, who were 28-point favourites, had got to the handicap mark by the 36th minute. However, the final score ended up 34-6 as coach Tony Smith reshuffled the pack to the chagrin of those punters who had fancied the Rhinos to run up a cricket score.

But then two days later, Hull, who were similar handicap jollies to bash Widnes, refused to rest on their laurels and won 70-4 despite leading by just two more points than Leeds were ahead of Salford at half-time.

It's difficult enough trying to pick winners at the best of times so don't make life more difficult by trying to work out the players' mentality unless there is an obvious reason why a team might hold back – an important Cup match being next up, for example.

It is generally best to stick to the more competitive fixtures where the handicap line gives the impression both teams will be trying until the 80th minute.

IT'S A KNOCKOUT Betting on the Super League Grand Final has been quite profitable for punters who like trends. Coming first in Super League is a massive advantage and no table-topper from 1996 to 2003 failed to make the final at Old Trafford.

In fact, only Wigan in that period managed to finish outside the top two and make the campaign finale. That's largely because having to play in consecutive weeks, usually away from home, is a massive disadvantage for those who finish down the pecking order.

The biggest showpiece occasion for rugby league is the Challenge Cup final but don't let the romance of the competition lead you to believe the underdogs will have their day. They don't.

Only once, when Sheffield were successful in 1998, has the cup not gone to Wigan, Leeds, Bradford or St Helens in ten years between 1994 and 2004, while London (1999) are the only other team outside the big four in that period to even make the final.

Picking between the quartet is never easy and punters should beware of lumping on any team in a cup competition where the draw is random and you could find your selection paired with a daunting away trip due to an unlucky draw.

Once we reach the final, there is always a huge amount of markets available, with the Lance Todd Trophy (the man of the match as voted for by rugby league journalists) the most prestigious.

Between 1994 and 2004, just two favourites were successful (Sean Long and Henry Paul) and it is fairly safe to assume half-backs are by far the most likely winners.

LOWER LEAGUES Away from the glamour and glitz of Super League, a number of firms bet on the two divisions of the National League. These games are not shown on

betting on rugby league

 **Time for
half measures**

the tie handicaps punters

The dreaded handicap tie swells bookmakers' profits and is something both rugby league and union punters have had to put up with for far too long.

Instead of offering half-point handicaps, as they do for American football, the vast majority of UK layers offer whole-point starts, whch throw up the possibility of a tie. Indeed, the handicapper's intention is for the tie to occur as frequently as possible.

With the teams priced at 5-6 and the tie a 14-1 or 16-1 chance, it is obvious just how disadvantaged rugby punters on both codes are compared to their gridiron counterparts, who generally get 10-11 both teams and no chance of a tie.

Thankfully, Betfair offer half-point handicaps, as do most Australian layers. And, after promptings from the *Racing Post*, a handful of British firms are now issuing half-point handicaps so hopefully the day will soon come when handicap ties, which invariably end up as massive winners for bookmakers, will be consigned to the dustbin once and for all.

television so any guide must be either through the form book, reading match reports or going to the games to formulate your own impressions of teams.

It's not an ideal situation, particularly for those who live in the south, miles away from the grounds, while team news is the key factor for punters and bookmakers alike.

You may have to spend hours trawling through local newspaper websites, official team sites and fan forums to pick out the nuggets of injury news which could be the difference between striking a winning and losing bet but it is worthwhile in the long run. As with all forms of sports betting, there is simply no substitute for hard work.

Long-range advice is difficult to give with team news such an important factor in National League betting, but do be wary of teams who are forced to play three times in a week due to fixture congestion. Most squads are only part-time and it's not uncommon for players to work during the day before rushing to a game in midweek and,263 naturally with the travelling involved in away trips, fitness often plays a massive part in proceedings.

DOWN UNDER It is generally accepted that Australian rugby league leads the way in terms of quality and excitement, but punters have been deserting the NRL in their droves due to the unpredictability of the results and the lack of difference of opinion as nearly all the British bookmakers copy the line from the Aussie bookmakers.

Match and handicap betting is available, and unlike Super League, the 80-minute market is one to get stuck into with teams often evenly matched due to the NRL's salary cap guidelines, which mean that all sides have a more equal chance of securing the services of the best players.

One plus is the fact teams have to be announced by the middle of the week, but the downside for those based in the United Kingdom is that the vast majority of teams can all beat each other on any given day and form rarely seems to count for much.

Sure, it makes for greater viewing – and Sky's frequent live NRL coverage is a bonus – but a proven adage in betting is that the best games do not always produce the best bets. For those who do want to try their luck on the NRL, rleague.com and NRL.com offer the best news, statistics and information service.

INTERNATIONALS Unlike rugby union, there is little in the way of interest in the international scene, which Australia dominates, so representative rugby is confined to the Stage of Origin (Queensland v New South Wales) which sees Australians fight it out on behalf of the state of their birth.

These games are often keenly-contested encounters and points are usually at a

betting on rugby league

 Bookmaker's view

unfashionable = underrated

Mike Triffitt of Skybet says:
Generally people like to back the big four teams blindly, particularly Leeds and St Helens, but it's the unfashionable teams I like to get with because they seem to be underrated most weeks.

I would never go near a line when it is around the 30 mark but punters like to back the favourite, which is great for the company – you have to lay those bets. I just don't know how people can have such a strong opinion on a game in which it's impossible to judge whether or not the better team will take their foot off the gas.

Shrewder clients wait until the weather and team news are known, probably the one advantage they have on me. I have to price the weekend games up on a Thursday and can't really rely on the long-range forecast.

There are three people who do rugby league handicaps for Skybet but the final decision rests with me. The standard way to begin is to offer four points for home advantage and then go with my gut feeling. I don't understand those who use ratings in rugby league because the teams change so often – plus the weather may be having an effect. It's much better to price it up as you see it.

While Super League is the most popular betting medium, the National Leagues have their loyal following and this is where the money really talks. Team news is far more important at this level, with clubs having small squads and the players often being only part-time. That's why we have a minimum-doubles stipulation but you have got to admire those firms who stick their neck on the block by offering singles.

The Australian Rugby League betting is dead. All the layers stick to the Australian line so you don't get any crazy handicap differences and, to be honest, turnover has been very disappointing. Mind you, it's no surprise punters leave it alone when you see how many weird results there are from one week to the next.

Super League is becoming an increasingly popular betting medium with each passing year, but while our turnover has increased the punters are gradually starting to knock down our profits.

However, we always get a few handicap ties in a season and they are complete skinners. I know from when I bet how frustrating the tie can be but as a layer they are a right bonus. Stanley have started offering half-point handicaps and if any of the Big Three firms followed suit I suppose we would have to, but for the moment, getting a handicap tie is so profitable that we are not looking to change things.

premium in the best-of-three series. One trend that is worth bearing in mind is just how tight the opening match normally is.

Over the 16 years between 1988 and 2004, the average points total was just 25.6, so selling the total points or going under the fixed-odds

betting on rugby league

 Scant in-running action

look to draw with fancy prices

Unfortunately, rugby league is one of the few sports with little in-running liquidity on Betfair, though a number of markets are open to trade on.

The best advice is to ask for outrageous prices about the draw on the match betting market. You can often back it at around the 40 mark (normal bookies usually go 16-1) and will often be able to get out of the bet with a tidy profit at some stage in the final 20 minutes

if the game remains tight.

Apart from looking to have the stalemate on your side, the best advice is to sit tight and see how a match is panning out, though if a team manage to get a fresh set of six tackles in the opposition's half they are far more likely to score a try, so backing a side who have just forced a goalline drop-out, with the option of trading out of your position, could be a sound move.

points line has been a licence to print money. Another stat worth taking into consideration: between the years of 1981 and 2003, the series went to the team which won the opener.

SPREAD BETTING The rise in the variety of rugby league markets available to trade on has grown with every that year that the sport establishes itself as one of the most popular on our screens.

Supremacy, total points, tryscorers' shirts, team tries, team points, team performances, team hotshots plus individual players' try minutes are part and parcel of the package offered to spread punters for every live game, while Sporting and IG offer win indices, mini-performances and a whole lot more.

However, just because there is plenty of variety to spice up a bit of TV viewing (a truncated service is available on non-live matches) it does not mean value is to be had every week. It sounds obvious but being disciplined is the only way to go. If the supremacy and total point lines are where you would expect, the corresponding team markets will be too.

If a firm is out of line, ask why. One spread trader once told me on the day of a game that two players from a high-profile team would not be playing and one star man would be used out of position to fill one of those vacancies. I went through every available internet site and a few club sources to check the story but this information was nowhere to be found. Lo and behold, the trader was right.

The moral of this story is that spread traders are shrewd and usually well-informed. They are always more likely to be on the ball than their fixed-odds counterparts and more often than not they play a numbers game rather than just go on their own opinion.

That's not to say they don't make ricks, it just means we have to be even more selective. One trader once told me – and this applies to other sports as well – that selling is invariably where the best value is.

Whether it be points (particularly in wet weather), hotshots or tryscorers' shirts, the price is artificially high because casual punters want to buy. They want to see points and tries and they are invariably the sort of customers spread companies welcome with open arms.

However, selling is not for everyone, and punters can be put off. You sell hotshots week-in, week-out and nick a few points here and there and then you get whacked when the nominated players embark on a try rampage. It happens to the best of traders but in the long run selling is still, by and large, a winning strategy.

Player try minutes are becoming increasingly popular with small punters and they can provide 80 minutes of entertainment for a small buy. However, you should be aware that traders know people like to buy these markets and you guess the rest . . . the price is artificially high as a consequence. ▪

it's not just about wimbledon

SERVE IT UP
TO LAYERS

FOR MOST PEOPLE IN BRITAIN
betting on tennis, like watching tennis, starts
and stops with Wimbledon fortnight, with the
turnover the bookmakers report throughout
these two weeks of the summer far
outweighing the combined levels of trade
on the other three Grand Slams.

However, tennis betting is not just about
Wimbledon. Although in turnover terms it is
still something of a minority sport, the diverse
range of markets available in this sphere of
sports betting caters for most gambling tastes,
while with pro-tennis bookmakers like Stan
James pricing up all the events on the men's
ATP tour, a continuous stream of action is
guaranteed throughout the year.

Match betting offers the prospect of a speedy
return on your investment, but it is not for
the faint hearted, as huge momentum swings
can occur.

Backing players to win tournaments falls
at the opposite end of the gambling spectrum
to match betting as it takes days rather
than minutes to determine the fate of your
bet and offers punters a chance to bag a
weighty return from a small outlay. These
markets are most appealing to patient and
disciplined punters with an affinity for trends
and statistics.

By JAMES PYMAN

Andy Roddick in action at Flushing Meadows: more to life than SW19

Tennis betting is also growing in popularity, especially on the exchanges, where big matches are now attracting millions of pounds of trade.

MATCH BETTING Betting on the outcome of matches is the most popular type of tennis betting in terms of turnover, with Stan James's tennis compiler Gordon Caskie reporting that, in an average year, their turnover on match betting is about ten times greater than on their outright markets. When several bookies are involved, margins can be favourable, with the layers betting to just over 100 per cent. With an increasing number of firms pricing up matches it makes sense to shop around.

There is the option to have a single bet on a player, or to perm numerous selections, but big-hitters tend to stick to singles and Stan James say they have laid bets of up to £200,000 in the early rounds of Grand Slams.

Stan James say they are most reluctant to take large singles on matches in nondescript events played in remote locations where

betting on tennis

 Know the terrain

surfaces so important

The type of surface a tournament or match is being played on cannot be ignored, as players' games are more suited to some surfaces than others. The speed of the surface, the style of play to which it is more conducive, and the height and consistency of the bounce are the main factors that need addressing before having a wager.

Few players are capable of producing their peak form on all surfaces and players' form can dip or improve dramatically when making the transition from one type of terrain to another.

Therefore, spotting players whose games translate surprisingly well on to a surface that is foreign to them can bring massive rewards,

with improving players with plenty of ability being the most likely candidates.

The obvious example in recent times is David Nalbandian. In 2002 the Argentinian's baseline game proved to be extremely effective on pace-laden grass courts and consequently allowed him to reach the final at Wimbledon in what was his first ever ATP tour grass-court event.

Although it would have been impossible to have foreseen Nalbandian doing so well before Wimbledon, a few shrewd punters latched on to him when it was clear that he was not there for the strawberries and cream after impressing in the early rounds.

punters may have access to information, such as weather reports and injury news, that they cannot easily obtain.

Multiple bets are most popular in the early rounds of Grand Slams when the high number of matches gives punters plenty of choice. For example, in the first round of the 2001 US Open, Stan James took a wager from one tennis enthusiast who had strung together 47 short-priced selections into a monster accumulator.

It looked as though the firm would have to pay out around £2,500 to the punter, who had staked just £10, when incredibly the first 46 picks all won. But he was cruelly denied by Thomas Enqvist's failure to beat Bjorn Phau in the 47th and final leg.

At the back end of big events, when matches are less frequent, the layers, in an attempt to get punters to part with their hard-earned, will price up a whole manner of match related markets, ranging from the score in sets to more obscure markets such as the number of double faults or tie-breaks.

Caskie admits that his company can make errors when compiling markets on some of the more unpredictable aspects of tennis and consequently, in the past, have been picked off by shrewdies who specialise in these niche areas, with the number of double faults being a good example. Windy conditions on court make accurate serving difficult and therefore when blustery weather prevails the number of double faults can go through the roof.

A sudden influx of turbulent weather before a match can rubbish bookmakers' quotes, allowing the few punters who are aware of these climatic changes to take advantage.

During Grand Slam and Masters Series events the spread betting firms like to get a piece of the action. Those punters who wish to play the variety of markets offered by these firms should stick to the well-touted precept of buying low and selling high.

Set supremacy markets are desirable to punters who are wishing to oppose jollies as selling the hot favourite on these markets usually carries little downside, with the market leader often needing to win in straight stets to inflict serious damage.

Punters are always eager to buy the total number of games in matches at Wimbledon, the French Open and the Australian Open as players do not play a tie-break in the fifth set at these events, so buying games in a match that develops into a five-set marathon can yield a sizeable return. Game buyers hit the jackpot in the 2003 Australian Open when Andy Roddick defeated Younes El Aynaoui 21-19 in the fifth set.

Selling games resulted in a catastrophic loss to others, though, further underlining the perils associated with spread betting in tennis.

THE KEY VARIABLES A catalogue of variables can influence the outcome of a tennis match. However, with most playing only minor roles, this section looks in detail at the key variables that must be considered, and how they can be analysed to find value.

ABILITY This has a bearing on the outcome of all matches and consequently bookmakers' match odds are largely a reflection of the difference in ability of the two players. Ability can be measured in many ways, although ratings are probably the most commonly used method. In the men's game, the ATP use two systems to rate players based on their performances on the tour which punters can therefore use to quickly assess the respective abilities of the two players contesting a match.

The Entry Points system takes into account players' displays over a rolling 52-week calendar, with more weight given to their displays in Grand Slams and Masters Series events. Players are ranked depending on the number of points they have amassed and the ATP deploys these rankings to iron out issues such as which players will be granted automatic places in events and who will be seeded. This system is also used by the WTA to rank the top women's tennis players.

The Champions Race system is based on performances in that year. Players start at zero in January and accumulate points throughout that season.

Both systems have their strengths and weaknesses. The Entry Points system takes into account the results of players over a longer time frame, so is a more reliable indicator of ability. The Champions Race is largely a form-related rating, especially in the early part of the year when players have appeared in few tournaments. Some of the other criteria

betting on tennis

 Head-to-head hoodoos

John McEnroe once said that most tennis matches are won or lost in the mind, and head-to-head records between players provide evidence to support this view.

There are endless examples of players who can never find a way of beating a particular opponent, a good one being Wayne Ferreira, who between 1994 and 2003 lost all 11 of his matches with Andre Agassi.

These situations usually develop as a result of a player's failure to cope with his opponent's style and consequently ability and form bear no significance on the likely outcome of the match.

Head-to-head records therefore carry greater significance in matches involving well-established players, who are unlikely to have made any wholesale changes to their playing styles.

Improving, unexposed players are more likely to overturn losing records against their adversaries.

commonly used to assess a player's ability are how many career titles they have won or the number of Grand Slam titles they have captured.

PLAYER FORM Winning tennis matches instils confidence and generates rhythm in players' games and this can offset a gulf in ability between two adversaries. Every season players of differing abilities are able to string together lengthy winning sequences, while others will suffer long losing runs. Form is much harder to quantify than ability and therefore bookmakers have problems factoring its influence into their prices.

Statistics are commonly used to approximate form, although watching matches can also provide visual clues to a player's current well-being.

Win-loss records, games difference and players' positions in the Champions Race are just a few examples of form-related statistics, but, with so many available, it's best to be selective and analyse just one or two.

PHYSICAL FACTORS A player lacking fitness or carrying an injury will not be able to produce his A-game so this will greatly reduce his chances of winning. It can therefore pay to oppose players who you know are suffering from an ailment or are short of match fitness.

However, obtaining up-to-date injury news can be problematic for punters as players are coy about the state of their fitness, because revealing that they are not in supreme condition can hand an advantage to their opponents.

Visual clues such as strapping are obvious signs that a player is carrying an injury, while the wearing of cycling shorts can be indicative of a thigh or hamstring problem.

Statistical evidence can also yield information. Lower serving speeds than normal can mean a player has a shoulder or rib injury, while a sudden increase in unforced errors can be an indication of fatigue.

Stamina is more important in energy-sapping clay court tennis when the rallies are long and arduous, and also in tournaments played at altitude where the lower levels of oxygen in the atmosphere force players' cardiovascular systems to work much harder.

OUTRIGHT MARKETS It is essential to adopt a long-term approach when having an outright bet on a tennis tournament. While the high levels of uncertainty attached to a tournament involving up to 128 players breeds value in these markets, you must be prepared to accept the fact that you will back more losers than winners.

The less glamorous tournaments are a breeding ground for big-priced winners, as these events often lack strength in depth and therefore don't take a lot of winning. To generate publicity the sponsors know they must attract a few choice names, and therefore lure the top players with hefty appearance fees. But the ranking points and prize money attached to these events are not considerable so, after scooping their appearance money, the big names who have little to gain from staging a title bid frequently fall by the wayside in the early rounds. Even in Grand Slams it is not uncommon for a big-priced outsider to land the spoils, with Goran Ivanisevic's Wimbledon win in 2001 being a classic example. The Croat was a 150-1 chance before the event.

However, punting on tennis tournaments can also be one of the most demoralising forms of gambling.

Picture the following scenario; you have spent three years tracking the career of a precocious 16-year-old Swedish baseliner, who

betting on tennis

 In-running boom

beware volatile markets

The introduction of the exchanges is revolutionising tennis betting and there is an in-running betting boom.

Millions of pounds are now being matched during live games in feature events. In-running betting on tennis can be extremely volatile so punters wishing to get involved must do their homework or they could suffer heavy losses.

Arming yourself with relevant statistics can improve your chances of returning a profit from these markets.

For example, information on players' five-set records, the number of matches they have won in straight sets that season or their strike-rate in tie-breaks can all help you make unbiased, calculated decisions rather than acting on impulse or leaving lady luck to seal your fate.

---

has been touted by his local tennis club as being the next Bjorn Borg.

Finally your man pockets enough ranking points to secure a place in the main draw of some tin-pot clay-court event in the far reaches of Macedonia, which has been targeted by a wave of washed-out veterans looking to rekindle their declining careers.

You skim over the Pricewise box in your *Racing Post* and feel a little deflated to see the first firm you come to offering 16-1. However, as you move your eyes across the page the hairs suddenly jump off the back of your neck when you realise you can back him at 100-1 with Bet7daysaweek, and you develop a smug grin after managing to get on £50 each-way before the firm falls into line with their competitors.

Your man gets off to a flying start and when the draw opens up for him after the top-seed crashes out in the first round, he races through to the semi-finals.

Mini Borg is now the tournament favourite and you've already spent the winnings a thousand times over in your head, with him

betting on tennis

 Player interviews

how to filter out the flannel

Players are obliged by the ATP to conduct a minimum number of interviews with the press before, during and after tournaments.
It is possible to ascertain players' playing styles, preferences for different surfaces and fitness status from these transcripts, making them potentially one of the most useful sources of information available.

However, extracting relevant information from these noisy data sources often requires a great deal of filtering and can be extremely time-consuming.

The quality and integrity of the information is very much dependent on the relationship that the player has with the press, and whether the interviewing journalists ask questions that yield useful information to punters, because often they are more interested in a player's recent appearance on a prime-time TV show or an alleged relationship with a Hollywood star.

The following points are worth considering when analysing player interviews: during tournaments players are often cagey and unresponsive as they do not want to hand their opponents any advantage by revealing their strengths and weaknesses.

Interviews that take place within minutes of the match are usually unreliable sources as they are emotionally charged and contain biased opinions. For example, victors will often massage their ego by praising the opponent they have just defeated.

Opinions expressed before and after tournaments are invariably unbiased and more genuine.

needing to net just one more win for you to land the place part of your each-way bet.

But it all goes pear-shaped when your fancy is on the receiving end of an inspired performance from one of those washed-out veterans, who had been training behind closed doors for six months for this event which he won ten years ago, leaving you £100 out of pocket.

All those hours of research have been a complete waste of time and now that the world and his wife are aware of Mini Borg's talent, a week later he starts a stronger event at grossly deflated odds.

THE DRAW The draw is central to finding value in outright markets and therefore needs

betting on tennis

 Getting your information

A mine of information can be unearthed on the internet. The best sites for scores, statistics and news are www.atptour.com www.itftennis.com www.wtatour.com www.stevegtennis.com www.tenniscorner.net While for the latest betting try www.betfair.com www.stanjames.com www.racingpost.co.uk and odds comparison site www.bestbetting.com

to be studied in meticulous detail. The men's game is so competitive that even the top players struggle to overcome difficult draws.

The purpose of the seeding system is to distribute talent throughout the draw, but this system based on rankings has its limitations. Therefore, it's not unusual to find most of the big names housed in the same section.

Consequently, you will find compartments of the draw with very few title candidates and the better players in these weaker sections can be value each-way betting propositions.

These players may have a bit to find in ability terms on their more fancied rivals in the stronger sections, but their favourable draw gifts them a passage to the later stages, where they are required to win just one or two matches to yield an each-way return.

It is much harder to profit from these situations on the outright indices compiled by spread betting firms as the influence of the draw is usually factored into these markets.

TRENDS IN OUTRIGHT MARKETS

When analysing the outright betting for a tournament, punters are advised to look at previous results from this event. Once a player finds the winning formula in a particular venue or city they will target future events at these locations. A return to familiar surroundings brings out the best in certain players who, year after year, make a big impression in the same tournaments. For example, Yevgeny Kafelnikov won the Kremlin Cup at Moscow five times in a row from 1997 to 2001.

Even if a player is out of form, revisiting the scene of a successful title bid can bring about a reverse in their fortunes.

And the chance of a defending champion, who has a mountain of entry points to defend, must be respected as failing to reach the later stages will cause them to crash down the rankings.

find the potters under pressure

CUEING UP FOR CASH

THERE OUGHT TO BE TWO CHAPTERS on betting on snooker – one for how things were in the early 1990s, and one for the state of play by the end of the 2003-04 season.

By PAUL KEALY

By then, years of mismanagement by snooker's governing body, the WPBSA (now the WSA), had left the sport with an ever-shortening number of tournaments, most of them unsponsored.

Indeed, it is questionable whether the term 'season' was the right one to use for the 2003-04 campaign. It implies a time of year devoted to a regular activity, but nine tournaments spread over 223 days at random intervals and comprising just 12 weeks – not including qualifiers – of action can hardly be called regular.

So what has any of this got to do with how to approach betting on snooker? More than you might think.

THE FLAWS IN FORM Anyone who punts on sport should do their best to have a complete knowledge of the discipline they are following, and it is doubly important in snooker that you understand how the game is structured so that you can comprehend what the players are facing up to.

One of the main reasons for this is that current form can be almost worthless in the

Extremes: Matthew Stevens's 2003-04 season showed how form can fluctuate

stop-start campaigns that have been prevalent from 2000 onwards.

Form is hard to pin down because the timing of events is so irregular. For instance, there was a gap of one month between the first event of the 2003-04 season, the LG Cup, and the second, the British Open. The gap between the British Open and the UK Championship was two days, but then there was a wait of two months until the Welsh Open.

Opposing player A because he played like a prune two months ago can hardly be considered a particularly shrewd idea on its own as there is no knowing what he has been up to since. The same goes for backing player B on the grounds that he was in scintillating form the last time you saw him.

Once again, the point needs making that this was not always the case, as the more tournaments there are, the more evenly spread they are likely to be. If the snooker calendar is replenished to its former levels, feel free to give more weight to the most recent form.

But there was little sign at the end of the

2003-04 campaign that things were going to get much better in a hurry and with snooker seasons as disjointed as they regularly are, form rarely gets a chance to settle down. Players, therefore, drift from one extreme to the other even more often that you would expect. Matthew Stevens making the semis of the British Open, winning the UK Championship a fortnight later and then losing in the first round of the European Open after a break of 60 days is just one of many examples from 2003-04.

FEELING THE PRESSURE

We often talk about pressure at the business end of sporting events, but there are no easy rides for snooker players. It is cut-throat stuff from the off.

Lack of tournaments mean a dearth of earning opportunities, while the absence of sponsorship affects the levels of prize money that can be won from those limited opportunities. Three average golf tournaments on the European Tour would more than cover the entire prize fund for a snooker season.

It is a fact that the Embassy World Championship accounted for more than 25 per cent of the total prize money pool in snooker's eight world ranking events in the 2003-04 season.

In all, there was just under £5m for the 128 main-tour players to aim at, but almost £1.7m went to the top ten on the one-year ranking list. The rest was shared between the other 118 professionals at an average of £27,000 per man.

If you took the next ten on the one-year list they would take another sizeable chunk out of the pool and it soon becomes apparent that a large proportion of players are earning peanuts in terms of prize money and clearly not enough to make a decent living.

Unlike golf, where you can earn millions

without ever threatening to actually win a tournament, there is no comfort zone in snooker.

Another form of pressure facing certain players is the ranking system. While a full field of the 128 players on the main tour is the perfect number for a straight Grand Slam-style knockout event, that is not how it works, possibly because of the logistics of playing 127 matches at one venue, but more probably because TV stations do not want to be faced with a string of unknowns when the cameras finally arrive. And in best-of-nine frame matches, that would always be possible.

What happens is this; the top 16 do not come into tournaments until the last-32 stage, while those ranked from 17-32 enter at the last 48 stage, and so on. It is a form of protection, but it comes at a price.

At the more advanced stages of qualification, anyone who loses their first match receives only half the ranking points of someone who goes out at the same stage but has already won a match to get there in the first place. In many cases a top-16 player losing his opening match can earn less ranking points than someone who goes out of the event two rounds earlier.

Armed with this knowledge, you should be able to spot a number of players who are facing more than usual pressure from the start of the season. Some will be able to cope with it, but many will not and they will soon present themselves to you – every year you will soon latch on to a few players who suffer a string of defeats. Bookmakers may also know this, but they find it hard to make the sufficient reaction in their odds.

INFORMATION SOURCES Everything else you need to do in order to maximise your potential for profit in snooker would apply to any other sport.

betting on snooker

 Oddsmaker's view

Keep up with the qualifiers

Roger Tull, Ladbrokes' main snooker odds-compiler, says punters play into their hands by continuing to take short prices.

He said: "The standard between the top 16 and the rest has dramatically narrowed over time, but we still see huge numbers of accumulators on all the supposed first-round 'good things'.

"Best-of-five frame matches are so unpredictable, but in these days of no tax punters are now prepared to have £10,000 to win £1,000 and those are the types of bets you have to lay."

And Tull believes even the longer matches seen at the UK and World Championships are becoming tougher to call.

"There is no doubt that the class players used to come to the fore in those events," he said. "We would go into every World Championship aware that we were almost certain to lose to accumulator punters in the first round as the hotpots would virtually always win. But times are changing. Even though I would expect one of the big guns to come out on top in the end, very few matches are won easily at the Crucible. Snooker has become a really competitive sport, far more so than in the 1980s."

Tull's main piece of advice for punters is to keep up to date with all the qualifying action.

"We approach snooker the same way as any other sport, with current form seen as the most important thing," he said.

"Qualifying form is also very important, especially at the start of the season when you can't be sure how much practice the more established players have been putting in. The qualifiers will head into the tournament match fit and that can give them a big advantage. There also tends to be another batch of qualifiers just after Christmas and punters should keep an eye on those as well."

Put simply, you must do your homework. Study, study, then study some more. Devour every piece of snooker information that you can get your hands on, whether it be from press cuttings or the internet, personal visits to competitions or sitting in front of the TV.

Actually, you won't find a great deal when it comes to press cuttings because the vast majority of newspapers (basically all bar the *Racing Post*) pay only lip service to the sport. You will rarely find anything other than a few paragraphs when the big names are in action.

However, there are alternatives, with one of the best of these the WSA's own website, worldsnooker.com.

There may be some notable omissions, like a yearly money-list table (probably too embarrassing to put on show), but otherwise it is jam-packed with most of the information you need.

Snooker Scene, edited by Clive Everton and with reports from the excellent Phil Yates, who often commentates for Sky Sports, is the best of the magazines, but the problem with periodicals is that you often receive the reports after another tournament has already started.

The web is the best place to go, but don't waste your time on individual player sites as they rarely tell you anything other than what starry-eyed fans want to hear.

There is no substitute for watching the action unfold, whether it is at the venue or on TV. Actually, in the days of interactive digital services, TV makes more sense (nowadays the atmosphere is roughly the same anyway, regardless of the arena).

Particularly relevant on worldsnooker.com are the results and reports, especially for the qualifying stages, which appear pretty much as and when the action finishes. It is wise to keep cuttings, or at least refer back to the website, for players' quotes, etc, as they give some idea of how the victor or vanquished will approach the rest of the season or even their next match. Are they on borrowed time after a lucky win or are they full of confidence?

It's an important point as you will find that a player performing poorly is more likely to remain vulnerable for the rest of their stay in any single tournament.

An obvious example of this would be David Gray at the Crucible in April 2004. Never will a professional play so badly and reach a World Championship quarter-final. In the last eight he faced Graeme Dott, an opponent whom the rankings and, just as importantly, the bookies, said was roughly the same player. Dott had clearly played the better snooker of the two, but was still rated the underdog by some layers. The Scot won 13-7 and anyone who had watched the two in action would have considered Dott at evens as buying money.

Also on worldsnooker.com is the provisional rankings list, which will give you an idea who the players are that are facing a desperate struggle to retain their status in the top 16, 32, etc.

Confidence can make a huge difference in a game where the class differential between a top player and a qualifier is narrowing all the time, especially when you allow for the fact that most matches are contested over the best of nine frames. Usually there are a handful of players who can rightly be considered different class to the chasing pack, but the gulf in ability between players ranked from, say, ten-32, is not so great.

MATCH AND TOURNAMENT BETTING

Most of your betting on snooker will centre round individual matches, as that is where the best value tends to be. With several bookmakers fighting for your money and the exchanges another option, you will often find that you can bet with virtually no bookmakers' profit margin to contend with.

Of course, with matches you are invariably punting at short odds, but there is always the option of betting on the tournament outright.

As a youngster I was taught that the best way to approach a snooker tournament is to work out what an accumulator would pay in the worst-case scenario of any individual having to face the best player possible in each section of the draw. If the accumulator would

betting on snooker

 Watch out for first-round shockers

duck the early knockout

A point about tournament betting is that you must have a very strong view about your selection getting past the first round. That sounds ridiculously obvious, but the opening round of snooker events features more shocks than any other.

Part of this can be put down to the fact that qualifiers are more match-prepared than those coming in cold, but not all events are preceded by the qualifiers so the added pressure of defending ranking points must also be taken into account.

Whatever, over the two seasons from September 2002 to May 2004, almost 50 per cent of matches were won by the lower-ranked player. Most of them would have been odds-against and a healthy profit would have been made simply by backing the lower-ranked player.

Indeed, it seems little has changed on that front since the mid-1990s. Back then, it was shown in the *Racing Post* that backing the underdog blind at every stage of a tournament throughout a whole season would have made punters a profit, and that even took into account the nine per cent betting tax.

Yet the fact that there are so many shocks in the game seems lost on most punters if their betting habits are anything to go by.

pay less than the outright odds available, you have then got a value bet.

It sounds okay in principle and may even have worked in the days when bookmakers did not take sports betting that seriously, but it is actually nonsense now. It implies, of course, that bookmakers are not looking at the draw themselves, which they sure as hell are.

Try it. I doubt you will come up with a bet more than once every five years, and even then it will mean taking 400-1 on Betfair about a genuine 200-1 chance. And given that your 200-1 shot will on average win once every 20 years over a ten-tournament snooker season, the method looks increasingly flawed however plausible it might initially sound.

The good news, of course, is that worst-case scenarios rarely happen anyway because shocks are commonplace in snooker. Being able to identify vulnerable players is something that will make you plenty of money on the match-betting front and it can also help you with outright tournaments.

Each time you assess a competition you should sift through the draw and underline every player you consider likely to under-perform. You won't get it right all the time, but you will find sometimes that certain sections of the draw feature an unusually high proportion of players begging to be taken on.

However you choose to bet, the one golden rule is that you must get into the habit of pricing up everything yourself, whether it is the tournament as a whole or an individual match. And always do it to a 100 per cent book. For example, if you rate a favourite at 1-2, the outsider must be 2-1, not 6-4 as a bookmaker would go.

If you see a bigger price either way, the chances are you have a value bet, although don't make the mistake of just piling in straight away in the belief that the layer has got it wrong.

Remember, these people are being paid to price up the events. They do make mistakes, but only rarely, so before stepping in you should go back over your prices and make sure you have not missed anything. Only once you are confident in your own assessment should you strap those betting boots on.

INTEGRITY With prize-money levels so low, snooker would have to be seen as being a sport most in danger of match-fixing. If the financial rewards for winning can easily be surpassed by those for losing, the temptation to throw a match could become very high.

However, a couple of things prevent widescale corruption in snooker, the first being the players themselves.

Thankfully, the vast majority are desperately trying to make a living out of a sport they love and deliberately losing a match is not

betting on snooker

 Table spreads

assess the early action first

Spread betting can provide punters with the best way to oppose the favourites, whether it is on the outright front or in matches. Most firms offer an index (with varying scoring systems) on every tournament, but if you are opposing (selling) even the market leader you must always bear in mind that you are betting at odds-on.

There is nothing wrong with punting at odds-on, but I often feel that spread betting tempts you in to having bets that you almost certainly would not consider if you were presented with a fixed-odds equivalent. The best example of this is in spread match bets, where the firms offer ten points for a win and three per frame won by.

A 1-7 chance will be quoted at something like 13-16 in a best-of-nine frames match. A lot of people will see only the potential nine-point profit for a whitewash win and not the 41-point downside if it happens the other way. And remember, even defeat in a tight match leads to hefty losses.

There are plenty of other markets for snooker punters to latch on to, like match 50-ups (aggregate points scored in a break over 50), ton-ups and performances and the advice here is to keep an eye on the early action before getting involved.

Conditions can vary at any event, whether it is down to humidity in the arena or the tables themselves (there were complaints from players about conditions at at least three tournaments in the 2003-04 campaign) and this can make a huge difference to the scoring potential.

Remember, though, that the layers will be watching as well and will make adjustments to their markets if necessary.

something that is going to help them move up the rankings. The second is that snooker remains a minority betting sport, which means unusually large wagers, especially in the early rounds when any skulduggery is likely to happen, would not go unnoticed.

Ladbrokes's Roger Tull has no concerns about the integrity of snooker. "It's a very clean sport," he insists. "I would certainly say that I didn't see one suspicious match in the 2003-04 season. And anyway, we can react quickly if anything starts to look a bit iffy, either by changing prices dramatically or simply suspending betting. I really don't think there is a problem with snooker."

punters needn't get carsick

WINNING FORMULA

FORMULA ONE MIGHT NOT APPEAL to those who see it as betting on technology rather than a true sporting occasion but it offers everything punters could want – competition, changing fortunes and the chance to make a profit.

Yes, even a great driver cannot win a race in a terrible car, although he can still wring a better lap time out of it. Just as importantly, a bad driver won't necessarily win in a good car.

So what factors, other than the surname Schumacher, should be considered in the search for a grand prix winner?

HORSES FOR COURSES Knowing the relative strengths and weakness of the competing cars (there are currently ten teams of two cars of the grid) is paramount.

Do not make the mistake of thinking that the teams finish in the same order at every event because one car is faster than another every time. Certain tracks suit certain cars better than others and knowing who should prosper at which venue is a great path to finding winners.

Try to get to grips with the make-up of the circuits. Those with long straights separated only by chicanes such as Montreal

By PHIL AGIUS

City limits: the Monaco circuit makes unique demands on car and driver

in Canada and Monza in Italy will play into the hands of teams with the most powerful engines – aerodynamic brilliance will not matter much when you are not going around fast corners.

At the other end of the spectrum is the historic Monte Carlo street circuit, venue for the Monaco Grand Prix. There, grip and acceleration away from the painfully slow corners are far more important than a car's top speed.

For example, in the 2004 season Ferrari and BAR had cars which worked well at most circuits. Williams had plenty of power but took their time getting their aerodynamic performance together. Renault were quick and nimble but lacked top-end speed early in the season and former giants McLaren were saddled with an uncontrollable machine which proved neither fast, easy to handle nor reliable.

Bookmakers can be very slow to react to a change in the status quo, particularly when a midfield team makes genuine improvement.

Have confidence in your own views and make them pay.

Simply assessing the prevailing conditions at the start of a meeting can narrow your race selection down to three or four likely candidates even before the first car has left the garage.

The horses for courses principle applies to drivers as well as their machines. All competitors have their own individual driving style – Rubens Barrichello always goes well in Japan for example, while Jarno Trulli is a master at Monaco. Listen out for interviews where drivers mention if they either love or hate driving at a circuit – it can make a big difference. Otherwise, past form is a valuable tool, particularly if, for example, a driver has dragged a poor car into the points at a circuit which he will now be tackling in a better machine.

WHO REIGNS IN THE RAIN? The only guaranteed way to ensure an F1 race is not a procession is for the heavens to open. Driving talent, rather than car performance, comes to the fore in the wet. Get to know which drivers go well in the wet and you could pull off a big-priced shock.

Olivier Panis was 300-1 when he survived a treacherous Monaco Grand Prix in 1996, when only four drivers completed the course, and the chaos that rain can bring is the ideal opportunity to back a big-priced driver to find a way through the field courtesy of multiple pitstops, collisions and cars going off the circuit. Michael Schumacher is known as the Regenmeister for his prowess in the wet while Barrichello, Giancarlo Fisichella, Kimi Raikkonen and Mark Webber are similarly fearless on slippery tracks.

QUALIFYING Betting on Formula One qualifying is an ever-changing discipline as

betting on formula one

 A tyresome business? Far from it

It's a dull subject best left to the petrolheads to discuss, but if you want to stay in profit you'll need at least a passing knowledge of the current state of the tyre war. In a situation where even the fastest and slowest cars are separated by only two or three seconds over a lap, how each company's tyres perform at each circuit can make a major difference.

The situation came to a head in 2003, when there was a stark contrast between the performance of Bridgestones, which worked best in wet and cold conditions and Michelins, which stood out when the sun shone. This led to world champion Michael Schumacher, on Bridgestones, suffering the indignity of being lapped and finishing behind seven Michelin racers in scorching Hungary. By the following season, the two camps were far more evenly matched. Keep an eye out for early signs of either manufacturer gaining an edge.

betting on formula one

 Clock the early clues

practice makes perfect

By the time a grand prix starts the competitors will have been on track no fewer than six times already – in four practice sessions and two periods of qualifying.

If your course form has identified a big value bet, by all means take a chance and step in as the price may contract rapidly once the cars have been tested against each other on the track.

Otherwise, keep a close eye on all the preliminary action to hone your impression of who is ready to shine.

Fast free practice times are not the be-all and end-all. Pitfalls to avoid are teams trying to impress their sponsors or engine manufacturers by running very light on fuel in a bid to gain an artificially fast lap time.

However, by the time qualifying starts you should have a fair idea of which cars are suited to the track and which need to make further adjustments to be competitive.

The bare results of practice sessions are available in national newspapers but these do not tell the full story. For real insight, punters can log on to the sport's official website www.formula1.com and view live timing from all sessions from the track computers exactly as the teams themselves see it. This tool enables you to see exactly what the situation was when each driver set his fastest time – was he the only one to improve his best lap while others were struggling? Did he post a disappointing time while others were all going faster?

the sport's ruling body, the FIA, is constantly tinkering with the format in an attempt to improve the show for TV viewers.

In July 2004, the sport scrapped a plan to replace the stilted one-lap format in favour of two free-for-all sessions, with a driver's aggregate time for the two used to determine grid positions. A return to the traditional 'pure' qualifying where the driver to post the fastest lap at any time in qualifying claims pole position could still happen at any time.

If it does, punters will be delighted to again know that all cars will be running the same fuel load in qualifying again (ie, very little). The 2004 rules force teams to qualify using the fuel they intend to start the race with.

Note that the main qualifying market is now usually called fastest qualifier rather than the traditional pole position. This is due to the possibility of drivers being demoted on the grid from the position their time would otherwise have earned because they changed the engine in their car during race weekend.

The main difference in selecting a driver to back in qualifying as compared to the race is that you can completely ignore reliability. While the likelihood of a temperamental engine giving up the ghost in a cloud of smoke is a major consideration for those betting on a two-hour race, even the most problematic machine should keep going long enough to complete one flying lap.

Bear in mind that some drivers are more adept at qualifying than others. Jarno Trulli, for example, has a reputation for being a great qualifier who can often look lacklustre over a race distance. His Renault team-mate, Fernando Alonso, often plays second fiddle on a Saturday only to storm past his colleague in Sunday's race.

And Mark Webber has dragged the unreliable Jaguar to the front row of the grid at big prices before without getting a blow in over a race distance.

Most firms bet win-only on qualifying, although some are beginning to come over to the concept of each-way wagering.

Qualifying match bets, both fixed and spreads, are always worth consideration. Many firms annoyingly pit team-mates against each other, which rules out the prospect of taking advantage of any of the technical issues discussed above. Focus on those matches where the contestants are from different teams and, preferably, on different tyres and you could be in business.

GO GO GO Sunday afternoon is the focus of the weekend but who is really worth backing once the grid order has been decided?

Again, the track plays a part in determining

betting on formula one

 The layer's view

crucial to get off to a flier

Jody Orgee of Sporting Index says: The beginning of the year is critical. If you make a mistake it can be very hard to get it back, particularly on the long-term markets.

For example, before the 2004 season, there were reports that Jenson Button was flying in testing, but the temptation was to think they were running him light on fuel to gain publicity. Of course, after his performance in the first race, you knew the speed was for real.

Similarly, anyone who sold Michael Schumacher's points in 2004, maybe thinking that Ferrari's Bridgestone tyres would let him down, never had a chance to get out of trouble. You are effectively betting on last year's form, so I'd be very wary about having big bets before seeing the cars on the track.

On a race-by-race basis, we can sometimes find qualifying more difficult to price up than the race, but we do our best to stay on top of the technical news and you should never discount course form. We know, for example, that Trulli loves Monaco and Fisichella enjoys racing at Hungary, which punters should take advantage of if a bookmaker has not factored it in.

Match betting is a shrewd route to F1 punting success. Reliability is the key. In 2004 Renault were finishing every race at the start of the season, while McLaren had mechanical trouble. If drivers of the two teams were paired together in any matches, it was an ideal opportunity to pounce.

In-running betting is extremely popular, particularly when an unexpected driver is leading. Our busiest race by far in 2004 was Monaco, where Jarno Trulli led throughout and, more importantly, Michael Schumacher did not.

There are also opportunities to profit on markets such as numbers of finishers. Knowing the tracks is important on this market. For example, the cars are flat out for much longer than usual at Indianapolis, which puts more strain on the engines and causes retirements. Because reliability had been so good in the opening races, we overestimated the number of finishers in the 2004 US Grand Prix and should have taken more account of the history of the race. Only nine cars finished.

Sometimes the prices on some special markets can be simply wrong. For example, Michael Schumacher has a remarkable reliability record, and the prices for him to finish each race, although short, are often nowhere near short enough.

how far down the field you should look for a winner. At places like Monaco, overtaking is impossible except off the startline and during pitstops. Take note of the positions past winners of the race have come from. Bear in mind that some cars get off the startline better than others. In 2003 and 2004 Renault

betting on formula one

 Making podium profits

champagne charlies

Punters who are not fans of each-way betting can effectively bet place-only on races by backing a driver for a podium finish, which is to finish in the first three. This market is particularly useful in races with a clear favourite, which happens so often in the Schumacher era, although at times the layers will even offer betting without the favourite.

The points finish market makes every car in the field a potential source of profit. This pays out on all points-scoring drivers in the race, ie. the first eight home. Even teams like Minardi, who are pretty much there to make up the numbers, can enter your betting strategy here.

The poor relations of the grid may find their drivers on offer at 25-1 and 33-1 to score a world championship point but such an occurrence is not impossible – the unheralded Zsolt Baumgartner got his name on the scoreboard at Indianapolis in 2004 when only nine cars were still running at the finish.

There is usually no particular edge to be gained from betting on which driver will post the fastest lap of the race, as this tends to occur when cars are light on fuel just before a pit-stop, although first retirement can be worth a punt if one car or other has had engine trouble during the weekend in particular. A first-corner incident makes that market far more random, however.

were the undoubted masters of the fast start and regularly made up positions before the first corner.

Tyrewear is an important factor over a race distance and check for consistent lap times over long runs in Friday practice, when teams are usually testing out their set-up for the race. Comment on websites and in the press gives immediate feedback on drivers' thoughts about their chances and over time you will learn how to screen out the corporate speak and, by learning their personalities, evaluate the competitors' true opinions of their prospects.

TEAM TACTICS F1 teams have been banned from actively preventing free competition between their drivers, but it would extremely naïve not to take the possibility

betting on
formula one

 Get your facts right

Motor sport enjoys excellent international press coverage and it is well worth taking out subscriptions to weekly magazine *Autosport* or glossy monthly *F1 Racing*, which provides opinion, reports and previews plus valuable insight and analysis. The FIA's official magazine *F1* is also worth a read, but lacks the same irreverent spirit and sense of humour. Watch as much of the ITV coverage as you can, particularly at the races where they show the qualifying sessions live (some early morning events and those which clash with soap operas are shown on tape-delay only).
Online resources are plentiful. www.formula1.com not only provides the valuable live timing but its historic database includes session-by-session times.
The Formula 1 Database at www.f1db.com also has the statistical records and acts as a news portal to a host of other sites.

of a manufactured result into account when betting. Hopefully the darkest days of drivers openly moving over for team-mates, or the ridiculous attempted dead-heat staged by Ferrari at Indianapolis in 2002 are behind us, but it's still very likely that drivers from the same team will be under unspoken orders not to race each other after the final pitstop, for example, in order to prevent the possibility of an accident which knocks out one or both. When backing Ferrari No. 2 Rubens Barrichello for example, be aware that he will probably only have a chance to win the race if some misfortune befalls team leader Michael Schumacher.

WE ARE RACING When the red lights go off to start the race, the opportunities to profit are far from finished. In fact, motor racing is an excellent sport for in-running betting, either with fixed-odds firms, spread companies or, most lively of all, the betting exchanges. Keep an ear out for teams' likely fuel strategies and you might be able to create a handy position. Better still, monitor the in-race data from www.formula1.com and see who is putting in fast lap times or slowing dramatically – it will give you a major advantage over those who have only the television pictures to work with.

ANTE-POST ACTION Long-term fixed-odds markets on the drivers and constructors' titles can be painfully dull and tie your money up for long periods without promising any huge gains. Pre-season testing can be particularly misleading and waiting until the first three or four races have gone before taking an interest is a sensible precaution.

Of slightly more interest are the drivers' points and various spread indices, where careful monitoring of teams' progress and prospects can bring about profitable portfolios.

punch your weight with layers

BOXING CLEVER

IT IS PROBABLY FAIR TO SAY THAT boxing is one of the harder sports for casual punters to get a handle on.

By PAUL KEALEY

Sure, there is plenty of information out there, but there is no substitute for first-hand knowledge of fighters and their styles. The problem is that despite the efforts of TV companies like Sky, a big chunk of bouts that British bookmakers ask you to bet on will feature a boxer you have never heard of before, let alone seen. So, like it or not, second-hand info becomes king.

It is the same for bookmakers, of course, which leads to hope that the punter prepared to put the work in can get an edge, but those few firms who price up lower-profile contests tend to use extremely defensive profit margins, thus doing their best to ensure ricks are at a minimum, while squeezing any value out of the market at the same time.

Victor Chandler's Ivan Stojanovic highlights the problem for all concerned, saying: "Boxing is undoubtedly very, very difficult. A lot of the time all you have to go on is stats. Most of the time you won't have seen one of the boxers and sometimes you won't have seen either. There are magazines you can go to get archive footage, but even they are only the key fighters who you have probably seen anyway. Unless

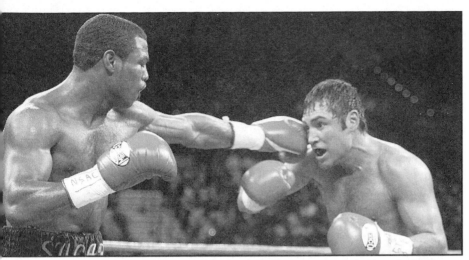

Don't believe the hype: Shane Mosley beats Oscar de la Hoya in 2003

you know both fighters well it is impossible to make an opinion on your own."

Boxing may once have been the noble art, but it lost the right to boast such a tag long ago and for many years the game has been about who you know and not what you can do in the ring.

Politics, not talent, dictates champions and there are very few genuine best-against-best title fights in any one year. The rest feature a long odds-on belt-holder against a challenger who has been on the rent-a-bum circuit beating up stiffs unlikely to hold their own with your local nightclub bouncer.

INFORMATION SOURCES Your quest for a more intimate knowledge of the boxing world should start with a subscription to *Boxing News*, a weekly (hitting the streets every Friday) publication packed with reports, previews, news from the big dates coming up and plenty more.

In any sport, when it comes to punting the last thing you should do is consult someone who idolises the subject in question and while

Boxing News is aimed obviously at fight fans, the great thing about their writers is that they refuse to be drawn in by the hype.

Ask boxing promoter/manager Frank Warren who is going to win, his fighter or his opponent, and he will back his own man to the hilt whatever odds and logic might say. That's his job.

The job of *Boxing News* fight previewers is to give a balanced view. As experts they are able to convey to you something that an untrained eye may have missed and, just as importantly, they have more access to information about boxers than you could hope to amass on your own.

What you must remember, though, is that their fight previews are written without the consideration of the odds. Follow them blind and you will invariably back the favourite and lose in the long run.

Just like reading a Spotlight for a horserace in the *Racing Post* is one way of assessing the merits of a potential bet, a *Boxing News* preview – or any preview of any sport you care to read – is just one part of the key to unravelling the puzzle.

When it comes to punting there are very few people it pays to follow blind, so being led by a publication that has no interest in betting would be financial suicide.

But the advantages of *Boxing News* don't end there, as the reports can provide gems of info such as a fighter's susceptibility to a certain type of punch, or a particularly good weapon likely to prove effective against a subsequent opponent. Keep records, either by storing all back copies, or by building your own files.

ON THE NET A lot of the information you require can easily be found on the internet. Just enter the word boxing on any internet search engine and you will be directed to a vast array of websites. It's a case of trial

betting on boxing

 Archive to end 'em all

the complete online record

Boxrec.com is an absolute must for anyone seriously interested in boxing and, from a stats point of view, is one of the best around. Just search for any boxer's name and at the click of a button you are taken to a complete history of the fighter in question.

The record gives the date of every fight (important so that you can easily cross reference reports that you have kept) in his CV, weights of both fighters (in most cases), venue, win record of opponent plus a link to his full breakdown and, of course, the result.

The archive goes back years. Anoraks can, for instance, access the full 129-fight record of Jack Johnson from his first bout in 1894 to his last in 1938.

Interestingly, Boxrec.com has its own ratings for all divisions and these are simply the result of all boxers' records being fed into a computer.

No outside opinion is involved. They can give you an idea of how a title challenger rates – if he doesn't appear on the first page you can be sure there is little substance in his record.

There is also a forum where you can pick the brains of fellow fans plus a link to the latest news on the Boxing-central website.

and error to see which ones serve you best, but the following is a short list that should prove very useful.

Fightnews.com – in-depth reports from all the big fights, links to news from all over the world, upcoming fight schedules, plus the latest rankings from the four most recognised (WBC, WBA, IBF and WBO) organisations along with fightnews.com's own ratings on the same page.

If nothing else the rankings page at fight-news.com gives you an idea of what a sad state boxing is in. At the time of writing 30 different names featured among the four big organisations' top-15 rated super-middleweights. They each ignored the other bodies' champions and none could come up with an even remotely similar top five.

Lasvegassun.com is a long way from a dedicated boxing site, but worth a look all the

betting on boxing

 Alphabet soup leaves sour taste

just who are the champions?

The number of titles on offer prevents decent competition. While there used to be eight weight divisions, there are now 17 and where there used to be eight world champions, there are now well over a hundred boxers who, however ludicrously, can lay claim to a world title, whether it be one of the four recognised versions (WBA, WBC, IBF, WBO) or some of the more obscure (IBO, IBC, WBU, WBF – there is no need to apologise for missing anyone out) championships.

Unfortunately, a lot of what you will see on your screens in Britain is the latter bunch, plus fights sanctioned by the WBO, generally considered the least prestigious of the big four.

Come fight night what you are quite often faced with is a 1-20 chance plus a string of unappetising round-by-round odds about a fighter you think you know all about against one whose name meant nothing to you until a few moments ago.

Nine times out of ten you will find there is no accessible video footage of the challenger, so what do you do?

It goes without saying that you should record as much action as you can, but you will still be left short more often than not so you simply have to rely on people in the fight game to supply you with the missing pieces of information you need. Fortunately there is plenty of it about.

same. Boxing columnist Dean Juipe can be amusing and clearly knows his way around the odds.

Eastsideboxing.com has all the news you can get from any other site, but also features a link to the latest odds in Las Vegas, has an interview archive and some excellent columns in the Time Tunnel section.

Britishboxing.net is well worth a look given that the large majority of fight betting in Britain features British boxers. Plenty of fighters' records, rankings, news and views can be found here.

Compuboxonline.com is a favourite of Chandler's Stojanovic, who says: "This is the best site for stats on American boxing. There are some terrific previews and the statistical breakdown does a lot of the work for you."

WEIGHING IT ALL UP Once you have digested all the information you can handle, there is still the question of translating it all into odds. As with any other sport you are interested in betting on, you should really have a go at pricing up boxing matches yourself.

It is far from easy, which probably explains why so few bookmakers are prepared to bet on anything other than the really big fights where they can be guided by Vegas lines.

There are three main considerations that will help you gain an edge when it comes to betting on boxing and they come under the following headings . . .

HYPE Bookmakers do not fall for hype, yet they know full well that the majority of their customers do, so a talked-up Briton will be a good deal shorter in the market than he deserves to be purely because the layers expect that is where the money will go.

One of the best examples of an over-hyped boxer is Prince Naseem Hamed, a three-weight world champion, who made a career out of boxing past-their-prime opponents. Of the 37 opponents Hamed faced, only five stepped into a ring with an unbeaten record. One of those was at the start of his career and turned out to be useless; the other four had never fought at world level before.

The first really big world name that Hamed took on was Tom Johnson in 1997, but Johnson turned pro in 1986, was 35 at the time and ready to be taken out, as a subsequent record of seven defeats in 14 fights up to his 2002 retirement would show.

The only time he took on a genuine at-his-peak world-class boxer, Hamed was completely out-boxed, in April 2001, by Marco Antonio Barrera.

A year earlier Barrera had lost a decision to Erik Morales, another truly world-class boxer, in a verdict that amazed most experts.

Outboxed: Naseem Hamed suffers at the hands of Marco Antonio Barrera

When the odds were first issued for Hamed-Barrera, Hamed was 2-9 and Barrera 3-1 with Hills. If you had watched tapes of Barrera-Morales and any of Hamed's most recent contests and been unaware of each fighter's reputation, you would have defied anyone to make Hamed favourite.

Hype gives you the impression that a boxer is better than he actually is and punters, particularly patriotic ones, will fall for it most of the time. It can work in your favour in more ways than one. If a boxer has been fed a diet of stiffs there is a fair chance that he will have a good knockout rate and that his punching power will be vastly overstated.

Hamed provides yet another glaring example. One-punch knockouts always look impressive and the Prince had plenty to his name. But when a boxer steps up in class the competition he faces tends to be better able to withstand an opponent's power, even if they aren't good enough to win.

In these instances it is well worth considering backing a prohibitively-priced favourite to win on points. There are very few really explosive punchers at the highest level, whatever their records would suggest.

Of Hamed's last eight fights, two were against boxers who should not have been allowed in the ring. One went 11 rounds and the other five were decided on points. So much for explosive power.

Now that you can bet in-running on the likes of Betfair, you can take advantage when others get sucked in by the hype.

No-one is immune from falling for hype, and that includes TV commentators. In September 2003, Shane Mosley fought Oscar De La Hoya for the second time in an eagerly-awaited clash at the MGM Grand in Las Vegas.

Sky covered the fight, and commentator Ian Darke, clearly expecting to be dazzled by the skills of Golden Boy De La Hoya, gave one of the most biased commentaries you will ever hear, repeatedly talking of how De La Hoya had 'done a number on Mosley'.

Of course, nearly every viewer on Sky agreed judging by the uproar when Mosley was awarded the decision, but most ringside observers that night thought Mosley was the rightful winner.

It may well have been a controversial decision, but it was never a landslide, yet Betfair's in-running market would have reflected what Darke was seeing rather than what was actually happening.

Darke, who is generally excellent, is far from the only commentator to fall for the hype (in 2004 Eammon Dunphy eulogised about Audley Harrison's brilliant defensive work – against Julius Francis!) but that was a startling example.

CONDITIONING One of the most important times for punters is the weigh-in, because it can tell you so much about how a boxer has prepared for a fight. Early in 2004, American broadcaster ESPN released the results of a study it compiled called 'Degree of Difficulty: Sports Rankings'.

An eight-member panel, comprising academics who study the science of muscles and movement, members of the US Olympic Committee and journalists, convened with a view to finding the sport that 'demands the most from the athletes who compete in it'.

Sixty sports were judged in ten categories (agility, analytic aptitude, durability, endurance, flexibility, hand-eye coordination, nerve, power, speed and strength) with marks awarded from 1-10.

Boxing topped the list with an overall mark of 72.37 and was the only sport to score eight or above in five categories. In fact, no others managed to score eight in four categories. The top ten were: 1 boxing (72.37), 2 ice hockey (71.75), 3 American football (68.37), 4 basketball (67.87), 5 wrestling (63.50), 6 martial arts (63.37), 7 tennis (62.75), 8 gymnastics (62.50), 9 baseball (62.25), 10 football (61.50).

Whenever a boxer fails to make the weight it should set alarm bells ringing. Not only is it a psychological blow to the fighter concerned, who must then go away and try to sweat off the excess, it may also tell us something about how his preparation has gone. Something has usually gone wrong if a ten-week training regime results in failure to qualify to fight at the first time of asking.

Weight variation in heavyweights must also be monitored. One of the glaringly obvious examples was James Buster Douglas, who weighed just under 232lbs when shocking Mike Tyson in Tokyo in 1990, but was a stone heavier when losing to Evander Holyfield eight months later (Douglas really went on a burger-spree after his three-round defeat, ending up at more than 400lbs before getting

Weighty matters: slimline 'Buster' Douglas beats Tyson. He later ballooned

his act together for a short-lived comeback in 1996).

Bookmakers will also be aware when the difference is so obvious, but the discerning punter can unravel a few gems just by looking at fighters' past weight-records. For example, Lennox Lewis only twice turned out at more than 250lbs in his career. Even more idiotically, the first time (253lbs) was at altitude against Hasim Rahman in South Africa, where he was knocked out in five rounds.

Lewis was 6lbs lighter when gaining impressive revenge just months later, but was 256.5lbs as his career drew to a close with a lucky six-round victory over Vitali Klitschko. He was well behind when Klitschko was stopped due to cuts.

Just a few pounds can make a difference in such a demanding sport, and you should also be wary if a heavyweight comes in unusually light. A heart defect was given as the reason for Evander Holyfield's defeat to Riddick Bowe in 1992, but it could easily have been down to over-training.

Under-prepared: Lewis was unready for Rahman, who floored him

Holyfield weighed 206lbs for that fight, his lightest for four years and a mark he never approached again.

STYLES Styles make fights. It's probably the oldest sporting adage around, but it still rings true. It would be madness to claim that nearly all rematches are won by the victor of the first fight because you could cite any number of recent examples (Lennox Lewis against Hasim Rahman and Oliver McCall, Marco Antonio Barrera against Erik Morales) to prove otherwise but it will still pay in the long run to back the previously successful man if you do your homework.

You need to be sure, however, that the first fight resulted in a genuine, clear-cut victory with no excuses for the loser. Rahman, for instance, beat Lewis because Lewis was under-prepared, McCall won with a fluke punch, while Barrera and Morales were so evenly-matched you would have struggled to pick the winner of their second meeting.

Fight history is littered with examples of boxers having the Indian Sign over a particular opponent. A couple of examples: few people would rate Junior Jones in the same league as Barrera when it comes to lifetime achievement, but Jones beat the Baby-Faced Assassin twice in the space of five months in the mid-1990s and was a big underdog each time. And Barrera was never ill-prepared for a fight.

The career of Jose Luis Castillo provides some superb examples. The Mexican, twice WBC lightweight champion, had lost six and drawn one of his 57 fights by June 2004. Two of his defeats came to Floyd Mayweather Jnr in 2002, which is hardly surprising.

Two more, however, came at the hands of another man much earlier in his career. In 1994 Castillo fought Javier Jauregi for the Mexican lightweight title and was stopped in the tenth round. Two years later they squared up again for Mexican honours, and Castillo was stopped in the tenth round.

And we're not finished yet. In 2000 Castillo pulled off what *Ring* magazine called the upset of the year by out-pointing Stevie Johnston for the WBC lightweight crown. One of the judges that night gave the fight as a draw, as did two of the judges when Johnston and Castillo went head-to-head for the second time three months later.

You have to feel sorry for Johnston. He was originally awarded the second fight until it was realised that the scorecards had been incorrectly counted. Castillo only found out when Johnston knocked on his dressing room door to hand him back the belt.

Obviously with Johnston the result wasn't the same but the point is worth making. If one fight is very close and there are no excuses on either side, the rematch will almost certainly be equally tight, irrespective of how the bookies bet. And that's important because sometimes an upset winner (or someone beaten in a tight contest) will be allowed to go off at a big price for a rematch. ∎

super bowl not just a lottery

GRIDIRON GAMBLES

PUNTERS BETTING ON AMERICAN football might be forgiven for soon thinking that the odds are stacked against them.

Firstly, the National Football League (NFL) operates with a goal of parity – the concept that all 32 competing teams should have as equal a chance of possible of success. The buzzphrase is that on 'any given Sunday' any team can beat any other.

And secondly, the most popular form of gambling on the sport, the handicap line, or points spread, gives the oddsmakers a chance to even up the chances of any two competing teams on any day.

So why bet on a discipline that would appear to be something of a lottery? Well, for starters, attempting to make all teams equal and actually doing so are very different. Injuries, coaching and personnel management are the three main factors which will sort the successful sides from the failures.

The last two of those are crucial to finding a potential Super Bowl winner at the start of the season.

ANTE-POST ACTION Look at any preseason list of Super Bowl odds and you will see the previous year's play-off teams at the top, the teams who had a bad year at the

By PHIL AGIUS

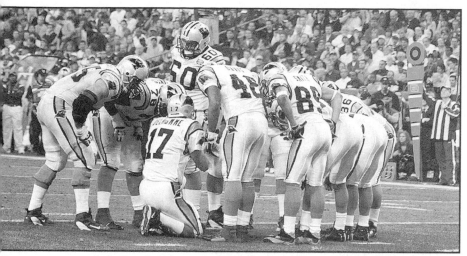

Level playing field? Some teams are more equal than others in gridiron

bottom. Bookmakers, maybe because they are keyed into thinking of British football, seemingly assume that changing the status quo is more difficult than it really is and the recent run of big-priced Super Bowl winners should be a salutary lesson that there is nothing absurd about taking a punt on an ante-post outsider.

St Louis were 150-1 when they won the Vince Lombardi Trophy on the arm of zero-to-hero former shelf-stacker Kurt Warner in 1999. Baltimore were 80-1 shots the following year, New England 50-1 when they won in 2001 and 20-1 two years later, while 2002 champs Tampa Bay were the shortest-priced winners of recent seasons and even they were a juicy 18-1.

Common factors among those champions? None had a premium quarterback, all were well-coached and played to their strengths and few people saw them coming.

Don't be drawn into backing teams solely because they have a big-name quarter-back. Assuming a team shares possession in a game, and that, say, 40 per cent of a team's offensive plays are rushes, even the most talented QB will only be able to influence 30 per cent of a match with his passing skills. Don't put too much faith in one member of a 53-man roster.

Look for teams who improved towards the end of the previous season, as the momentum of a strong finish can often be carried over. Carolina, who had showed steady signs of improvement under first-season coach John Fox at the end of 2002, were a classic case of this in 2003, when they reached the Super Bowl as unconsidered 100-1 shots.

It's always worth assessing the relative strengths of a team's division (the sides they place twice) and the apparent strength of schedule they face (teams don't all play each other and some fixtures on a team's schedule are decided by the position in their division they finished the year before) but remember that what appears a tough slate of games at the start of the year can soon prove very different as teams' fortunes rise and fall sharply.

HANDICAP BETTING The main market on **NFL** matches is the handicap line. Most bookmakers will offer a number of points' start to one team, which when added to the match result provides the handicap result. The majority of bookmakers will use half-point handicaps, which rules out the possibility of a tie.

When full-point handicaps are on offer, most firms void bets on handicap ties. Many firms will offer 10-11 each team on this market, and betting with those who persist in money-grabbing 5-6 offers is not advised unless the handicap itself is way out of line. The days of minimum trebles restrictions are just about a thing of the past now, with singles allowed across the board. All of this makes American football a fundamentally more punter-friendly

uncommon knowledge

**Draft system
a side issue**

raw recruits need time

Don't be blown away by the draft. It is a fatal error to place too much store in how a team fared in the NFL draft – the process by which teams are allocated the cream of the college players each April – when selecting a Super Bowl side. It really is a side issue, at least for that year's event.

The success or otherwise of a draft can only really be assessed around three years later, by which time the pedigree of player each team selected can be gauged after they have had time to adapt to the pro league.

Only one or two players in each side, usually those selected in the first two rounds, are likely to even have a shot of making their team's starting line-up in their first season.

sport than rugby union or league, where handicap ties still occur to make a regular number of matches virtual skinners for the bookies.

Las Vegas oddsmakers are extremely good at handicapping the sides and most British firms will take a position close to the prevailing US price, known as the Vegas line, albeit a little to either side if they have a strong opinion or position. Some firms change their handicap as betting progresses in the lead-up to the game, while others hold their lines and change the odds on each team.

Over the course of the 2003 season, the US handicappers were so accurate that virtually 50 per cent of games saw the favourite cover the handicap (win by more points than they were penalised in the market) with the other 50 per cent of matches favouring those who backed the underdog (matches in which either the favourite won by fewer points than the handicap line or the underdog won the match outright).

It is all too easy to assume that the supposedly better team will win a game and be sucked into fancying too many

betting on american football

 Key starters matter

team news you can trust

Team news is important, even in a sport where each team has 45 active players on match day. Teams provide official injury reports to the league throughout the season, listing players as probable (75 per cent chance of starting), questionable (50 per cent), doubtful (25 per cent) or out. Coaches are not allowed to bend the truth with these assessments. How UK football punters would love such cast-iron team news.

These injury bulletins are available from a number of online sources. Try to acquaint yourself with the teams well enough to know when a key starter – the quarterback, running back or a starting cornerback for example, will not play and also look out for situations where a team has lost several players at one position.

Three or four injuries at the same time to offensive linemen, for example, will severely weaken a team's chances of running the ball well or protecting its quarterback.

Teams can deal with one or two injuries but beyond that they will be forced to field inexperienced youngsters. If you fancy an underdog strongly, don't shy away from backing them to win the match outright on what some firms call the money line.

favourites. Yes, the better team might win, but will they win by enough to cover the handicap? It is an obvious point, but one which is worth emphasising.

Always remember that teams are not playing to cover the handicap. In the NFL all that matters is winning and losing. The margin of victory is inconsequential. This can lead to the infuriating situation known to all NFL punters of a team which, for example, needs to win by seven points to cover the handicap line, holding a six-point lead and having the ball at their opponents' goal line with one minute to play, yet making no attempt to score what to the punter is the most important point of all and meekly allowing the clock to run down to zero.

To a coach it is simple. He needs no more points – running up the score to win by wide margins is in fact not the done thing – and to run more offensive plays would

american football

Crucial coaches

A coach and a general manager who know what they are doing are essential to success in the modern NFL era. All teams must operate within a strict salary cap which brings about tough decisions each off-season. That is why teams cannot stay at the top for long any more, as the 49ers, Cowboys and Packers did when building successful so-called dynasties in the past. Success means veteran players must be paid more, which in turn means teams must jettison some in the free agency market in order to stay within their financial limitations. Having a coach who can make silk purses out of players others deemed sow's ears, such as Patriots coach Bill Belichick, is a major help.

jeopardise his guaranteed victory by risking a fumble or interception if his team went for a touchdown or a blocked field-goal attempt was returned for a touchdown.

Always check how the teams match up against each other tactically. Ranking of teams' relative strengths at running and passing the ball and stopping those actions defensively are available and mismatches can occur. NFL coaches spend hours studying videotape of each others' games and will exploit it ruthlessly. If something works – for example putting their fastest receiver against a cornerback who simply can't cope with his pace – they will go at it again and again until the defensive team finds a solution.

If there is not much difference between one team's offensive rushing ranking and their rivals' defensive rushing rating, it should be competitive battle in that area.

If one is the best rushing team in the league, maybe due to the strength of their offensive line or the skill of their running back, and the other is ranked last at stopping the run, maybe due to defensive line injuries or bad tactics, for example, there is every reason to expect that team to move the ball easily.

TOTAL POINTS If the tightrope walk of handicap betting does not appeal to you, the second most popular form of American football wagering – the total points line – may well.

In the same way as the handicap, the Vegas gurus set their idea of the total number of points scored in each game and punters bet either over (more points than the nominated figure) or under (fewer points).

For successful totals bets, keep defences and weather at the forefront of your thinking.

Like football and rugby, pitch conditions and the prevailing temperature, precipitation and wind can have a dramatic effect on the number of points scored in a game.

Extreme conditions are the most obvious route to profit. In the infamous Snow Bowl AFC Championship final between Oakland and New England, the eventual total of 29 points (overtime is always included in total points and handicap bets) was about the most the two sides were ever going to produce in a virtual snowdrift, while Oakland's farcical 24-0 victory over Kansas City in a paddy field was another victory for those who noted the extreme forecast and played the under.

Forecasts for all US cities are widely available on the net and www.weather.com even has a dedicated page with links to the expected conditions for all the week's contests. Do not underestimate the impact high winds can have on a total either, as gusts can make long passes more difficult and also reduce the prospect of kicks being converted.

It's also handy to be aware which teams play indoors – don't put the farm on the under in snowswept Minneapolis while the Vikings are involved in a shootout in their cosy Metrodome home.

Defences, rather than offences tend to be the key factor in determining the points total and this is where punters can find an edge. That is to say good defensive players, organised by a shrewd coach, can stop anyone from scoring – witness the way Baltimore, Tampa Bay and New England have ground their way to Super Bowl success with dour safety-first offence and a stifling rearguard.

Similarly any team will find a way to score against a bad defensive team – receivers don't have to be that good to break free from a slow defensive back who can't cover well, and nor do running backs have to be that prolific to blast past linebackers who can't tackle.

The only word of warning when seeking out top defences in order to bet the under is be

betting on american football

 Handicap hints

learn how to tease the line

Three and seven are the magic numbers when looking at handicap lines. They are the number of points scored for a field goal and a converted touchdown and are also the margins by which many games are settled.

With this in mind, it is always worth visiting Bet365's website, where the firm allow you to choose your own handicap line on a game, with the price adjusted accordingly. But think of the difference you can make to your chances of collecting by teasing, as it is known, the line down from minus seven to minus 6.5.

This might force you to take odds of 4-5 or 8-11 rather than 10-11 but means you have a winner if the common scoreline of the favourite by seven comes in. Which price you take depends to a great extent on your personal attitude to risk and there is no real right or wrong answer.

aware that defences score points too, through interception returns and fumble recoveries.

OTHER MARKETS Bookmakers will price up a wide variety of player markets, which they may call props (short for propositions) such as a quarterback to throw more than 14.5 completed passes in a match, or a running back to gain more than 97.5 rushing yards, and spread firms will offer similar markets in their own style.

Plenty of information is available on player statistics at nfl.com and other sites but it is applying the basic player history to the game in question that can pay off. For example, it would be foolish to take the over on a rushing back's yardage gained without checking the success level the opposing defensive line has had in limiting similar players in recent games.

And don't forget that if you know something, the coaches in the game will know it too. What happened in the past does not govern what will happen in the game you are betting on.

The best example of this is the NFC Championship game of 2000, when many punters thought the conservative New York Giants offence would be outgunned by the pyrotechnic attack of the fancied Minnesota Vikings.

The Giants had other ideas though and came out with an explosive passing game they had never before demonstrated. This caught the Vikings on the hop and the Giants trounced them 41-0 (another example of a good defence beating a good offence).

First touchdown scorer generally offers bad value except for very rare occasions when market-makers have missed a likely tactical change or a piece of injury news. With so many runners, what might look an appealing price compared to a football first-scorer market is no such thing.

Bookies often price up highest scoring team markets from a selected band of six or eight clubs (spread firms offer similar indices) and these can be boiled down to a couple of potential bets using the steps described in the total points discussion.

INFORMATION SOURCES Basic information required for American football betting can be found on the league website nfl.com, where you'll find live play-by-play scores, player profiles and major news, plus links to all the individual team websites. Live internet match commentaries are available for a reasonable subscription.

The weekly magazine First Down caters well for UK fans of the sport and offers insights from weekly columnists and match previews.

British bettors with digital TV access are also well advised not only to watch the excellent coverage of both Sky Sports and five, but to subscribe to NASN, which screens the major NFL preview shows, a source of valuable tactical analysis and news.

american football

 Mythical matches

Spread bettors can tailor bets to their own tastes with Sporting Index, who offer a Create Your Own supremacy market, where punters can pit one team they really fancy against one they want to oppose in a mythical match.

Correct-score betting on matches is done in six-point bands (Dallas to win by 1-6 points, by 7-12 points etc) and can be a particularly useful option when your opinion on a handicap is marginal. For example, rather than agonise over whether to take Philadelphia -3.5 points or Seattle +3.5, instead take Philly by 1-6 points and collect if the result falls close to the handicap line either way. That said, waiting for a game on which you have a stronger opinion might be an even better course of action.

betting on american football

 The oddsmaker's view

shrewdies prosper on points

Paddy Power compiler Craig Mucklow says: Sharp punters are better off avoiding the handicap market, where many favourites are poor value.

Match handicaps are a marvellous market for bookmakers because of the parity in the NFL. I would only ever back underdogs I fancied on the market and always oppose teams who are favoured by 14 points or more – it is too much to ask and teams just don't need to win by that many.

Shrewder punters prosper on first-half handicaps and, more usually, total points. When the Vegas line moves because of weather news, for example, we just know our customers will all bet the same way. I would never have a bet on first touchdown scorer, it's just too easy for the bookmakers to clean up on it. For some reason punters often get the edge over us on player props, no matter how much work we put in.

When betting on the Super Bowl market, I would rule out all teams at 25-1 or shorter. They are just poor value in a league which changes rapidly and I would oppose all the previous year's divisional winners for the same reason.

But to really get inside the game, keeping tabs on the major US sports portals for up-to-date news, analysis and opinion is advised. Here are some of the best:

www.espn.com

www.cnnsi.com (Sports Illustrated)

www.cbs.sportsline.com

www.usatoday.com

For detailed betting statistics, sites such as www.covers.com provide details of teams' records against the spread and discuss matches from a betting perspective.

Other useful sites include www.pro-football-reference.com, which has details of all past match results, league tables and play-offs, while www.marasoft.com/newspapr.htm, an offshoot of a premium betting site, provides links to the local newspapers of all 32 NFL teams. Fans of in-depth statistical analysis and intellectual comments should look no further than www.footballoutsiders.com. ■

put a spoke in bookies' wheels

IT'S NOT ALL UPHILL

CYCLING IS A LONG WAY FROM being the most popular betting medium in the sporting world, but that is not to say it does not represent a decent window of opportunity for profitable punting.

By BRUCE MILLINGTON

You are not going to make a living as a professional cycling punter. There simply aren't enough races priced up for that to be considered remotely viable.

But therein lies its advantage. Cycling, like other fringe betting sports, is such an insignificant factor in the overall scheme of things that no bookmaker can afford to employ a dedicated cycling expert.

Thus, the punter need not feel he is gravely disadvantaged when he has a cycling wager just because he does not devote his entire life to following the sport. The person who is setting the odds does not either.

That said, it would be an error to underestimate the ability of the part-time cycling compilers. No bookmaker would release prices on anything unless they had reasonable faith in the person chalking up the odds.

But I have had numerous conversations with these people down the years to convince me that, shrewd though they are, they can be beaten where cycling is concerned.

As with all sports these days, it is harder

Good thing: but there are plenty of bets to be had besides Lance Armstrong

and harder to offer laughably wrong prices. Not only does the internet afford ample research and verification opportunities – www.cyclingnews.com is among the best sites – but Betfair provides an established market from which the compiler can always cross-check his prices.

Additionally, a number of European bookmakers are usually up and running with cycling markets – don't forget, the sport is far more popular on the continent – well before the UK compiler needs to release his prices.

This means that chaotic situations like those which used to exist before the Tour de France's team time trial stage are now increasingly rare, more's the pity. In 2001, the prices, both fixed-odds and spreads, for the team time trial were all over the place.

This was perfectly understandable. The team time trial is a rare and extremely specialised discipline. Some Tour de France teams practise them with supreme thoroughness, while others just go out there with a vague gameplan not to haemorrhage

betting on cycling

**Rare, but
profitable**

look out for emerging stars

It was not my biggest ever win but my each-way punt on Miguel Indurain at 16-1 in the 1991 Tour remains one of my very favourite bets of all time. I had noticed Indurain performing heroically to support his then Banesto team leader Pedro Delgado in the mountains the previous year and could not believe how effortlessly he tackled the highest and most savagely gruelling roads in Europe.

Coming into the 1991 race Delgado was still numero uno at Banesto but the right to be team leader carries no automatic guarantee once the race is in progress and I hoped a bold show from Indurain in one of the early mountain stages would enable him to quit his subservient role to Delgado and give him the green light to instead attempt to dethrone 1990 champion Greg Lemond.

Sure enough, he grasped the Tour de France by the scruff of the neck and did not let go until he dramatically cracked on a mountain pass five years later.

In 2004 the tactic of backing an emerging talent to usurp his established team leader and win a major stage race paid dividends again when 22-year-old Daniel Cunego came of age with an authoritative display to wrest leadership of the Saeco team from Gilberto Simoni and register a handsome win, again at 16-1, in the Tour of Italy.

It must be stressed, however, that breakthrough triumphs like Indurain and Cunego's are reasonably rare in the main three-week races, especially in the biggest betting event of them all, the Tour de France.

too much time. But when the priceboxes for the stage appeared in that morning's *Racing Post*, seemingly every arb-hunter in the world rushed to snap up all the value.

ONCE, odds-on with one firm, opened at 6-1 with another, while on the spreads the same team was quoted at 8-11 on one index while on another, with an identical scoring system, they were as high as 35-38, easily the most dramatic example of an arb I have seen.

IG Index, responsible for the 8-11 quote, came up with a novel way of ensuring the genuine cycling punters were accommodated at the standout prices while the arbers were rebuffed. Clients coming on looking to buy ONCE were refused if they pronounced it 'wunce' as in one time, but were allowed to trade to small stakes if they used the correct pronunciation of 'on-say'.

Punters have been able to bet on cycling since the late 1980s, when Coral were among the first firms to price up the Tour de France.

FOLLOW THE MEN IN FORM Since 1989 only six men have won what I consider to be the most awesome sporting event of them all. And since 1999, of course, the race has belonged to one man – the remarkable Lance Armstrong, whose recovery from cancer that required brain surgery to win a record six Tours is probably the most incredible story in the history of sport.

The Texan began his epic sequence by making pre-race odds of 8-1 look stupid with a brilliant display in the first long time trial and by the time he had left his rivals spread-eagled in his wake on the opening mountain test he was virtually unbackable, providing further evidence to one of my principal rules of cycling betting – namely that if a rider shows form early on in the mountains, he must be treated with the utmost respect for the rest of the race.

That might sound obvious, but it is amazing how many punters prefer to assume that because a rider has given his all to win a particular mountain stage, he will pay a price for his exertions on subsequent hard days.

It tends not to work like that. If a rider shines in the first mountain test he is likely to retain a high performance level at high altitude simply because he is in form, just as a rider who toils from the word go is almost certainly struggling with his condition (and, let's face it, in a sport as tough as this, you cannot blame a guy for having a hard time) and will do very well to suddenly turn it around and start performing to a standard his pre-race odds might suggest he is capable of.

TAKING IT STAGE-BY-STAGE But while betting on the outright Tour de France winner is, or rather has been in the Lance Armstrong era, something of a fait accompli, there is still the daily business of unearthing the stage winner to concentrate on (stage betting on the tours of Spain and Italy is barely worth bothering about, with only negligible sums traded on Betfair). Tour de France stages fall into four main types.

THE FLAT STAGE These form the bulk of the early schedule of the race, which invariably starts in the north of the country or one of its neighbouring states and wends its way either clockwise or anti-clockwise south to the Alps and Pyrenees, where the key battles are played out before the traditional finish in the centre of Paris.

Flat stages usually mean a bunch finish, in which a small number of specialist sprinters contest the first prize. These men are protected in the early stages by their team-mates and then led through in the closing kilometres in the hope that their powerful late surge can bring them and their team glory.

You may think it strange that of a field of some 190 riders, the same half-dozen names always dominate the leaderboard when there is a sprint finish, but it is virtually impossible for a non-sprinter to get the better of the specialist fast men.

Picking the winner is still not easy, however, even when it becomes obvious that the finish will develop into a mass scramble for the line. Traffic problems and crashes are an ever-present hazard, and the timing of the late burst must be perfect to prevent a rival coming off one's wheel and getting up on the line. The threat to sprinters winning flat stages comes in the form of the breakaway. This tactic provides many of the field with their only chance of a stage victory. Early on, a group of riders will

betting on cycling

 Team tactics

The uninitiated will ask what a team can do to assist its leader, apart from to fetch and carry food, drink and spare parts.

The whole point is that drafting, the practice of riding directly behind the wheel of another rider, can help conserve energy by 30 per cent, as the team leader pedals through reduced air resistance caused by the effect of having another rider directly in front of you.

Thus, Lance Armstrong's team will comprise at least three capable climbers so that when it comes to the crucial mountain sections of the race he can ride in a team-mate's slipstream in the flat sections between the climbs, enabling him to conserve energy for the final ascent.

He will also have at least one high-quality ascender in his team who can set a furious pace at the front, to minimise the risks of other riders attacking Armstrong and to burn off the lesser climbers who remain in the leading group.

normally break clear of the pack, often with its consent. The group will work together even if they are from rival teams, taking turns at the front and conserving energy by riding in the slipstream of the others the rest of the time in a bid to put as much distance as possible between them and the peloton.

The sprinters' teams then come under pressure to lead the main field in pursuit of the break. Their sponsors do not take kindly to the limelight being taken by brave have-a-go heroes. Often the breakaway merchants will eventually be hunted down, but there are times when they manage to stay away, much to the bookmakers' delight.

A successful break will usually throw up an unheralded, and unbacked, winner. Punters who bet on flat stages in-running should be aware that if the peloton works together to chase down a break, it can usually pull back a minute every ten kilometres.

The best guide to whether the break will stay away comes in the form of a field price quoted by IG Index when they bet in-running on flat stages. Each of the main sprinters will be quoted on an index which awards 50 points to the stage winner, 30 to the runner-up, 20 to the third rider home and ten to the man who finishes fourth, with the rest lumped together as the field. If the field looks like being swallowed up, the price will fall and vice versa.

THE INTERMEDIATE STAGE These occur mostly in the rolling terrain between the Alps and the Pyrenees and feature ascents that are tough but far shorter than the brutal climbs of the high mountains.

In terms of profile, they are similar to the one-day spring classics that traditionally favour high-quality Belgian, Dutch and Italian cyclists who have neither the speed to contest the sprinters nor the pure climbing ability to play a major part in affecting the overall classification by dominating in the mountains.

These are not the best betting events because so many different riders can feasibly win, although they can offer reasonable in-running opportunities once you get the chance to assess which of a breakaway group has the form and pedigree to prevail.

You can also use internet sites like letour.fr and cyclingnews.com to check the credentials of the breakaway group to see which riders have previous form when it comes to winning stages of this nature.

MOUNTAIN STAGES Wonderfully stirring to watch – I can willingly spend seven hours glued to Eurosport's coverage – and the stages that usually decide who will win the yellow jersey. Time-trialling is almost as crucial, but if you cannot climb, you cannot win the Tour, whereas the late Marco Pantani showed it is possible to be champion without being top-class against the watch.

Most mountain stages comprise at least three major climbs, sometimes as many as seven, and it is not uncommon for a big-priced rider to go well clear early on. These are usually wiry men who can have the odd big day in the mountains but lack the quality to challenge for overall honours and are therefore left to go about their business.

Very occasionally, they will stay out in front if the race principals play too much of a cat-and-mouse game with each other before the final climb, but more often than not their early prominence is inspired by an attempt to get TV exposure and some king of the mountains points.

TIME TRIALS You can split these into four kinds. The prologue, a short test of less than eight kilometres, always starts the Tour and is a difficult betting puzzle because, even though relatively few riders can win, the

betting on cycling

 Stage management

Backing a rider who has already shown strength in the mountains has already been pinpointed as a wise move, but you must also bear in mind that for many riders, a stage victory in the mountains is of secondary importance to ensuring the best possible place on the overall standings.

That was the case when Armstrong and Pantani went pedal-to-pedal up Mont Ventoux in the 2000 Tour. Armstrong was interested solely in preventing his adversary eating into his race lead and, having refused to buckle as Pantani desperately tried to shrug him off, he let the gutsy Italian cross the line in front.

Pantani was unhappy at being given the victory and Armstrong's sportsmanship also went down badly with those who had backed him for the stage.

margin of success is measured in seconds so the odd misjudged turn can be crucial.

The longer, flat time trials are seldom won by anyone other than a market leader, most of whom will be the favourites for outright victory or specialists like Britain's David Millar who you seldom hear about for the rest of the race as this is all they are good at.

Mountain time trials are equally uncompetitive, with fewer than five men likely to triumph. And then we come to the team time trial, an absurd concept as it handicaps certain riders' bid for overall glory just because they belong to a relatively weak outfit that simply cannot keep up with those of the other star names.

An early start is necessary for punters on team time trial day as there is usually plenty of value around, for reasons explained at the start of this chapter.

WORTH REMEMBERING The best Tour de France pointers are not the Tours of Italy or Spain, but previous Tours de France and the Dauphine Libere, a stage race which many of the main Tour contenders ride in.

When spread firms operate limited-runner indices for intermediate stages that comprise the likeliest breakaway merchants, check out where these guys usually finish in stages when the field crosses the line en masse.

Some will happily end up at the back of the bunch while others push for the best possible placing. In the 2004 Tour, it paid to buy one such rider, Laurent Brochard, in the hope that there would not be a breakaway and he would win the index as none of his rivals on the lists were remotely bothered whether they were 15th or 150th.

Although certain mountain stages begin as early as 9am UK time, bookmakers will generally carry on betting until the riders come to the first big climb of the day.

parallel worlds of darts

HITTING THE BULL

THE GOLDEN AGE OF DARTS WAS IN the late 1970s and early 1980s when if you peered through the smoke haze on stage you could just about discern giant figures in ill-fitting shirts throwing slivers of tungsten at a wall 7ft 9-and-a-quarter inches away.

By STEVE DAVIES

From a betting perspective, however, the golden age is unfolding right now thanks to Sky TV's coverage of a sport that had fallen into decline. Relics of the past like John Lowe and Cliff Lazarenko are still on the circuit along with a new breed of star names, while five-time Embassy world champion Eric Bristow is a mainstay of a Sky commentary and analysis team that majors on betting.

Bristow is a punter so a main task in his darting afterlife has been to offer match-betting advice during the handful of tournaments that Sky broadcast so impressively, and that's largely because the Professional Darts Corporation's three flagship events that Sky cover are sponsored by bookmakers.

In mid-summer there's the Stan James World Matchplay from Blackpool, then the Paddy Power Grand Prix in Dublin followed by the blue riband competition in the PDC calendar, the Ladbrokes.com World Championship from the Circus Tavern in Purfleet.

Power play: Phil Taylor has dominated the PDC for more than a decade

The patronage of Sky and the bookmakers has been crucial to a sport that was in danger of retreating back into the pubs and clubs in the early 1990s, with new money and new players ready to entice a new generation of youngsters on to the oche.

Throw in the fact that the BBC also cover the rival British Darts Organisation's two key tournaments – the Lakeside (formerly Embassy) World Championship and the Winmau World Masters – and darts punters have never had it so good.

THE TOURNAMENTS TV executives and the game's governing bodies must be congratulated on ensuring every competition is different.

Partisan punters can never therefore complain about lack of opportunity for a bet and the following is a rundown of the major tournaments and their differing formats.

Ladbrokes.com World Championship The PDC's New Year spectacular where the world's top 32, plus eight wild cards and eight qualifiers, do battle over sets, culminating in a best-of-13 set final.

Lakeside World Darts Championship The BDO's flagship, once known as the Embassy and played at the widely acknowledged 'home of darts', the Lakeside Country Club in Frimley Green, Surrey. Also contested over sets between the BDO's top 25 players plus qualifiers.

Budweiser UK Open Back to the PDC and their FA Cup of darts. Seedings are decided by performances in qualifiers and not the world rankings with 128 players competing in legs-only straight knockout.

Las Vegas Desert Classic To Nevada where a series of eliminators earn 16 play-off winners and four North American qualifiers the right to join the top 12 in a knockout competition over sets.

Stan James World Matchplay High summer in Blackpool and the PDC's top 28, plus four qualifiers, toe the oche in a legs-only shootout.

Paddy Power Grand Prix Dublin in the autumn for the PDC's top players, plus qualifiers from Britain and Ireland, to compete for the only title in which legs are double-in, double-out.

Winmau World Masters A colossal event featuring more than 150 players from all over the world, separated into 16 groups with one of the BDO's seeds per section. Knockout from the last 16 onwards.

The different formats may mean a slight tweak to the darts punter's shortlist or his staking plan, though by and large it's the same figures who attract the money and the only discernible adjustment the layers make depending on how each tournament is devised is to ease Phil Taylor in what are perceived to be slightly more random, short-format events.

BETTING WITHOUT PHIL TAYLOR

EVERY silver lining has a cloud attached and that definitely applies with Taylor.

betting on darts

 **BDO v
PDC**

when two tribes go to war

FOR the unintiated, the sport of darts is run by two distinct ruling bodies and it has a significant bearing on how and when you bet.

The PDC was born out of the World Darts Council, which was a body that initially looked after the interests of 16 top players, among them Lowe, Bristow, Dennis Priestley and Phil Taylor, who broke away from the British Darts Organisation in January 1992.

Their grievance was that the BDO wasn't aggressive enough in marketing the sport at the highest level while the BDO countered that it had obligations to hundreds of thousands of players all around the world at grass-roots level.

The split was acrimonious and there were rights and wrongs on both sides, but the upshot is two separate governing bodies.

Plenty of players, lured by the exposure Sky can offer, have since crossed the divide including John Part, who like Taylor and Priestley is now a world champion on both sides, Steve Beaton, Ritchie Burnett, Ronnie Baxter, Kevin Painter and many more.

You'd think it would weaken the BDO's standing but there is a reservoir of talent ready to come out of the Super Leagues and county circuit to take their places. They may get chalked up at big prices in the few events that the BDO get screened on television, but these boys are no mugs as a glance at the county averages will highlight.

From a betting standpoint, it means that for more than a decade the BDO have run highly competitive events open to all, devoid of many star names but jam-packed with value - and over the same period the PDC has been dominated by one Phil Taylor.

While Sky and the game's backers are to be applauded for the way they have dragged the game into modern times, his emergence has ruined it for many small punters.

'The Power' is the best darts thrower there has ever been. Or ever will be. It's as simple as that. Even in a game as competitive as this with tens of thousands of participants and a stack of world-class names, Taylor has always been in a class of his own.

Since he won his first Embassy title in 1990, slaughtering his mentor Bristow 6-1, he has dominated like no other sportsman or woman has dominated his or her own field.

He has claimed 11 world titles – including

eight in a row between 1995 and 2002 – and has mopped up Matchplays and Grands Prix as if they were bread-and-butter exhibitions down at the Dog and Duck.

He doesn't play much in lesser-ranking events but when he does he invariably wins them, and for many years now The Power has habitually gone off at odds-on – he actually took to the stage at the 2002 Las Vegas Desert Classic at no bigger than 2-7.

Big-hitters filled their boots but Taylor had taken the fun out of outright betting for the small-timers who would have otherwise fancied a bet on a tournament he was likely to boss at skinny odds.

Finding ways to bet without or oppose Taylor in PDC competition had therefore become a central strategy for those with limited funds who wanted to take a view on the outright market. Obviously with Taylor taking so much out of the book there were decent prices to be had further down the field, so enabling punters to consider an each-way bet on a player from the other half of the draw.

Betting on who wins each quarter is another market which one or two firms have started pricing up, which means punters can either latch on to players who are masters at reaching the semi-finals of tournaments but seem to crumble near the winning post, or they can identify one of the rising stars that the game throws up from time to time.

And, of course, there is handicap betting, especially in legs-only heats, meaning even games in which Taylor has gone off a 1-16 shoo-in can be traded on.

Now there are signs that Taylor's crown is slipping – Part has started scalping him regularly while Painter and Wayne Mardle represent a newer breed of younger recruit from the BDO who are far less daunted by taking on the game's legendary superheroes and are freely to be found talking up their own

betting on darts

 Edge it on the spreads

Spread betting centres around match supremacy. All the firms use the same rules – ten points per match win, three points per leg or set won by – and sellers normally trip over themselves to bin the favourites in the early stages of short-format events like the UK Open, where the early rounds are chaotic with so many arrowsmiths involved, conditions that could favour the unheralded club players.

The spread firms devote most of their efforts to just a handful of competitions where their customers can trade on markets like number of maximums, maximum supremacy, checkout ton-ups and each player's high checkout as well as supremacy. Bear in mind with spreads, as with all forms of darts betting, that no bookmaker has the resources to employ a full-time arrers expert so the clued-up punter is entitled to feel he has an edge.

betting on darts

 Taylor's (almost) perfect ten

Between 1999 and 2002 Phil Taylor produced his most dazzling run of success with ten wins in the 11 premier category events Sky televised at the time.

Punters who backed 'The Power' to win each of those competitions would have returned a profit of £44.06 to a £10 stake. Such a spell of dominance will surely never be repeated again.

1999 Grand Prix
WON (10-11)
2000 World Championship
WON (4-6)
2000 World Matchplay
WON (Evens)
2000 Grand Prix
WON (1-2)
2001 World Championship
WON (4-9)
2001 World Matchplay
WON (8-15)
2001 Grand Prix
LOST R1 (1-3)
2002 World Championship
WON (2-5)
2002 Las Vegas Desert Classic
WON (2-7)
2002 World Matchplay
WON (1-3)
2002 Grand Prix
WON (1-3)

games. It has meant Sky's events are slightly more open though the bookies are naturally reluctant to lay Taylor at big prices and rack up heavy liabilities.

THE EMBASSY This was the championship that superseded the News of the World as the big one in darts.

Not any more. Since the split the Embassy has struggled to capture the imagination with fewer and fewer household names taking to the stage in Frimley Green. Now it hasn't even got Embassy after the Government changed the rules on tobacco sponsorship.

But what the Lakeside World Professional Darts Championship does have is betting opportunities galore and with Taylor so dominant across the rubicon, this is the tournament where darts shrewdies would hope to make big profits.

Since Taylor won his second Embassy title in 1992, there have been ten different winners of the crown ranging from 4-1 favourite Ray Barneveld to John Walton (50-1), John Part (66-1) and Tony David (66-1). Part, Les Wallace and Andy Fordham took glory despite not being seeded.

David was a classic example of a player who the bookies simply couldn't evaluate. The Australian arrived with little more than decent form but while he was in England awaiting the start of the Embassy he threw superb darts at league level – performances that went unseen by the odds-setters.

Those with an ear to the ground got on and got rich, those who didn't were left to wait for another chance.

And given that of the 32 players who take to the Lakeside stage probably about three-quarters of them could win it – in stark contrast to PDC events – no wonder this is the tournament that the value-seeking darts punter cannot wait for.

POINTERS Darts isn't a sport where trends or pointers are obviously helpful for punters. Apart, of course, from the obvious trend that Taylor usually wins everything he enters.

Talent and bottle are the two ingredients that separate the best from the rest, while Taylor's obsessiveness and work ethic is what has given him that little bit more.

But there are one or two rules, some set in stone, others more contentious, that punters might like to think about before a tournament.

Stage v floor The majority of the season is spent playing Open competitions, which carry fewer ranking points, less prize money and have monstrous fields. Also, these events are played on the 'floor', ie not on a stage, or at least not until the latter stages. Without the pressure of TV cameras, burning stage lights, dry ice and a live audience of many hundreds, decent league players can prosper. But that doesn't necessarily mean they will do well come the big events.

Backing outsiders over short distances The Grand Prix is the classic tournament where upsets tend to happen early over a shorter format. In 2001 three of the then top four in the world – Taylor, Peter Manley and Ronnie Baxter – were toppled in rapid-fire three-set matches. The better players prefer longer matches and there are upsets to be had in early skirmishes over a short course.

Natural actions When Marko Pusa was blitzing his way through the 2001 Embassy field, fellow pro Wayne Mardle predicted an almighty fall, suggesting the Finn's manufactured action wouldn't hold up under pressure. Come quarter-final night against John Walton, Pusa was on first, lost a couple of legs and completely lost his rhythm. He was thrashed 5-0.

Ill health Seedings and protected ranking points mean some players are guaranteed

betting on darts

Home advantage

Farnworth lad Paul Williams reached the semi-finals of the highly-competitive UK Open in Bolton in 2003 and reckoned playing in front of a partisan local crowd made a big difference. Colin Monk, a perennial campaigner at the Lakeside, just a few miles up the road from home town Basingstoke, is equally convinced that those extra friendly decibels improve his prospects. Ray Barneveld is almost unbeatable in Holland where his fanbase is colossal. Those examples are rare, however, and let's face it, one board is much like any other.

places in competitions even when they aren't feeling quite right. Hence, Cliff Lazarenko met Richie Burnett in round one of the World Matchplay in 2003 and would normally have fancied his chances against the out-of-sorts Welshman. Lazarenko having just undergone shoulder surgery, however, Burnett was a shoo-in. The bookies won't always be privy to that sort of information in a sport that gets virtually no national newspaper coverage, so the informed punter can get an edge.

TYPES OF BET Unrestricted singles have changed the face of football betting, but arrers fans like nothing more than an acca to keep them interested during a session. The big tournaments can have anything from three to eight matches billed for any one session, numbers that lend themselves to multiple bets.

A few firms have added set betting to their portfolios – the firms represented at darts venues do it as a matter of routine though their margins aren't always the best – and those same companies tend to provide other opportunites such as over-under betting on high checkout, winning checkout, total maximums and so on.

Another popular bet is quarter betting, especially in events run by the PDC which are so dominated by Taylor and, to a lesser extent, John Part. Those two are rarely out of the last four so rather than feel compelled to oppose the two tungsten titans, punters can concentrate on the identity of the remaining two semi-finalists.

More and more fixed-odds firms also offer specials and novelty markets, especially bookmakers in tournaments that they sponsor.

Specials being specials, the value is rarely great, but if you want to bet on the possibility of a nine-dart finish, nationality of the winner, best-placed qualifier and more, the opportunities do arise.

betting on rally is growing

CARS FOR COURSES

THE WORLD RALLY CHAMPIONSHIP By ADAM SCRIVEN
began in 1973, and was designed to provide
the ultimate test of drivers, cars and
mechanics. Over the course of a season, which
currently runs from January to November
and comprises 16 events, the teams will
compete on asphalt, gravel, mud, snow and
ice; on mountain roads, forest tracks and public
highways. The winner of each event, which
typically spans three days, will spend between
four and five hours driving competitively, but
much more than that travelling between
the stages, which must also be done in the
competition car. And at the end of a gruelling
season, the teams have only eight weeks to
recover before it all starts again.

Initially, it was never a betting sport, but in
recent years a growing number of bookmakers
have got involved, and the WRC is now a
regular item on the sports betting menu.

TYPES OF EVENT Although each of the 16
events that comprise the World Rally
Championship is unique and takes place in a
different country, they can be grouped into
three main categories – fast gravel, slow gravel
and asphalt. To be fast on each of the event
types demands very different requirements
of driver and vehicle, and for this reason course

Flying high: the WRC is now a regular on the sports betting schedule

specialists often crop up who win a particular event year-in, year-out, while in another type of event they will not figure.

The majority of the season's rallies fall into the fast gravel category, and are generally run through forest areas. The gravel is often quite smooth, and there is a considerable disadvantage to running first on the road as the earlier cars on the stage tend to sweep the slippery top-surface gravel away to leave a grippier surface for the later cars. From a betting point of view, attrition is a lesser concern in these rallies, so the form is more likely to work out reliably.

Fast gravel rallies: Mexico, New Zealand, Finland, Japan, Wales, Sardinia, Australia. In 2003 the average winner's SP in fast gravel events was 2-1.

Slow gravel events are prevalent in Mediterranean countries such as Cyprus and Greece, and take place primarily on twisty mountain tracks. The surface on these kind of rallies is usually much rougher than in the forests, and loose rocks often prove hazardous, making freak results more common.

Slow gravel rallies: Cyprus, Greece, Turkey. In 2003 the average winner's SP in slow gravel events was 16-1.

Asphalt rallies take place mostly on public roads, and require a totally different driving style to gravel rallies. Whether on fast, straight roads such as in Spain, or in the mountains which await the crews in Corsica, the same drivers tend to come to the fore. While these events are not traditionally hard on drivers or machinery, the weather and choice of tyres are factors which can strongly affect the outcome of these rallies.

Asphalt rallies: Germany, Corsica, Spain. In 2003 the average winner's SP in asphalt events was 10-1.

DRIVERS AND TEAMS
Drivers come and go with the passing of time, but they have fairly long careers so the following guide to the men behind the wheel, compiled in July 2004, should still be pertinent for a number of years to come.

The very different nature of the individual rallies means that certain drivers adapt much better to some than others, and course-specialists frequently emerge. Here is a brief summary of the leading current drivers, and their attributes:

Marcus Gronholm Twice World Champion despite never having won on asphalt. Very fast but prone to errors, and excels in fast gravel events and in Sweden.

Sebastien Loeb Youngster who was very much an asphalt specialist when he first arrived on the stage. He has developed into a real all-rounder but like most French drivers remains very tough to beat on the smooth and finished first on the road in the Monte Carlo Rallies from 2002-04.

Petter Solberg World Champion but with only

---

betting on rally

 Snow fun in Sweden

The events in Monte Carlo and Sweden do not really fall into any category, the former seeing the drivers faced with a number of different types of surfaces throughout its length, and the Scandinavian event traditionally being run entirely on a thick covering of snow.

These events often produce unusual results which do not stand up as formguides for the rest of the season. As of 2004, no eventual winner of the championship since Tommi Makinen in 1999 was on the podium in Monte Carlo, while until 2004 no non-Scandinavian driver had ever taken victory in Sweden.

one asphalt victory under his belt. Excels in all gravel events.

Markko Martin A champion of the future, the Estonian came of age in 2003 by winning the gruelling Acropolis Rally and later outbattling Marcus Gronholm in an epic in Finland. He is consistent, and best on gravel.

Carlos Sainz Veteran Spaniard, twice world champion in the early-1990s. Team-mate of Sebastien Loeb, he can be relied upon to pick up a couple of podiums and make his experience count in the slower gravel events.

BETTING ON THE CHAMPIONSHIP The drivers' championship is traditionally a fiercely competitive affair, and as such provides some good betting opportunities. With little to choose between the performance of the cars of the main contenders, and with such a short gap between the end of one season and the beginning of another, the previous season's form can be taken quite literally when planning an ante-post bet. If this is your cup of tea, look for a driver with proven ability who underperformed in the previous season for some legitimate reason.

Maybe he was spending the year settling into a new team. Perhaps mechanical problems or accidents early in the season cost him his championship chance, but he finished the year strongly.

Certainly there is little point backing the ante-post favourite, as due to the schedule of the season – as we mentioned before it starts with two one-off events which traditionally bear little relevance to the rest of the year – it is highly likely that a better price will be on offer later on.

Throughout the year, the drivers market will fluctuate greatly, and canny punters can build up a portfolio which should guarantee a profit come the end of the year. There are a few things to watch for if this is your aim.

Teams don't generally start the season with the latest development of their car – rather they will use the one they finished the previous season with.

Unfortunately, exchange punters have not really taken to rally betting yet, but if and when they do this is just this sort of thing that will make it popular with traders.

FINDING THE VALUE The bookmakers tend to price up rallies on the strength of past results. Nothing unusual about that you may think, but in this sport the final result rarely tells anything like the whole story of the event.

Quite often the best formguide to come out of a rally is the number of stage wins picked up by each driver, but you should also take into account such factors as the order in which the drivers ran on the road, any non-terminal mechanical problems, and time penalties picked up (a far from infrequent occurrence).

The winner of the event is there for all to see, but the point of the above is to pinpoint drivers who could have won under other circumstances, or at least whose performances were much better than the final result would suggest.

Such information is readily available from a quick study of www.rally-live.com or www.wrc.com or by watching the one-hour show on ITV on the Sunday of each rally.

Make a note of an eye-catching performance and try to work out when it can be used to your advantage as a punter. Because of the nature of the season, it may be necessary to wait a while before the information in your armoury becomes useful. Pointers gathered from a rally will only be relevant in a similar event and may not work out in the following rally on the calendar.

For example, on the 2004 schedule the New Zealand Rally is followed by Cyprus, Greece, Turkey and then Argentina. New Zealand

betting on rally

 Cars key to success

When a new car is introduced, it can greatly boost its driver's championship hopes, and reduce his odds. In 2003, the new Ford Focus proved very quick when it first arrived on the scene, but reliability problems prevented it from being a winner straight away.

Once the technical niggles were fixed, the team's lead driver Markko Martin scored two wins in four rallies, the first of his career, and put himself right in the championship picture (although he would ultimately end the season disappointingly).

In 2004, Petter Solberg was unlucky not to make amends for a poor start to the season by winning with the debut appearance of his new Subaru, but the layers did not react and he was still available at 11-2 to retain his world title. Next time up the Norwegian did the business, and it took a run of three non-finishes from July onwards before he approached that price again.

is a fast, flowing gravel rally, and form pointers gleaned from there are unlikely to be of use in the following three low-speed, twisty road events run on a very rough surface. Our advantage is that when the circus arrives at Argentina, most layers' prices will probably be heavily influenced by the results in the three previous events, while in reality the New Zealand form is likely to prove more relevant.

This sort of thing is also responsible for the wide difference in opinion observed between the different bookmakers, and you will quickly learn which layers are more prone to make an oversight and offer inflated, value prices.

Similarly, towards the end of the season, the fast gravel event in Sardinia is followed by a pair of asphalt rallies where the Italian form will be of little use, but punters could find it worth consulting for the season-ending Australian Rally.

TYPES OF BET Unfortunately, the only bets readily available on the WRC are win and each-way, both on the title race and on the individual rallies. Some bookies are beginning to offer match bets between individual drivers, but there is rarely value to be found here and with the minefield of hazards facing the combatants, these can be something of a lottery.

A sensible approach to the individual rallies is to back one of the leading contenders, whose prices usually range up to about 6-1, and to invest each-way in a podium candidate at around 14-1 or 16-1 to cover your stake if he makes the podium. The advantage of this approach is that if your win bet makes an early exit, his demise should at least boost the each-way option's chances of reaching the top three.

Spread firms offer indices on all rallies and also drivers' points spreads at the start of the season.

tv helping speedway to star

BET WITH THE ELITE

BOOKMAKERS ARE TAKING MORE and more interest in the world of speedway, as can be seen by the fact that the 2004 Elite League was sponsored by Skybet. With television coverage on the increase, solely down to Sky – and how many sports can we say that about? – there is a variety of markets, such as outright score, handicap score, heat winner and forecast, for the discerning punter to get involved in, particularly when matches are televised.

However, it is not all good news for speedway punters as the days of the Stan James longlist, when all Elite League matches for a week would be priced up several days before, are long gone. To be fair, you cannot really blame the odds-compilers for their caution. This is a sport where team news is all-important, and where competitors are only 60 seconds away from serious injury.

With most top riders plying their trade in Poland on Sundays and Sweden on Tuesdays as well as in this country – notwithstanding the grand prix series – last-minute team changes are part and parcel of the sport. Consequently, most bookmakers tend to price up Elite League matches – even the televised ones – only on the day of the meeting.

The use of squad systems in the Elite

By ANDY SMITH

Tricky business: betting on speedway means keeping well up to date

League this season has not helped either. The choice of reserves can often make the difference between success and failure and most teams in 2004 have used several different rider combinations in the two berths, depending mainly on availability and sometimes suitability to a track.

What can we bet on then? Well, at the start of the season most of the major firms will price up the Elite League and the outright grand prix champion, and when the individual grands prix come along – a nine-round series in 2004 – they will furnish prices for them.

DOMESTIC ACTION Picking the Elite League winner in March is never easy and with the use of a play-off system designed to keep as many teams as possible in the hunt for the title, you can pick a team which finishes top of the league at the end of the season but is not crowned champions, due to the play-offs. Another thing to bear in mind is that it is difficult to gauge the effects of the inevitable rule changes that may be made to the sport during the close season.

Poole cleaned up in 2003 primarily because they had both Tony Rickardsson and Leigh Adams in the same side, thereby making them practically unbeatable in the decisive late heats. However, a grading system was introduced the following season, which effectively meant only one top rider was available for each side.

It is difficult to make hard and fast statements as to what you should be looking for when making your investment on a side for the League as the rules may alter again next year.

In 2004, I selected Poole and Wolverhampton on the basis that I thought both would be hard to beat at home, and could provide enough firepower on their travels to pick up vital bonus points. I also liked the look of Wolverhampton's reserve options.

Both sides went on to enjoy considerable success. However, when those selections were made Tony Rickardsson was one of the main reasons for tipping Poole, and he quit the club in May, while Wolverhampton's latest star reserve Freddie Lindgren was not even in their side.

THE GRAND PRIX SEASON Luck also plays a significant part in the determining of the grand prix champion, even though you would think it would even itself out over a long series. I cannot remember how many times I have mentioned Jason Crump and black cats in the same sentence over the past few years in grand prix copy, but for him not to have won the title thus far is a travesty.

With gate positions being massively influential on most tracks, the lottery of backing short-priced runners is there for all to see as the draws for the semi-finals and finals are done randomly. A rider could have ridden brilliantly but then get drawn in gate three, from which no winner has come from all night. He bows out while the guy

betting on speedway

 Keeping in touch

it's easy to stay informed

Speedway is well served by websites. All the Elite League clubs have their own sites, official and unofficial, while speedwayworld.tv is excellent for checking out what's been happening in Poland and Sweden, as well as in the UK. Most of the top riders have their own sites while *Speedway Star*, a weekly magazine, gives full match reports on all the various leagues as well as an array of statistics and quotes which I find invaluable.

Speedwaybet.com is a tote system where you can bet on forecasts and tricasts on selected Elite League and Premier League matches as well as the grands prix. However, bear in mind that the pools do not tend to be particularly large so it is best to keep your bets small. Betfair also have plenty of speedway markets available, but the amount of money traded on them is not large.

Finally, some tracks have a bookmaker in attendance for meetings. Occasionally, they will make a rick but my experience is that they bet to ridiculous percentages so those occasions are few and far between and you are probably better off keeping your money in your pocket.

he has beaten three times that night spawns the inside gate in both semi-final and final and emerges as the winner. Is it fair? Does luck even itself out?

Someone once told me it doesn't matter whether you are a good punter or a bad punter, what's important is that you are a lucky punter. I think it is probably the same if you are a grand prix speedway rider.

However, before you decide never to have another speedway grand prix bet again, here are a few things I look for. Some riders really struggle on one-off tracks – Tomasz Gollob springs to mind. Others are practically unbeatable around a particular circuit – Gollob at Bydgoscz, for instance. How has a rider gone at this track in the past? How does he go on similar tracks? Is he in form? Is it a track which is hard to win on if you are not seeded through to the latter stages? Is the rider fully fit? Is it the wrong price? These are some of the thought processes I use. ■

bowls ain't bowls without a bet

NUB OF
THE GREEN

THE LINK BETWEEN THE SPORT

By RON WYLLIE

of bowls and betting may not quite date right back to when Sir Francis Drake ignored the advancing Spanish Armada to finish his game on Plymouth Hoe, but it is certainly centuries old.

History does not record whether Drake had a flutter, but further north from the Devon coast, in what is regarded as the heartlands of crown green bowling in Lancashire and Yorkshire, a match has long not been considered a match without a bet.

However, where the flat green code is concerned betting has also proved popular, particularly in traditional strongholds such as Scotland, where in the former mining communities bowls is next only to horse and dog racing when it comes to punting.

THE REVOLUTION

While this interest is hardly a new innovation, it is highly significant that in the early years of the 21st century a revolution in bowls betting has taken place, especially in relation to the major televised competitions which attract most attention from the bookmakers and general public.

In 1997, the year 'new' Labour came to power, bowls saw its own 'new' order take over when the World Bowls Tour assumed control

betting on bowls

Super bowls deceptively popular

Bowls might not attract the media attention that other sports do, a fact which is a bone of contention with its most enthusiastic advocates, but it remains one of the most popular participatory activities in the UK – allegedly second only to angling in its appeal. Ironically, at a time when TV coverage is being reduced, it attracts viewing figures among the highest recorded for any sport on the BBC – much greater than many higher-profile activities such as rugby and athletics which at certain times of the year enjoy almost blanket coverage.

of the key events in the indoor calendar, which attract the most betting attention. One of their early initiatives was to reduce the length of matches from the best of five sets to the best of three sets with the third set merely a tiebreaker, which lasted just three ends.

Over the longer haul favourites usually held sway. However, since the change of format radical differences in results have been noted with lesser players able to win a set, particularly earlier in a game, which means they can then take their chance in what is virtually a sudden death shootout.

There is little doubt that backing outsiders, though not long-priced ones, has proved more profitable over the past five years and this should continue to be the case with television companies, who are known to have insisted on shorter games for viewing purposes, certain to stick to their guns in the immediate, and probably long-term, future.

Followers of the *Racing Post*'s selections since 2001 will testify to the good sense of investing in outsiders, especially if the price is between evens and 2-1, and those who have done just that have shown a small but still significant profit by following this advice.

TOURNAMENT MARKETS Ante-post betting has long been a feature of the sport, though selecting winners at such an early stage of any bowls event is extremely difficult. Arguably the field for a major competition such as the World Indoor Championship or the BUPA Open is similar to a sprint handicap in horse racing but, of course, without the handicap. That makes the draw vitally important since you have a field of 32 or 48 challengers, almost all of whom are capable of defeating each other on their day and normally do just that on a fairly regular basis.

Therefore it pays to look closely not just at the formlines but also at who certain players will encounter at what stage of the championships and try to pinpoint those whom the draw favours. Ante-post favourites are rarely priced at less than 4-1 and it hardly ever pays to side with contenders as short as that in a sport where winners are invariably on offer at much longer odds.

The best advice that can be given at the ante-post stage is to hedge your bets and merely enjoy a modest flutter unless the draw suggests that a particular individual looks a banker for an extended run. It is also important to remember that each-way betting usually relates to the first two in any competition rather than the first four. Most bookmakers offer half the odds to reach the final, which may be rewarding if it comes up but is quite a difficult feat to accomplish.

LANDING A TOUCH Over the years there have been tales of major gambles succeeding, especially when little-known outsiders who have caught the eye of bowls-watchers are concerned. More than one layer has had his or her fingers burnt by offering generous odds against someone who has shown form quietly but effectively away from the spotlight of major events.

Almost all bowls betting relates to individuals and televised championships since team games are not as attractive a proposition to the bowls punter. This is because such is the dominance of the major players like England and Scotland at international level that prices offered at this level would not tempt most of those who enjoy a bet on the sport.

If anything betting has proved, certainly at the highest level, that bowls is an honest sporting activity as borne out by events at the world indoor championship at Potters in 1999. Ladbrokes, who were the bookmakers on site, offered odds of 9-1 against each of three singles matches one particular day ending in straight-

betting on bowls

 Venue bias seldom vital

While there have been significant gambles down the years, there is a big difference from, for example horse racing, in that runners are not laid out for a specific events.

While players at the top level are known to favour certain events and venues, the effect of this is not as marked as in other sports, though twice world title holder Hugh Duff was honest enough to write off his chances at Potters Leisure Resort in Norfolk, the home of the world indoor championships since 1999, on the grounds that he was easily distracted by the social attractions of the east coast venue!

sets victories for the underdog – that was, at the time, three sets to nil. Several discerning enthusiasts considered this a good bet and sums of between £1 and £30 were invested on what was a 1,000-1 treble to the extent that liabilities were over six figures.

The first two contests duly ended in straight sets but the final one saw the favourite take a set to sink some hefty bets. Some might say those involved in the gamble were naive since they could have 'looked after' the favourite with considerably more cash than he would have collected in prize-money!

Relief was the order of the day where Ladbrokes were concerned as their on-site manager had failed to notice their liabilities and would have arrived at work the next morning to one almighty shock!

GROWING BETTING INTEREST In the early years of the 21st century Stan James is the company which has established itself as the leader in bowls betting, having courted the sport assiduously since the 1990s. However, Bet365 have emerged in recent times as a rival as internet betting takes a grip in the way it has done with so many sporting activities.

In common with any sport there are countless anecdotes about gambles won and lost with as many relating to individual betting with the parties concerned as to those enjoyed with the major bookmakers.

Betting undoubtedly adds to the appeal and popularity of bowls yet is considered by many to be an area whose potential has yet to be fully exploited. The sport's hierarchy are all too aware that added publicity is gained by generating greater interest in bowls betting and fully intend extending and expanding opportunities in future years. I wonder if Sir Francis Drake fully realised all those centuries ago just what he was starting!

be one jump ahead in athletics

RUNNING PROFIT

THE NAME STEVE PREFONTAINE will ring a bell with most track and field devotees but it strikes a deafening and particularly painful chord with William Hill media relations director Graham Sharpe.

By STEVE DAVIES

Prefontaine was an American middle-distance runner, who would have been among the favourites for 5,000m Olympics gold at the Montreal Games in 1976. The all-American boy was already a national record holder at every distance from 2,000m to 10,000m and a bright future awaited.

Just a few days after the 24-year-old had won the NCAA 5,000m race in 1975 he was killed in a car accident – though the news obviously didn't filter through to Hills, who priced him up for a forthcoming race.

"With so much access to information these days I doubt anything like that will ever happen again," said Sharpe, as the cold sweat was replaced with a dry smile.

If nothing else, this tale proved that pricing up what is effectively still a minority sport like athletics is nowhere near as straightforward as football, cricket or rugby.

At least the Prefontaine episode wasn't a costly one, though that hadn't been the case a few years earlier when a clued-up gang of Scandinavian punters emptied the tills of

Lasse comes home: shrewd Swedes filled their boots at the 1972 Olympics

many British high street bookmakers.

Going into the 1972 Olympics dozens of Swedish shrewdies knew that long-distance machine Lasse Viren was virtually unbeatable over 5,000m and 10,000m. Many of those canny Vikings flew over to England specifically to back the Finn and filled their boots when their man broke the tape at odds of 6-1 for the shorter distance and 9-1 for the 10,000m.

Four years later at the Montreal Games the bookies were yet again caught unawares as the Swedish gang profited once more from their in-depth knowledge of track and field, a knowledge way beyond that of the odds-makers.

"Sophisticated punters would have had a big advantage over us in those days when 95 per cent of our ante-post department was geared to horse racing alone," Sharpe said.

Times have changed, but while a deceased runner is unlikely nowadays to feature in a book, athletics remains a sport where the very shrewd and very knowledgeable can still find an edge and layers are understandably wary.

That explains why, with the very odd

betting on athletics

 Crime pays

drugs can damage your wealth

The spectre of drugs looms over athletics. Performance enhancement, by fair means or foul, is the name of the game and ever since Ben Johnson's spectacular fall from grace after the 1988 Olympics, big names are continuously getting caught out.

British sprint ace Dwain Chambers and world 100m champion Kelli White are two of the highest-profile crop of current transgressors and no matter how committed the authorities are to cleaning up the sport, there will be many more.

There is nothing bookies can do about paying out on a druggie who crosses the line first, and athletics punters are also well aware of the risks of betting on a sport where cheats really can prosper.

But the fact is that athletics is that rarest of sports where, with disciplined research, the punter can give the bookmaker a real run for his money.

exception, the only time you can bet on athletics is at the really big events such as the World Championships, the Olympic Games and the Commonwealth Games, and even then you rarely find books on every discipline.

Stan James are an honourable exception. As something of an authority on track and field they price up, for example, Golden League meetings, which in 2004 consisted of six well-represented international meets across Europe culminating in the final in Monaco.

The caveat is that they offer only group betting on events, though Chris Edwards, one of the firm's two front-line athletics compilers, insists that it isn't out of fear of being chinned.

"The fact is that we don't always know who is going to be taking part because of injuries, late withdrawals or any number of other factors," he said. "But we offer the service because we like to think we know what we're doing. You've always got to be wary of the specialists having better inside knowledge, but it's a chance we're prepared to take, and we can always limit our liabilities.

"The beauty of something like Golden

League competitions is that generally everybody is off because the prizes are so great, so the events tend to be genuine."

The Olympic Games is inevitably where the odds-setters get more jittery than usual. It's no formality deciphering the heats in track and field events and there is the added complication of how to weather the patriotic plunges on favoured British performers.

Athens 2004 was no exception. Despite Britain winning only two individual gold medals and despite Paula Radcliffe, one of the hottest home favourites, flopping in floods of tears in the marathon, the bookies still had sweaty palms.

The culprit was Kelly Holmes, the new golden girl of British athletics following her wonderful 800m/1,500m double. Saturation coverage – on terrestrial telly rather than satellite – meant millions of people took 'Our Kelly' to their hearts, punters among them.

Steve Freeth of Bet365 said: "When Holmes went to the line for the final of the 800m she was 12-1 to win the 1,500m. But by the time of that second final a few days later she was as short as 1-2."

Overall, though, most bookmakers registered profits and the pick of their successes was the 100m final.

Maurice Greene and Asafa Powell were deemed the big two and most of the money was for them whereas unheralded American, Justin Gatlin, was a 14-1 outsider before the first heats. By the time of the final there was still a belief that the jewellery was heading for the necks of Greene, Powell, another American, Shawn Crawford, or Francis Obik-welu. Gatlin went off at 25-1 and 9.85 seconds later it wasn't only the 22-year-old New Yorker who was doing cartwheels.

"When you get a skinner in the biggest event you're well on your way to making a profit," said Nigel Seeley of Stan James.

novelty bets can lead to profit

REALITY CHEQUES

AS IF THE PUNTER DID NOT HAVE
enough raw material to bet on within the
burgeoning sphere of sport, he now finds
himself bombarded with opportunities of a
different kind.

The novelty market, once restricted to Miss
World and the Eurovision Song contest, is
expanding rapidly as the nation graduates
from trying to get six balls up in the National
Lottery to more puzzling tests like who will
prove the best of a collection of very minor
celebrities at poaching eggs under the watch-
ful eye of an abusive chef (Hell's Kitchen) or
how many days an attention-seeking illusionist
can spend suspended in a perspex box above
the River Thames (David Blaine).

Bookmakers are now as likely to issue prices
on the Cheltenham Gold Cup as they are
on which member of a popular boy band
will be the next to release a solo single.

It all started with the 'Who Shot JR?'
market. Younger readers may be unaware
that Dallas, a US drama series about a dynasty
of mega-rich, mega-promiscuous Texan oil
barons, was the most popular thing on TV in
the late 1970s and early 1980s.

The public's obsession with the programme,
in which it was obligatory for all female
cast members under the age of 50 to wear

By BRUCE
MILLINGTON

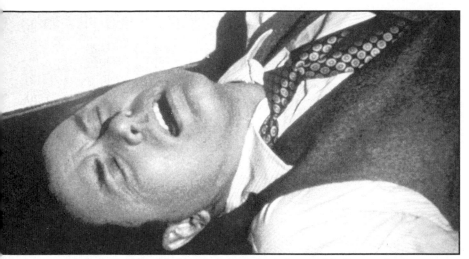

Who started novelty betting? JR Ewing's incapacitiation sparked a craze

dresses with absurd shoulder pads and sleep with a different man every two episodes, reached a frenzied climax in 1980 when the central character, JR Ewing, was shot and critically wounded (he miraculously recovered, of course).

The question of who fired the gun gripped Britain and with supremely canny opportunism, Graham Sharpe, William Hill's PR supremo, offered prices on who pulled the trigger.

Interest was huge, and the company gained enormous publicity during the eight months it took the viewing public to discover that JR's sister-in-law Kristen Shepard was the gunwoman.

Since then odds-compilers have constantly tested their powers of ingenuity in an attempt to conjure up new markets that generate business and, equally importantly, headlines in the national press.

Hills apart, one of the most successful companies in this aspect is Sporting Index, the spread-betting firm who have always had an eye for a catchy market.

'Nasty': Nick Bateman was exposed as a cad on Big Brother – to Craig's gain

They frequently dish up catchily-titled specials when a major event is on, often based on the performance of one particular team or player.

One that sticks in the memory was their Hot Totti market, based on the performance of Italian playmaker Francesco Totti during his side's 2000 European Championship semi-final against Holland.

Among the smuttier elements, heavily influenced by sexual innuendo (25 points for scoring, 10 for getting pulled off, etc) was a component that awarded points every time fellow Italy striker Filippo Inzaghi was caught offside, as frequently happened with this notoriously over-eager goal-getter. It was brilliantly entitled 'Your Mate's a Bit Forward'.

What really kick-started the current profusion of novelty bets was the advent of reality TV shows, and Big Brother in particular.

At the *Racing Post* we quickly picked up on the potential for the show to capture the betting public's imagination and gave it far

novelty markets

 Grave humour

not in the best possible taste

A very thin line separates good taste from bad, and one or two specials most definitely crossed it as far as some punters were concerned.

Sporting's desire to offer a headline-grabbing market when the OJ Simpson trial set the news agenda in 1995 saw them issuing prices on whether the former gridiron star was guilty or innocent.

While many consider this a perfectly valid means of satisfying a desire among those who were following the case to bet on its outcome, others took grave offence and for every account Sporting opened, another was closed in disgust.

"In the end, we came out about level," recalls the firm's Wally Pyrah. "All the Americans who were betting on it backed Simpson to be found guilty, while in the UK they were backing him to get off, which of course he did."

Paddy Power, another bookmaker with an eye for a market that will capture the public's imagination,

have since provoked similar outrage with a couple of risqué offerings.

In 2002 they opened a book on which of ten well-known figures would be the first not to be in their current job come the following Easter, which might sound innocuous enough except that one of them was the Pope, who was only ever going to stop being the Pope by dying. The market was taken down amid the furore (though not before the early 20-1 had been smashed in to 6-1).

Power do plenty of excellent, well thought out novelties, but they were way off target in 2003 when offering prices on which type of missile David Beckham would be struck with first when England ventured to Istanbul for a European Championship showdown against Turkey.

Among the objects being priced up were stones, a lighter, a kebab and a knife. Trading lasted barely an hour before the firm saw sense and took the market down.

more coverage than markets of this genre were previously awarded.

The response from the readers was mixed. Some shared our view that Big Brother represented a genuine, cerebral betting test based on one's character judgement, others considered it a sure sign of dumbing-down and resented what they considered to be televisual garbage being plastered over the back page of their favourite newspaper.

The show's producers were astounded that they had unwittingly created a thriving new betting market and yours truly, after a nervous screen test, was invited to appear on the first ever Big Brother eviction show.

Thus, I found myself sharing a sofa in a packed studio one sultry summer night with Davina McCall ('I only ever bet on the Grand National but the one I back always seems to die') and discarded hippy-chick Sada.

My ten-second update on the state of the Big Brother market was not sufficiently impressive to earn me a recall but it spread the word that betting was as integral a part of BB as housemates rowing over who had used the last of the lentils.

These days there are dozens of bookmakers offering all manner of markets on the show, from who will win to who will be the next evictee to who will go on to marry whom.

But does the programme represent a credible opportunity for profit or is it just a random contest that only a fool would dream of wagering hard cash on?

I firmly believe it is a potential money-spinner for the shrewd punter, especially now that Betfair has so much liquidity in its outright winner market.

There are some important rules when betting on the show, not least of which is that it is vital to keep tabs on what is happening. This does not mean quitting your job and watching live feeds 24 hours a day (although this obviously helps!).

What is does mean is that you should not leave money up to trade on Betfair unless you are happy that the price you are asking for or offering is still attractive to you if circumstances suddenly change.

The most seismic market move in Big Brother history remains the shortening of Craig in the very first series when the Scouse carpenter confronted 'Nasty' Nick Bateman over his scheming, cheating ways.

All of a sudden the muscly Craig went from

novelty markets

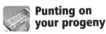 **Punting on your progeny**

kirkland snr hits back of net

Bad value, by and large, are the tailormade specials that generally take the form of a 30-stone woman having a tenner at 66-1 that she weighs less than Kylie Minogue by Christmas.

One such bet that bucked the trend, though, concerns Chris Kirkland, the Liverpool goalkeeper.

When he was 11, his father Eddie and nine friends each staked £100 at 100-1 that youngster would go on to keep goal for England by the time he was 30.

Eddie Kirkland was, by virtue of a few injuries to his son, still waiting at the time of writing, but Hills are not expecting to avoid having to cough up £100,000.

Which just goes to show that, sometimes, there is profit in novelty bets.

a peripheral, some might say boring, figure to a national hero who had bravely stood up to a man of greater intellect and exposed him as a cad and a rotter.

His price tumbled from 33-1 to around 4-1 in next to no time and he went on to win the title hands down.

Another key thing to remember is that it is the great British public that decides who is slung out and who ultimately emerges from the house tens of thousands of pounds richer as fireworks explode in celebration.

Thus, it is pointless betting on someone to win just because you happen to like them unless you consider yourself to be the most average Briton in the country.

I quite warmed to quirky boffin Jon Tickle in Big Brother 4, but there was no point having a penny on him. The average man or woman in the street was always going to get rid of him because they did not relate to his outlook on life.

And then there is the golden rule about avoiding backing people from ethnic minorities. For whatever reason – perhaps Britain is a more racially-intolerant nation than it lets on – non-white contestants rarely prosper and that goes for every form of reality TV show, not just Big Brother.

It is also unwise to back or lay a housemate on the simple basis that they remind you of someone who failed or succeeded in a previous series.

This may sound obvious but it is amazing how many punters I have heard say things like: 'Stuart won't win Big Brother 5. He is just like Alex in Big Brother 3.'

Their definition of 'just like' will consist of nothing more substantial than the fact that both went to university and both are considered good-looking.

Finally, always remember to look for someone who possesses the kind of basic human virtues we all admire deep down. Modesty, self-deprecation, humility, authenticity and kindness are always likely to stand a contestant in good stead.

Above all, though, remember that every time you bet on a reality TV show or, for that matter, a novelty market of any description, you are always at the mercy of the god of Bad Luck.

The purpose of these shows is to generate viewers and, by consequence, revenue from advertising and telephone votes. They may have also become fascinating betting events, but that is not their primary reason for being on our screens.

Thus, the scope for chaos and confusion is far higher than for an event specifically designed as a betting medium.

Using Big Brother as an example, you might find the 50-1 chance you backed on the first night has shortened to 2-1 favourite as the public and housemates alike have warmed to their charms. But you may then find that the customary nomination process is replaced by a game of spin the bottle, which

Dead horse: Shergar won't be turning up again – and neither will Elvis

results in your fancy being evicted.

Unlucky yes, but impossible no. There is no point crying to the host broadcaster, your bookmaker or anyone else in such instances. You just have to accept it as an occupational hazard of novelty betting.

That is not to say, however, that you should not complain if you feel your bookmaker has responded to an unscheduled and chaotic twist in the plot in an unfair manner.

If a firm seeks to exact profit out of a novelty event by pricing it up, it has an obligation to deal with unforeseen events fairly and responsibly.

Remember, too, that some novelties are simply headline-grabbers and should not be touched with a bargepole.

Anything to do with Elvis, Lord Lucan, Shergar and suchlike are devised with the intention of getting the bookmaker's name mentioned in the national press and never offer value simply because they cannot happen. ■

layers quick to refuse bets

PERILS OF WINNING

YOU HAVE FOUND WAYS OF GAINING the edge on the bookies, you are nicely in profit and you back far more winners than losers. You have cracked this sports betting lark, right? Not quite.

You might think you have done the hard part but being successful in betting stimulates a new hazard – how to get your bets on.

Bookmakers want you to bet with them unless your bets tend to be winners. And they have extremely simple methods of knowing whether you are a pesky winner or a welcome loser.

Every internet and telephone punter's betting history is logged by the firms and their profit/loss figures can be analysed at the touch of a keyboard.

And if the analysis shows that you are bad for business you will start finding yourself restricted to smaller stakes than you want and might even find your account closed completely.

Of course, many punters would be only too pleased to be knocked back by their book-maker simply because it would signify that, rather than continuing to back more losers than winners, they were actually enjoying some success in their betting.

But even habitual losers should aspire to

By BRUCE MILLINGTON

Your wad is growing: but will the bookies stop you in your tracks?

greater success and it is bad news for the punting fraternity as a whole that it is possible to be blacklisted for being profitable.

Playing devil's advocate, you would ask why, if you were a bookmaker, you would want to handle hot money. Why allow those who knock holes in your profits to continue to drain money from your coffers?

Whether or not you have a credible answer to that question, what is no longer open to debate is that most bookmakers are becoming increasingly shameless when it comes to saying no thanks to their successful clients or accepting a fraction of the wager they are requesting before offering them the balance at a vastly contracted price.

I know of a punter who has had an account closed after just two bets – and one of those was a loser!

He says his only chance of getting on at advertised prices for any worthwhile amount is with those layers who have realised he is of value to them in that if he is looking to back something, the team, horse, player or dog in question must be worth keeping on the right side of. What infuriates any punter who has had a bet rejected or an account closed is when he reads in the paper that the same firm has accepted a monster bet on a football team to win a match.

Many is the time I have fielded a call at the *Racing Post* from a disgruntled punter saying something along the lines of: "In your paper today it says such-and-such a bookie has laid £100,000 on England beating Greece, yet I tried to have £200 at 5-1 on so-and-so with them the other week and they said I could have £50 at the price and the rest at 3-1."

The only defence I can think of on the layers' behalf is that they may have been standing out at 5-1 and were restricting stakes in attempt to accommodate as many punters as possible before cutting the price.

But it is hard not to feel sympathy for punters who have been knocked back for fractions of some of the mega-wagers the large firms are so quick to report having absorbed.

The bottom line is that the major book-makers are now public limited companies or subsidiaries of plcs and must therefore answer to angry shareholders if profits start to dwindle.

And it is also probably true that the majority of knocking back concerns racing wagers rather than sport bets.

On high-profile football matches, when there is plenty of money changing hands and it is reasonably easy to lay a book, a firm is far less likely to restrict or refuse a bet than on a more obscure event.

Tennis springs to mind as a sport which generates more than its share of complaints about knockbacks. That is largely down to the fact that a relatively small number of book-makers get involved in tennis and those that do are extremely sensitive to the risks of having their trousers taken down by smart money from those in the know.

One way of avoiding a bookmaker knowing you are a winner is, of course, to be a cash customer in a betting shop. In theory this is failsafe, but managers get to know a face in the end and if they keep allowing shrewdies to put a dent in profits they can expect their superiors to have a stern word.

The spread betting equivalent of offering a shorter price than the one requested is known as calling a punter up or down.

Again, your betting profile is well known to the spread firms so if you ring up and ask for a shirt numbers quote on a live football match they know with reasonable accuracy whether you are likely to be looking to buy or sell. If you are a habitual buyer and the price on the teletext page or in the advert is 35-38, you may well be quoted 36-39 by the dealer. The simple way of avoiding the irritation of falling victim of being called up or down is to bet online, where there is no good reason why the price on the screen should not be the price you get.

A natural consequence of putting up the no-entry sign to clued-up clients is that smart money ends up on the exchanges, where the principles of supply and demand mean you can bet as much as you like until there is no money left to oppose your opinion with.

I have been told by one traditional book-maker that the established firms are perfectly happy for a lot of this money to be directed Betfair's way. "We are content to be left with the people who want a £20 acca on the football rather than a selective single on a winner," he said.

So if you want to gauge your success or otherwise at punting and have not been diligent enough to keep records, just remember that if you have not been knocked back you have probably got a fair way to go until you can consider yourself successful enough to quit your job and punt for a living.

beware the grave dangers

BETTING: THE RISKS

FOR THE VAST MAJORITY OF participants, betting of any sort, be it on football, horses, the National Lottery or cards, is one of life's pleasures, an antidote to everything work, the taxman and the public transport system can throw at you.

By BRUCE MILLINGTON

But with bookmakers reporting ever-increasing profits, someone has to pay. And nice though it would be to think that their wealth is simply the accumulation of wagers that punters can well afford to lose, the harsh truth is different.

It would be lovely to believe betting is a risk-free, if occasionally slightly expensive, hobby. But for some people it is a far more serious business, a curse that wrecks not just their lives but those of their families too.

It would be as irresponsible to produce a book about betting without acknowledging its ghastly potential downside as it would to write a book about the joys of whisky without pointing out that misuse can result in alcoholism, debt, violence and death.

Gambling, unlike booze and cigarettes, cannot give you cancer or heart disease (although excessive stress levels are good for nobody), but it can render the addicted punter a slave to the pursuit of winning money or, more pertinently, recouping losses.

I know of people whose lives have been ruined by betting. Their marriages have been wrecked, they have been forced to sell their houses. And in case you believe they must be weak and stupid to get themselves in such dire straits, that is not always the case. I'm talking about intelligent, educated men.

I believe for some punters the advent of internet betting has exacerbated the problem. Previously it was necessary to have some human contact when placing a bet, either in the form of a member of staff in a betting shop or a telephonist. But the facility to bet silently and anonymously can lead some punters to increase their activity and remove the subconscious brake that using another human to complete one's transaction can provide.

If you were ringing the same person every five minutes to have a punt, you may feel slightly sheepish, fearing they believe you to be a hopelessly addictive gambler. When it is just you, a PC and a mouse, it is far easier to allow your betting to spiral out of control.

Even the spread firms themselves warn you in the small-print never to bet with money you cannot afford to lose. It is imperative to heed the warning.

The only times we usually get to hear the heart-rending stories of crippled punters are when the victims are well known. Paul Merson, for instance, who admitted to being addicted to betting, drink and cocaine in 1995. Nearly a decade later he confessed: "I've stayed away from drink and drugs but gambling has beat me, spanked me all over the place."

Merson even had to cancel Sky TV, which he would watch for betting tips, and the mobile phone which he used to ring bookies had to be thrown away as well. But even then the wild punting continued.

"I was driving out to phone boxes at 11pm to put bets on. Then I was going home and five minutes later I was driving out again," he recalled. "I thought I was doing this in secret but my wife knew. I haven't really dealt with gambling since I came out of treatment nine years ago."

Willie Thorne, the snooker ace, is another well-known figure to succumb to the betting bug in a disastrous way.

"My life has been ravaged from wanting to bet," said Thorne. "Anybody who has been through the feeling of coming home potless will know exactly what I'm talking about.

"God knows, I regret my gambling. It's hard to put a figure on how much I lost but it's hundreds of thousands of pounds. And that doesn't take into account the hurt I caused people I love and who have always stood by me.

"Gambling made me moody. When I was winning it was the best feeling in the world. But when I was doing my brains I was the worst person in the world to be around."

While those two men deserve nothing but sympathy, imagine how many people have got themselves into similar trouble but do not have the earning power of a top-level sportsman to get themselves back on their feet.

Well-meaning organisations try to help, but what can they really do?

Gamcare (www.gamcare.org), for example, offers advice on responsible gambling and pledges not to take a judgemental approach to gambling. But the reality is that you are not going to seek help until you are so deeply in trouble that nobody but a sympathetic philanthropist can be of any practical use.

The writers of this book have striven to provide sound advice, but the most important piece of advice you will find anywhere is this: anyone can become a stricken gambler. A bookmaker may stop you betting when you are winning but will not when you are losing.

The consequences of allowing a gambling hobby to become a habit and then an addiction are truly dire. ■

INDEX